ISBN 978-1-333-24758-4
PIBN 10478290

This book is a reproduction of an important historical work. Forgotten Books uses state-of-the-art technology to digitally reconstruct the work, preserving the original format whilst repairing imperfections present in the aged copy. In rare cases, an imperfection in the original, such as a blemish or missing page, may be replicated in our edition. We do, however, repair the vast majority of imperfections successfully; any imperfections that remain are intentionally left to preserve the state of such historical works.

1 MONTH OF
FREE
READING

at

www.ForgottenBooks.com

———◇———

By purchasing this book you are eligible for one month membership to ForgottenBooks.com, giving you unlimited access to our entire collection of over 1,000,000 titles via our web site and mobile apps.

To claim your free month visit:

www.forgottenbooks.com/free478290

Early Western Travels
1748-1846

———

Volume XXX

Journal of Travels over the Rocky Mountains

To the mouth of the Columbia River, made
during the years 1845 and 1846.
By Joel Palmer

Edited with Notes, Introductions, Index, etc., by

Reuben Gold Thwaites, LL. D.

Editor of "The Jesuit Relations and Allied Documents," "Original
Journals of the Lewis and Clark Expedition," "Hennepin's
New Discovery," etc.

(Separate publication from " Early Western Travels: 1748-1846,"
in which series this appeared as Volume XXX)

Cleveland, Ohio
The Arthur H. Clark Company
1906

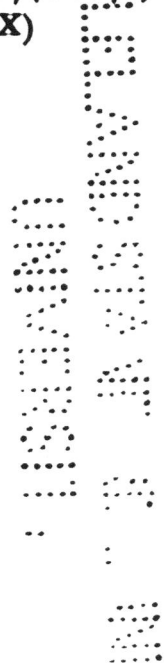

CONTENTS OF VOLUME XXX

ILLUSTRATION TO VOLUME XXX

PREFACE TO VOLUME XXX

In the wake of the pathfinders, fur-traders, Indian scouts, missionaries, scientific visitors, and foreign adventurers came the ultimate figure among early Western travellers, the American pioneer settler, the fore-runner of the forces of occupation and civilization. This concluding volume in our series is, therefore, fitly devoted to the record of an actual home-seeker, and founder of new Western communities.

The significant feature of American history has been the transplanting of bodies of colonists from one frontier to a newer frontier. In respect to the Oregon country, our interest therein is enhanced not only by the great distance and the abundant perils of the way, but also by the political result in securing the territory to the United States, and the growth of a prosperous commonwealth in the Far Northwest corner of our broad domain. In several previous volumes of our series we have witnessed the beginnings of Oregon civilization. Two of our travellers, Franchère and Ross, have graphically detailed the Astoria episode, giving us, not without some literary skill, the skeleton of facts which Irving's masterful pen clothed with living flesh and healthful color; in Townsend's pages we found an enduring picture of the régime of the all-powerful Hudson's Bay Company; De Smet, with faithful, indeed loving, touches has portrayed the vanishing aborigines, whose sad story has yet fully to be told — eventually, when the last vestige of their race has gone, we shall come to recognize the tale as the sorriest chapter in our annals; Farnham shrewdly narrates the sharp transition to American occupancy; but Palmer tells us of the triumphant progress of the conquering pioneer, and in his pages the destiny of Oregon as an American state is clearly foreshadowed.

"Fifty-four forty, or fight," the belligerent slogan with regard to Oregon, adopted in the presidential campaign of 1844, was after all not so much a notice to the British government that the United States considered the Oregon country her own, beyond recall, as an appeal to the pioneers of the West to secure this vast inheritance by actual occupation. As such it proved a trumpet call to thousands of vigorous American farmers, most of them already possessed of comfortable homes in the growing communities of the Middle West.

"I have an uncle," declared one of the pioneers to Dr. John McLoughlin, Hudson's Bay factor on the Pacific coast, "who is rich enough to buy out your company and all this territory."

"Indeed!" replied the doctor, courteously, "who is he?"

"Uncle Sam," gayly responded the emigrant, with huge enjoyment in his well-worn witticism. It was at the supposed behest of this same "Uncle Sam" that farms were sold, wagons and oxen purchased, outfits prepared, and long caravans of permanent settlers slowly and painfully crossed the vast plains and rugged mountains lying between the comfortable settlements of the "Old Northwest"— the "Middle West" of our

day — and the new land of promise in the Far Northwest of the Pacific Slope.

The emigration of 1845 exceeded all that had gone
before. That of 1843, eight hundred strong, had
startled the Indians, and surprised the staid officials
of the Hudson's Bay Company. That of 1844 had
occupied the fertile valleys from Puget Sound on the
north to Calapooia on the south. That of 1845 determined that the territory should be the home of Americans; it doubled the population already on the ground,
re-inforced the compact form of government, and laid
broad and deep the foundations of new American com-
monwealths.

Our author, Joel Palmer, a shrewd, genial farmer
from Indiana, was a leader among these emigrants of
1845. Born across the Canada line in 1810, he nevertheless was of New York parentage, and American
to the core. In early life his family removed to Indiana,
where Joel founded a home at Laurel, in northwest
Franklin County. By the suffrages of his neighbors
Palmer was sent to the state legislature in 1844, but
the following year determined to make a tour to Oregon
for personal observation, before deciding to remove his
family thither and cast his future lot with its pioneer
settlers. Arrived on the Missouri frontier, he found
that the usual wagon train had gone in advance. However, he overtook the great body of the emigrants in
time to assist in the organization of the caravan on Big
Soldier's Creek, in Kansas.

Gathered from all parts of the Middle West, with no
attempt at organization nor any pre-arrangement what-
soever, the emigrants, who had not yet forgotten the

frontier traditions of their fathers, proved to be a homo-
geneous body of about three thousand alert, capable
travellers, provided in general with necessities and
even comforts for the hardships of the long journey;
indeed, after the manner of their Aryan forbears in the
great westerly migrations of the past, they were accompanied by herds of cattle, to form the basis of agricultural life in the new land.   Each of the several
hundred wagons was a travelling house, provided with
tents, beds, and cooking utensils; clothing and food
were also carried, sufficient not only for the journey
out, but for subsistence through the first year, always
the crucial stage of agricultural pioneering.   The
draught cattle were largely oxen, but many of the men
rode horses, and others drove them with their cows
and bulls.

Aside from the duties of the nightly encampment
and morning "catch-up," life upon the migration progressed much as in settled communities.   There were
instances of courtship, marriage, illness, and death, and
not infrequently births, among the migrating families.
These, together with the ever-shifting panorama of
sky, plains, and mountains, made the incidents of the
long and tedious journey.   Occasionally there appeared
upon the horizon an Indian gazing silently at these
invaders of his tribal domain, and at times he came
even to the wagon wheels to beg or trade; the mere
numbers of the travellers gave him abundant caution
not to attempt hostilities.   The wagons were so numerous as to render a compact caravan troublesome to
manage and disagreeable to travel with.   The great
cavalcade soon broke into smaller groups, over one of

which, composed of thirty wagons, Palmer was chosen captain.

At Fort Laramie they rested, and feasted the Indians, who, in wonderment and not unnatural consternation, swarmed about them in the guise of beggars. Palmer afterwards harangued the aboriginal visitors, telling them frankly that their entertainers were no traders, they "were going to plough and plant the ground," that their relatives were coming behind them, and these he hoped the red men would treat kindly and allow free passage — a thinly veiled suggestion that the white army of occupation had come to stay and must not be interfered with by the native population, or vengeance would follow.

From Fort Laramie the invaders, for from the standpoint of the Indians such of course were our Western pioneers, followed the usual trail to the newly-established supply depot at Fort Bridger. Thence they went by way of Soda Springs to Fort Hall, where was found awaiting them a delegation from California, seeking, with but slight success, to persuade a portion of the emigrants in that direction. Following Lewis River on its long southern bend, the travellers at last reached Fort Boise, where provisions could be purchased from Hudson's Bay officials, and a final breathing-spell be taken before attempting the most difficult part of the journey — the passage of the Blue and Cascade ranges.

A considerable company of the emigrants, accompanied by the pilot, Stephen H. Meek, left the main party near Fort Hall, to force a new route to the Willamette without following Columbia River. The essay was, however, disastrous. Meek became bewildered,

and was obliged to secrete himself to escape the revenge
of the exasperated travellers, who reached the Dalles
of the Columbia in an exhausted condition, having lost
many of their number through hunger and physical
hardships.

Palmer himself continued with the main caravan on
the customary route through the Grande Ronde, down
the Umatilla and the Columbia, arriving at the Dalles
by the closing days of September. Here a new difficulty faced the weary pioneers — there was no wagon
road beyond the Dalles; boats to transport the intending colonists were few, and had been pre-empted by
the early arrivals, while provisions at the Dalles would
soon be exhausted. In this situation Palmer determined to join Samuel K. Barlow and his company
in an attempt to cross the Cascades south of Mount
Hood, and lead the way overland to the Willamette
valley. This proved an arduous task, calling for all
the skill and fortitude of experienced pathfinders. In
its course, Palmer ascended Mount Hood, which he
describes as "a sight more nobly grand" than any he
had ever looked upon. At last the valley of the Clackamas was reached, and Oregon City, the little capital
of the new territory, was attained, where "we were so
filled with gratitude that we had reached the settlements
of the white man, and with admiration at the appearance
of the large sheet of water rolling over the Falls, that
we stopped, and in this moment of happiness recounted
our toils, in thought, with more rapidity than tongue
can express or pen write." The distance that he had
travelled from Independence, Missouri, our author
estimates at 1,960 miles.

Passing the winter of 1845-46 in Oregon, Palmer made a careful examination of its resources, and in his book describes the country in much detail. The ensuing spring, after a journey to the Lapwai mission for horses, he started on the return route, arriving at his home in Laurel, Indiana, upon the twenty-third of July.

Palmer's experience, although trying, had been sufficiently satisfactory to justify his intention to make a permanent home in Oregon. In 1847 he took his family thither, the emigration of that year being sometimes known as "Palmer's train," he having been elected captain of the entire caravan, also in recognition of his great utility to the expedition. The new caravan had but just arrived in Oregon — now belonging definitely to the United States — when the Whitman massacre aroused the colonists to punish the Indian participants in order to ensure their own safety. In the organization of the militia force, Joel Palmer was chosen quartermaster and commissary general, whence the title of General, by which he was subsequently known.

He was also made one of two commissioners to attempt to treat with the recalcitrant tribes, and win to neutrality as many as possible. Accompanied by Dr. Robert Newell, a former mountain man, and Perrin Whitman, the murdered man's nephew, as interpreter, Palmer risked his life in the land of the hostiles, and succeeded in alienating many Nez Percés and Wallawalla from the guilty Cayuse. Thus was laid the foundation of that full knowledge of aboriginal character that availed him in his service as United States superintendent of Indians for Oregon.

To this difficult position General Palmer was appointed by President Pierce in 1853, just on the eve
of an outbreak in southern Oregon, and his term of
office coincided with the period of Indian wars. After
pacifying the southern tribes, Palmer inaugurated the
reservation system, removing the remnants of the tribes
of the Willamette valley and their southward neighbors
to a large tract in Polk and Yamhill counties, known
as Grande Ronde Reservation. This ended the Indian
difficulties in that quarter until the Modoc War, twenty
years later.

Palmer found the tribesmen east of the mountains
more difficult to subdue. Scarcely had he and Isaac
T. Stevens, governor of Washington Territory, made a
series of treaties (1855) with the Nez Percés, Cayuse,
Wallawalla, and neighboring tribes, when the Yakima
War began, and embroiled both territories until 1858.
During these difficulties the military authorities complained that Commissioner Palmer was too lenient with
former hostiles, and pinned too much faith to their
promises. Consequently the Oregon superintendency
was merged with that of Washington (1857), and James
W. Nesmith appointed to the combined office.

Retiring to his home in Dayton, Yamhill County,
which town he had laid out in 1850, General Palmer
was soon called upon to serve in the state legislature,
being speaker of the house of representatives (1862-63),
and state senator (1864-66). During the latter incum-
bency he declined being a candidate for United States
senator, because of his belief that a person already
holding a public office of emolument should not during
his term be elected to another. In 1870 he was Repub-

lican candidate for governor of the state, but was defeated by a majority of less than seven hundred votes. From this time forward he lived quietly at Dayton, and there passed away upon the ninth of June, 1881. His excellent portrait given in Lyman's *History of Oregon* (iii, p. 398) is that of an old man; but the face is still strong and kindly, with a high and broad forehead, and gentle yet piercing eyes.

One of Palmer's fellow pioneers said of him, "he was a man of ardent temperament, strong friendships, and full of hope and confidence in his fellow men." Another calls his greatest characteristic his honesty and integrity. Widely known and respected in the entire North West, his services in the up-building of the new community were of large import.

Not the least of these services was, in our judgment, the publication of his *Journal of Travels over the Rocky Mountains*, herein reprinted, which was compiled during the winter of 1846-47, and planned as a guide for intending emigrants. The author hoped to have it in readiness for the train of 1847, but the publishers were dilatory and he only received about a dozen copies before starting. The book proved useful enough, however, to require two later editions, one in 1851, another in 1852, and was much used by emigrants of the sixth decade of the past century.

Palmer makes no pretence of literary finish. He gives us a simple narrative of each day's happenings during his own first journey in 1845, taking especial care to indicate the route, each night's camping places, and all possible cut-offs, springs, grassy oases, and whatever else might conduce to the well-being of the

emigrant and his beasts. The great care taken by the
author, with this very practical end in view, results in
his volume being the most complete description of the
Oregon Trail that we now possess. Later, his account
of passing around Mount Hood and the initial sur-
vey of the Barlow road, produces a marked effect
through its simplicity of narrative. His incidents have
a quaint individuality, as for instance the reproof from
the Cayuse chief for the impiety of card-playing. No
better description of the Willamette valley can be
found than in these pages, and our author's records of
the climate, early prices in Oregon, and the necessities
of an emigrant's outfit, complete a graphic picture of
pioneering days.

In the annotation of the present volume, we have
had valuable suggestions and some material help from
Principal William I. Marshall of Chicago, Professor
Edmond S. Meany of the University of Washington,
Mr. George H. Himes of Portland, Dr. Joseph Schafer
of the University of Oregon, and Mr. Edward Huggins,
a veteran Hudson's Bay Company official at Fort
Nisqually.

With this volume our series of narratives ends, save
for the general index reserved for volume xxxi. The
Western travels which began in tentative excursions
into the Indian country around Pittsburg and Eastern
Ohio in 1748, have carried us to the coast of the Pacific.
The continent has been spanned. Not without some
exhibitions of wanton cruelty on the part of the whites
have the aborigines been pushed from their fertile seats
and driven to the mountain wall. The American
frontier has steadily retreated — at first from the Alle-

ghanies to the Middle West, thence across the Mississippi, and now at the close of our series it is ascending
the Missouri and has sent vanguards to the Farthest
Northwest. The ruts of caravan routes have been
deeply sunk into the plains and deserts, and wheel
marks are visible through the length of several
mountain passes. The greater part of the continental
interior has been threaded and mapped. The era of
railroad building and the engineer is at hand. The
long journey to the Western ocean has been ridded
of much of its peril, and is less a question of mighty
endurance than confronted the pathfinders. When
Francis Parkman, the historian of New France, going
out upon the first stages of the Oregon Trail in 1847
— the year following the date of the present volume —
saw emigrant wagons fitted with rocking chairs and
cooking stoves, he foresaw the advent of the common-
place upon the plains, and the end of the romance of
EARLY WESTERN TRAVELS.

Throughout the entire task of preparing for the press
this series of reprints, the Editor has had the assistance
of Louise Phelps Kellogg, Ph. D., a member of his staff
in the Wisconsin Historical Library. Others have also
rendered editorial aid, duly acknowledged in the several
volumes as occasion arose; but from beginning to end,
particularly in the matter of annotation, Dr. Kellogg
has been his principal research colleague, and he takes
great pleasure in asking for her a generous share of
whatever credit may accrue from the undertaking.
Annie Amelia Nunns, A. B., also of his library staff, has
rendered most valuable expert aid, chiefly in proof-
reading and indexing. The Editor cannot close his

last word to the Reader without gratefully calling attention, as well, to the admirable mechanical and artistic dress with which his friends the Publishers have generously clothed the series, and to bear witness to their kindly suggestions, active assistance, and unwearied patience, during the several years of preparation and publication.

R. G. T.

MADISON, WIS., August, 1906.

Palmer's Journal of Travels over the Rocky
Mountains, 1845-1846

Reprint of original edition: Cincinnati, 1847

JOURNAL OF TRAVELS

ROCKY MOUNTAINS,

TO THE

MOUTH OF THE COLUMBIA RIVER;

MADE DURING THE YEARS 1845 AND 1846;

CONTAINING MINUTE DESCRIPTIONS OF THE

VALLEYS OF THE WILLAMETTE, UMPQUA, AND CLAMET;

A GENERAL DESCRIPTION OF

OREGON TERRITORY;

ITS INHABITANTS, CLIMATE, SOIL, PRODUCTIONS, ETC., ETC.;

A LIST OF

NECESSARY OUTFITS FOR EMIGRANTS:

AND A

Table of Distances from Camp to Camp on the Route.

ALSO;

A Letter from the Rev. H. H. Spalding, resident Missionary, for the last ten years, among the Nez Percé Tribe of Indians, on the Koos-koos-kee River; The Organic Laws of Oregon Territory, Tables of about 300 words of the Chinook Jargon, and about 200 Words of the Nez Percé Language; a Description of Mount Hood; Incidents of Travel, &c., &c.

BY JOEL PALMER.

CINCINNATI:

J. A. & U. P. JAMES, WALNUT STREET,

BETWEEN FOURTH AND FIFTH.

1847.

TO THE

PIONEERS OF THE WEST,
AND THEIR DESCENDANTS,

THE BONE AND MUSCLE OF THE COMMUNITY,

WHO IMPROVE AND ENRICH THE COUNTRY IN PEACE,

AND PROTECT AND DEFEND IT IN WAR,

THIS WORK

IS RESPECTFULLY

DEDICATED.

PUBLISHERS' ADVERTISEMENT

In offering to the public a new work on Oregon, the publishers feel confident that they are performing an acceptable service to all who are desirous of obtaining full and correct information of that extensive and interesting region.

The facts contained in this Journal of Travels over the Rocky Mountains were obtained, by the author, from personal inspection and observation; or derived from intelligent persons, some of whom had resided in the country for ten years previously. It contains, as is believed, much very valuable information never before published, respecting the Oregon Territory.

Mr. Palmer's statements and descriptions are direct and clear, and may be relied on for their accuracy. He observed with the eye of an intelligent farmer the hills and valleys; timbered land and prairies, soil, grass, mill sites, &c.; all of which he has particularly described.

To the man about to emigrate to Oregon just the kind of information needed is given. He is informed what is the best season for setting out; the kinds and quantities of necessary outfits; where they may be purchased to the best advantage, so as to save money, time and useless hauling of provisions, and to promote comfort and prevent suffering on the long journey.

[vi] A particular account of Oregon city is given; the number of houses and inhabitants; the number

and kinds of mechanical trades carried on; and the prices current during the author's stay there.

The objects of natural curiosity on the route — the Solitary Tower — the Chimney Rock — Independence Rock — the Hot Springs — the Devil's Gate — the South Pass — the Soda Springs, and many others — are noticed.

The work is enlivened with anecdotes of mountaineer life — shooting buffalo — hunting bear — taking fish, &c.

Mr. Palmer made the ascent of one of the highest peaks of Mount Hood, almost alone, and with a very scanty supply of provisions. An extraordinary achievement, when the circumstances under which it was accomplished are taken into consideration.

Cincinnati, January, 1847.

JOURNAL OF TRAVELS OVER THE ROCKY MOUNTAINS

HAVING concluded, from the best information I was able to obtain, that the Oregon Territory offers great inducements to emigrants, I determined to visit it with a view of satisfying myself in regard to it, and of ascertaining by personal observation whether its advantages were sufficient to warrant me in the effort to make it my future home.[1] I started, accordingly, on the morning of the 16th of April, 1845, in company with Mr. Spencer Buckley. We expected to be joined by several young men from Rushville, Ind., but they all abandoned the enterprise, and gave us no other encouragement than their good wishes for our success and safety. I took leave of my family, friends and home, with a truly melancholy heart. I had long looked forward and suffered in imagination the pain of this anticipated separation; but I had not tasted of its *realities*, and none but those who have parted with a family under similar circumstances, can form any just conception of the depth and power of the emotions which pervaded my breast on that occasion. The undertaking before

---

[1] Oregon Territory, which under the treaty of 1818 was held in joint occupation by the United States and Great Britain, had been brought into prominence by the presidential campaign of 1844, and the belligerent message of President Polk at his inauguration in March, 1845. Emigration thither for the year 1845 exceeded that of any previous season and consisted of nearly three thousand persons, largely from Missouri and the frontier states of the Old Northwest.— ED.

me was arduous. It *might* and doubtless *would* be attended with various and unknown difficulties, privations and dangers. A doubt arose in my mind, whether the advantages, which were expected to result from the trip, would be likely to compensate for the time and expense necessary to accomplish it: but I believed that I was right, hoped for the best, and pressed onward.

We were favoured with a pleasant day and good roads, which tended in some degree to dissipate the gloom which [10] had weighed down my spirits upon leaving *home*. Our day's travel ended at Blue River, on the banks of which we encamped for the first time on the long and tedious journey before us.[3]

April 17. Arrived at Indianapolis, in the afternoon, where we expected to meet a number of persons, who had expressed a determination to join the party.[8] But here too, as in the case of our Rushville friends, we were doomed to meet disappointment; — not one was found willing to join us in our expedition. After having had our horses well shod, (we traveled in an ordinary wagon drawn by two horses,) and having laid in a supply of medicines, we put up for the night.

April 18. We this day had a sample of what might be called the *mishaps* of travelers — an encounter with a wild animal, the first which we met in our journey. One of our horses becoming lame, we were obliged to trade him away, and received in exchange one so wild,

---

[3] Blue River, in central Indiana, flowing through Rush and Shelby counties, is part of the White River system.— ED.

[8] For a note on the founding of Indianapolis see our volume ix, p. 190, note 100.— ED.

that it required the greatest vigilance and exertion on our part to prevent him from running away with our whole concern. We reached Mount Meridian after a day's journey of about thirty-four miles, during which we succeeded admirably in taming our wild horse.[4]

April 24. Reached the Mississippi, opposite to St. Louis, having traveled daily, and made the best of our time after leaving Mount Meridian.

April 25. We made a few purchases this morning, consisting chiefly of Indian trinkets, tobacco, powder, lead, &c. and, soon after, resumed our journey upon the road to St. Charles, the seat of justice for St. Charles county.[5] We reached this place at the close of the day, and encamped upon the banks of the Missouri, which appears to be about as wide as the Ohio at Cincinnati, in a fair stage of water; the current is quite strong; the water very thick and muddy. Here, we overtook a company of Germans, from St. Louis, who had started for California. The company consisted of four men, two women and three children; they traveled with a wagon drawn by six mules, and a cart drawn by two, — a very poor means of conveyance for such a long and tedious route. We traveled the same road until we reached Fort Hall.

April 26. At nine o'clock A. M. we crossed the river and traveled twenty-eight miles. The surface of the country is somewhat undulating; the soil, though poorly watered, appears to be good, and produces respectable crops.

---

[4] Mount Meridian is a small village in Jefferson township, Putnam County, Indiana. It was laid out in 1833 and at first named Carthage.— ED.

[5] For St. Charles see our volume v, p. 39, note 9.— ED.

April 27. We traveled thirty-one miles. The day was rainy [11] and unpleasant. The country through which we passed is a rolling prairie: some parts of it are very well timbered. On account of the scarcity of springs, the people rely generally upon their supplies of *rain* water. There we were joined by a clever back-woodsman, by the name of Dodson, who was making the best of his lonely journey to join an emigrating party at Independence; upon his consenting to bear an equal share in our expenses and outfit at that place, we took him in, and traveled together.

April 28. We started this morning at sunrise, and traveled to Lute creek, a distance of six and a half miles.⁶ This stream was so much swollen, in consequence of the recent rains, that we were unable to ford it, and were forced to encamp upon its banks, and remain all day. While there, we were greatly annoyed by the *wood-tick* — an insect resembling, in size and in other respects, the *sheep-tick*. These insects, with which the bushes and even the ground seemed to be covered, fastened themselves with such tenacity upon our flesh, that when picking them off in the morning, the head would remain sticking fast to the skin, causing in most cases a painful wound.

April 29. We traveled about twenty-six miles, through a gently undulating country: the principal crops consisted of corn, oats, tobacco and some wheat. We passed through Williamsburgh and Fulton. The latter town is the seat of justice for Callaway county.⁷

⁶ By the term "Lute creek," Palmer intends Loutre River, rising in north-east Callaway County, and flowing south and southwest through Montgomery County into the Missouri, at Loutre Island. See our volume v, p. 47, note 19.— ED.

⁷ Williamsburgh, a village in the township of Nine Mile Prairie, Callaway

April 30.   We made an advance of about thirty miles
through a well timbered country, and passed through
Columbia, the seat of justice for Boone county.   The
town is pleasant and surrounded by a fertile and attractive country.   We made our halt and encamped for
the night, five miles westward of this town.

May 1.   We started this morning at the usual hour,
and after a ride of eight miles, reached and re-crossed
the Missouri, at Rocheport, and continued our journey
until night, passing through Booneville, the county
seat of Cooper — a rich and fertile county, making in
all a ride of twenty-six miles.[8]

May 2.   Passed through the town of Marshall, the
seat of justice for Saline county.   The town stands
upon an elevated prairie, upon which may be found
a few groves of shrubby timber.   The country upon
this [the west] side appeared to be much better supplied
with water, than that upon the east side.[9]

May 3.   We traveled about twenty-eight miles, over
a thinly-settled [12] prairie country.   The crops, cultivated generally by negroes, consisted of hemp, corn,
oats, and a little wheat and tobacco.   The soil appeared
to be good, but the scarcity of timber will prove a serious
barrier to a complete settlement of the country.

May 4.   We traveled twenty-three miles this day,

County, was laid out in 1836.   For Fulton see our volume xxi, p. 131, note
7.— ED.

   [8] Columbia and Rocheport are noted in our volume xxi, p. 133, note 8;
Booneville, *ibid.*, p. 89, note 59.   Palmer probably crossed the Missouri at
Boonville.   Townsend went by a similar route from St. Louis to Boonville.
See his *Narrative* in our volume xxi, pp. 125-134.— ED.

   [9] Marshall was in 1839 set off as the county seat of Saline, and in 1900
had a population of 5086.   It was named in honor of the chief justice of the
United States, who died shortly before the incorporation of the town.— ED.

through a better improved and pleasanter part of Missouri, than any we have yet seen. The crops appeared well; there were fine orchards under successful cultivation. The country is well timbered, and there appears nothing to hinder it from becoming the seat of a dense and thriving population.

May 6. Reached Independence at nine o'clock A.M.;[10] and as the main body of emigrants had left a few days previous, we hastily laid in our supplies, and at five o'clock P. M., pushed forward about two miles, and encamped upon the banks of a small creek, in company with four wagons, bound for Oregon. From one of the wagons they drew forth a large jug of whiskey, and before bed-time all the men were completely intoxicated. In the crowd was a mountaineer, who gave us a few lessons in the first chapter of a life among the mountains. At midnight, when all were quiet, I wrapped myself in my blanket, laid down under an oak tree, and began to realize that I was on my journey to Oregon.

May 7. After traveling about fifteen miles we halted and procured an extra set of horse-shoes, and a few additional wagon bows. The main body of the emigrants is twenty-five miles in advance of us: we have now passed out of Missouri, and are traveling in an Indian country — most of which is a rolling prairie.[11]

May 8. We started at seven o'clock, A. M. and traveled about twenty miles. Towards evening we overtook an emigrating company, consisting of thirty-

---

[10] For Independence see our volume xix, p. 189, note 34. Gregg gives a much fuller description of this town as an outfitting place, than does our present author; *ibid.*, pp. 188-192.— ED.

[11] On the bounds of this territory, see our volume xxi, p. 50, note 31.— ED.

eight wagons, with about one thousand head of loose cattle, all under the direction of a Mr. Brown. We passed this company, expecting to overtake a company of about one hundred wagons, which were but a few miles before us. The night, however, became so dark that we were compelled to encamp upon the prairie. Soon after we had staked our horses, a herd of wild Indian horses came galloping furiously by us, which so alarmed our horses and mules, that they broke loose and ran away after them. Dodson and myself pursued, but were distanced, and after running two or three miles, abandoned the chase as hopeless, and attempted to return to the camp. Owing to the darkness, we [13] were unable to find our camp, until the night had far advanced; and when we finally reached it, it required all my logic, supported by the positive testimony of Buckley, to convince Dodson that we were actually there.

May 9. At daylight, Dodson and I resumed the search for our lost stock. After a fatiguing tramp of several hours, I came upon *one* of the mules, which being hobbled, had been unable to keep with the herd. Dodson was unsuccessful, and returned to camp before me; during our absence, however, the herd had strolled near the camp, and Buckley had succeeded in taking our two *horses*. Having taken some refreshments, we started again in search of the lost animals. As I was returning to camp, hopeless, weary and hungry, I saw at a distance Dodson and Buckley mounted upon our two horses, and giving chase to the herd of Indian horses, among which were our two mules. The scene was wild, romantic and exciting. The race was untrammeled by any of those arbitrary and useless rules with which the "knights of the turf" encumber their races, and was pursued on both sides, for a nobler purpose; it was to decide between the rights of *property* on the one side, and the rights of *liberty* on the other. The contest was for a long time doubtful; but the herd finally succeeded in winning the race, and poor Buckley and Dodson were compelled to yield; the former having lost his reputation as a sportsman, and the latter — what grieved him more,— his *team*; and *both* had ruined the character of their coursers in suffering them to be beaten. Sad and dispirited, they returned to camp, where, after a short consultation, it was unanimously resolved,— inasmuch as there was no *other* alternative, — to suffer the mules freely and forever to enjoy the enlarged liberty which they had so nobly won.

The day was nearly spent, but we harnessed up our team and traveled four miles, to the crossing of a creek, where we encamped for the night.

May 10. Re-considered our resolution of last evening, and spent the morning looking for the mules — re-adopted the *same* resolution, for the *same* reason, and then resumed our journey.

We advanced about eighteen miles through a very fertile and well watered country, and possessing, along the banks of the water courses, a supply of bur and white oak, ash, elm, and black walnut timber, amply sufficient for all practical purposes. In our travel, we crossed a stream called the Walkarusha, extending back from which, about two miles in width, [14] we discovered a fine bottom covered with heavy bur oak and black walnut timber. After passing through this bottom, the trail strikes into a level and beautiful prairie, and crossing it — a distance of four miles — rises gradually to the ridge between the Walkarusha and the Caw, or Kansas river.[12] We encamped upon the ridge, in full view of the two streams, which at this place are from six to eight miles apart. The banks of both streams, as far as can be seen, are lined, either way, with excellent timber: the country rises gradually from the streams, for fifteen or twenty miles, with alternate forests and prairies, presenting to the eye a truly splendid scene. I noticed here almost a countless number of *mounds*, in different directions — some covered with 'timber, others with long grass. The Caw or Kansas Indians dwell along these streams. Through this part of the route there are *two* trails, uniting near our camp; the difference in the distance is small.[13]

May 11. We traveled about twenty miles, and passed a company of twenty-eight wagons. The road runs upon the ridge, which after a distance of ten or twelve miles becomes a broad rolling prairie. As night came on, we came up with the company of one hundred wagons which we were in pursuit of: they were encamped upon the banks of a small brook, four miles from the Kansas,

[12] Walkarusa Creek rises in several branches in Wabaunsee County, and flows east through Shawnee and Douglas into Kansas River. The crossing of the Oregon Trail was almost directly south of Lawrence. The trail thence followed the divide between the creek and river to about the present site of Topeka. During the Free Soil troubles in Kansas, a bloodless campaign (1855) along this creek toward Lawrence was known as the "Walkarusa War."

Kansas River is noted in our volume xiv, p. 174, note 140.— ED.

[13] For the Kansa Indians see our volume v, p. 67, note 37; also our volume xxviii, p. 140, note 84. Wyeth notes their village in his *Oregon*, our volume xxi, pp. 48, 49.— ED.

into which it empties. We joined this company. At dark the guard was stationed, who becoming tired of their monotonous round of duty, amused themselves by shooting several dogs, and by so doing excited no small tumult in the company, which after some exertion on the part of the more orderly portion was quelled, and tranquility restored.

May 12. We traveled about four miles to Caw or Kansas river. This is a muddy stream, of about two hundred and fifty yards in width. We were obliged to be ferried over it in a flat boat; and so large was our company, and so slowly did the ferrymen carry on the necessary operations, that darkness overtook us before half the wagons had crossed the stream. Fearing molestation from the numerous Indians who were prowling about, we were compelled to keep a strong guard around our camp, and especially around our cattle; and when all the preliminaries had been arranged, we betook ourselves to rest; but our tranquility was soon interrupted by one of the most terrific thunder storms that I ever witnessed. It appeared to me that the very *elements* had broken loose, and that each was engaging madly in a desperate struggle for the mastery. All was confusion in our camp. The storm had so frightened the cattle, [15] that they were perfectly furious and ungovernable, and rushed through the guard, and dashed forward over the country before us: nothing could be done to secure them, and we were obliged to allow them to have out their race, and endeavor to guard our camp.

May 13. Early this morning we succeeded in finding and taking possession of our cattle, and by noon all our wagons had crossed the river. Soon after we took up our line of march, and after advancing about three miles, encamped near the banks of Big Soldier creek, for the purpose of organizing the company by an election of officers; the officers *then* acting having been elected to serve only until the company should reach *this place*.[14]   It was decided, when at Independence, that *here* there should be a thorough and complete organization. Great interest had been manifested in regard to the matter while upon the road; but *now* when we had reached the spot and the period for attending to the matter in earnest had arrived, the excitement was intense. The most important officers to be elected were the pilot and captain of the company. There were two candidates for the office of pilot,— one a Mr. Adams, from Independence,— the other a Mr. Meek, from the same place. Mr. Adams had once been as far west as Fort Laramie, had in his possession Gilpin's Notes,[15] had engaged a Spaniard, who had traveled over the whole route, to accompany him, and moreover had been conspicuously instrumental

[14] For this stream see De Smet's *Letters* in our volume xxvii, p. 197, note 74.— ED.

[15] This was probably a local publication of the journal or notes of William Gilpin, who went to Oregon with Frémont's party in 1843. Gilpin was a Pennsylvanian, appointed cadet at West Point in 1834. Two years later he became lieutenant in the 2nd dragoons, and saw frontier service, resigning from the army in 1838. He accompanied Frémont as far as the Dalles of the Columbia, and passed the winter of 1843-44 in the Willamette valley, returning overland to the states in 1844. As an intelligent observer his reports on the Oregon country were much sought (see *Niles' Register*, lxvii, p. 161). Gilpin afterwards served in the Mexican War, and earnestly urged the building of a Pacific railway. In 1861 he was appointed first territorial governor of Colorado, in recognition of "his services as an explorer of the Great West," and lived until 1894.— ED.

in producing the "Oregon fever." In case the company would elect him pilot, and pay him five hundred dollars, *in advance*, he would bind himself to pilot them to Fort Vancouver.

Mr. Meek, an old mountaineer, had spent several years as a trader and trapper, among the mountains, and had once been through to Fort Vancouver;[16] he proposed to pilot us through for two hundred and fifty dollars, *thirty* of which were to be paid in advance, and the balance when we arrived at Fort Vancouver. A motion was then made to postpone the election to the next day. While we were considering the motion, Meek came running into the camp, and informed us that the Indians were driving away our cattle. This intelligence caused the utmost confusion: motions and propositions, candidates and their special friends, were alike disregarded; *rifles* were grasped, and *horses* were hastily mounted, and away we all galloped in pursuit. Our two thousand head of cattle were now scattered over the prairie, at a distance of four or five miles from the camp.

[16] About two miles from camp, in full view, up the prairie, was a small Indian village; the greater part of our enraged people, with the hope of hearing

---

[16] Stephen Hall Meek was a brother of Colonel Joseph Meek so well known as an Oregon pioneer (see our volume xxviii, p. 290, note 171). Stephen began his career as a trapper under Captain Bonneville in 1832, and accompanied Joseph Walker to California in 1833-34. He was in the Willamette valley in 1841, where he purchased of Dr. John McLoughlin the first lot sold on the site of Oregon City. In 1842 he guided the emigrant caravan from Fort Laramie. His unfortunate experience in attempting a "cut off" with a party of emigrants in 1845 (related *post* by Palmer), discredited his abilities as a guide. At the time of the gold excitement (1848-49) he returned to California, where he made his later home in Siskiyou County.— ED.

from the lost cattle, drove rapidly forward to this place. As they approached the village, the poor Indians were seen running to and fro, in great dismay — their women and children skulking about and hiding themselves, — while the chiefs came forward, greeted our party kindly, and by signs offered to smoke the pipe of peace, and engage with them in trade. On being charged with the theft of our cattle, they firmly asserted their innocence; and such was their conduct, that the majority of the party was convinced they had been wrongfully accused: but one poor fellow, who had just returned to the village, and manifested great alarm upon seeing so many "pale faces," was taken; and failing to prove his innocence, was hurried away to camp and placed under guard. Meanwhile, after the greater part of the company had returned to camp, and the captain had assembled the *judges*, the prisoner was arraigned at the bar for trial, and the solemn interrogatory, "Are you guilty or not guilty," was propounded to him: but to this, his only answer was — a grunt, the import of which the honorable court not being able clearly to comprehend, his trial was formally commenced and duly carried through. The evidence brought forward against him not being sufficient to sustain the charge, he was fully acquitted; and, when released, *"split"* for his wigwam in the village. After the excitement had in some degree subsided, and the affair was calmly considered, it was believed by most of us that the false alarm in regard to the Indians had been raised with the design of breaking up or postponing the election. If such *was* the design, it succeeded admirably.

May 14. Immediately after breakfast, the camp was

assembled, and proceeded to the election of officers and
the business of organization.   The election resulted in the
choice of S. L. Meek, as pilot, and Doctor P. Welch,[17]
formerly of Indiana, as captain, with a host of subalterns;
such as lieutenants, judges, sergeants, &c.)

After these matters had been disposed of, we harnessed
up our teams and traveled about five miles, and encamped
with Big Soldier creek on our right hand and Caw river
on our left.

The next day we were delayed in crossing Big Soldier
creek, on account of the steepness of its banks; and
advanced only twelve miles through a prairie country.
Here [17] sixteen wagons separated from us, and we
were joined by fifteen others.

May 17. We traveled eighteen miles over a high,
rolling prairie, and encamped on the banks of Little
Vermilion creek, in sight of a Caw village.   The principal chief resides at this village.[18]   Our camp here replen-
ished their stores; and, although these Indians may be
a set of beggarly thieves, they conducted themselves
honorably in their dealings with us; in view of which
we raised for their benefit a contribution of tobacco,
powder, lead, &c., and received in return many good
wishes for a pleasant and successful journey.   After

[17] Little is known of Dr. Presley Welch save as related by Palmer — that he
was from Indiana, was chosen captain of the caravan, and was without authority
after the formation of the independent companies.   H. H. Bancroft (*History
of Oregon*, i, p. 612) notes that he was candidate for governor in 1846.
George H. Himes, assistant secretary of the Oregon Historical Society, writes to
the Editor: "In all my efforts to make a roll of Pioneers by years, I have not
so far been able to find anything about Dr. Welch; hence I conclude he either
left the country at an early date or died soon after his arrival here."— ED.

[18] For this stream see our volume xxi, p. 149, note 20.   Townsend also
describes the same Kansa village, *ibid.*, pp. 148, 149.— ED.

leaving them, we traveled about twelve miles over a
fertile prairie. In the evening, after we had encamped
and taken our supper, a wedding was attended to with
peculiar interest.

May 19. This day our camp did not rise. A growing spirit of dissatisfaction had prevailed since the
election; there were a great number of disappointed
candidates, who were unwilling to submit to the will
of the majority; and to such a degree had a disorderly
spirit been manifested, that it was deemed expedient
to divide the company. Accordingly, it was mutually
agreed upon, to form, from the *whole* body, three companies; and that, while each company should select
its own officers and manage its internal affairs, the
pilot, and Capt. Welsh, who had been elected by the
whole company, should retain their posts, and travel
with the company in advance.) It was also arranged,
that each company should take its turn in traveling in
advance, for a week at a time. A proposition was then
made and acceded to, which provided that a collection
of funds, with which to pay the pilot, should be made
previous to the separation, and placed in the hands
of some person to be chosen by the *whole*, as treasurer,
who should give bonds, with approved security, for
the fulfilment of his duty.

A treasurer was accordingly chosen, who after giving
the necessary bond, collected about one hundred and
ninety dollars of the money promised; some refused
to pay, and others had no money in their possession.
All these and similar matters having been satisfactorily
arranged, the separation took place, and the companies
proceeded to the election of the necessary officers. The

company to which I had attached myself, consisting
of thirty wagons, insisted that I should officiate as their
captain, and with some reluctance I consented. We
dispensed with many of the offices and formalities
which [18] existed in the former company, and after
adopting certain regulations respecting the government
of the company, and settling other necessary preliminaries, we retired to rest for the night.

May 20. We have this day traveled fifteen miles,
through a prairie country, with occasionally a small
grove along the streams.

May 22. Yesterday after moving thirteen miles
we crossed Big Vermilion, and encamped a mile beyond
its west bank; we found a limestone country, quite
hilly, indeed almost mountainous. To-day we have
crossed Bee, and Big Blue creeks; the latter stream
is lined with oak, walnut, and hickory.[19] We encamped
two and a half miles west of it. During the night it
rained very hard. Our cattle became frightened and
all ran away.

May 23. Made to-day but eight miles. Our pilot
notified us that this would be our last opportunity to
procure timber for axle trees, wagon tongues, &c., and
we provided a supply of this important material. Our
cattle were all found.

May 25. Early this morning we were passed by
Col. Kearney and his party of dragoons, numbering
about three hundred. They have with them nineteen

---

[19] The Big Vermillion is now known as the Black Vermillion, an eastern
tributary of the Big Blue, in Marshall County, Kansas. The usual crossing
was near the site of the present town of Bigelow. Bee Creek is a small stream
in Marshall County. The Big Blue is noted in our volume xiv, p. 185, note
154; also in our volume xxi, p. 142, note 15.— Ed.

wagons drawn by mules, and drive fifty head of cattle and twenty-five head of sheep. They go to the South Pass of the Rocky Mountains.[20] Our travel of to-day and yesterday is thirty-two miles, during which we have crossed several small streams, skirted by trees. The soil looks fertile.

May 26. Overtook Capt. Welsh's company to-day. We passed twelve miles through a rolling prairie region, and encamped on Little Sandy.

May 27. As it was now the turn of our company to travel in advance, we were joined by Capt. Welsh and our pilot. The country is of the same character with that we passed through on yesterday, and is highly adapted to the purpose of settlement, having a good soil, and streams well lined with timber.

May 31. In the afternoon of the 28th we struck the Republican fork of Blue River,[21] along which for

[20] For a biographical note on Colonel Stephen W. Kearny see our volume xvii, p. 12, note 4. In the summer of 1845 the general of the army ordered Kearny to take five companies of dragoons and proceed from Fort Leavenworth via the Oregon Trail to South Pass, returning by way of the Arkansas and the Santa Fé Trail. The object was both to impress the Indians, and to report upon the feasibility of an advanced military post near Fort Laramie. Leaving their encampment May 18, they were upon the Little Blue by the twenty-sixth of the month. See report in *Senate Docs.*, 29 Cong., 1 sess., 1, pp. 210-213. This was the first regular military campaign into the land of the Great West, and strongly impressed the Indians of that region. Kearny's recommendations were against the establishment of a post because of the difficulty of supplying it — advising instead, a biennial or triennial campaign similar to his own.— ED.

[21] By the "Republican Fork of Blue River" Palmer intends the stream known usually as the Little Blue. Republican River, farther west, is an important branch of Kansas River, and for a portion of its course nearly parallels the Little Blue. The Oregon Trail, however, followed the latter stream, and the distances given by Palmer preclude the possibility of a detour via the Republican River. The name of this stream, as well as that applied by Palmer to the Little Blue, is derived from the tribe of Republican Pawnee, for which see our volume xiv, p. 233, note 179.— ED.

fifty miles lay the route we were traveling. Its banks
afford oak, ash and hickory, and often open out into
wide and fertile bottoms. Here and there we observed
cotton wood and willow. The pea vine grows wild,
in great abundance on the bottoms. The pea is smaller
than our common garden pea and afforded us a [19]
pleasant vegetable. We saw also a few wild turkies.
To-day we reached a point where a trail turns from this
stream, a distance of twenty-five miles, to the Platte
or Nebraska river. We kept the left hand route, and
some nine or ten miles beyond this trail, we made our
last encampment on the Republican Fork.

June 1. We set out at the usual hour and crossed
over the country to Platte river; having measured the
road with the chain, we ascertained the distance to be
eighteen and a half miles, from our encampment of last
night. It is all a rolling prairie; and in one spot, we
found in pools a little standing water. Some two miles
before reaching the Platte bottom the prairie is extremely
rough; and as far as the eye can reach up and down
that river, it is quite sandy.[22] We encamped near a
marshy spot, occasioned by the overflow of the river,
opposite an island covered with timber, to which we
were obliged to go through the shallows of the river
for fuel, as the main land is entirely destitute of trees.
Near us the Platte bottom is three and a half miles

---

[22] There were two routes across from the head of Little Blue River to the
Platte. The first left the trail near the site of Leroy, Nebraska, and came in
to the Platte about twenty miles below Grand Island; the second continued
farther west, about ten miles, then crossed northwest to the Platte near the
site of Fort Kearney. See military map of Nebraska and Dakota, prepared
in 1855-57 by Lieutenant G. K. Warren of the topographical engineer corps.
For the Platte River see our volume xiv, p. 219, note 170.— ED.

wide, covered with excellent grass, which our cattle ate greedily, being attracted by a salt like substance which covers the grass and lies sprinkled on the surface of the ground. We observed large herds of antelope in our travel of to-day. In the evening it rained very hard.

June 2. Our week of advance traveling being expired, we resolved to make a short drive, select a suitable spot, and lay by for washing. We accordingly encamped about six miles up Platte river. As I had been elected captain but for two weeks, and my term was now expired, a new election was held, which resulted in the choice of the same person. The captain, Welsh, who was originally elected by all the companies, had been with us one week, and some dissatisfaction was felt, by our company, at the degree of authority he seemed disposed to exercise. We found, too, that it was bad policy to require the several companies to wait for each other; — our supply of provision was considered barely sufficient for the journey, and it behooved us [to] make the best use of our time. At present one of the companies was supposed to be two or three days travel in the rear. We adopted a resolution desiring the several companies to abandon the arrangement that required each to delay for the others; and that each company should have the use of the pilot according to its turn. Our proposition was not, for the present, accepted by the other companies. While we were at our washing encampment one [20] of the companies passed us, the other still remaining in the rear.

June 3. Having traveled about eight miles, we halted at noon, making short drives, to enable the rear company to join us. We have no tidings of it as yet. We met seventy-five or eighty Pawnee Indians returning from their spring hunt.[28]

June 5. Yesterday we traveled about twelve miles, passing captain Stephens, with his advance company. To-day we traveled about the same distance, suffering Stephens' company to pass us.[24] At noon they were delayed by the breaking of an axletree of one of their wagons, and we again passed them, greatly to their offence. They refused to accede to our terms, and we determined to act on our own responsibility. We therefore dissolved our connection with the other companies, and thenceforward acted independently of them.

June 6. We advanced twenty miles to-day. We find a good road, but an utter absence of ordinary fuel. We are compelled to substitute for it buffalo dung, which burns freely.

June 7. We find in our sixteen miles travel to-day that the grass is very poor in the Platte bottoms, having been devoured by the buffalo herds. These bottoms are from two to four miles in width, and are intersected, at every variety of interval, by paths made by the buffaloes, from the bluffs to the river. These paths are remarkable in their appearance, being about fifteen inches wide, and four inches deep, and worn into the soil as smoothly as they could be cut with a spade.

We formed our encampment on the bank of the river, with three emigrating companies within as many

[28] For this tribe, see our volume vi, p. 61, note 17; also our volume xv, pp. 143-165; and xxviii, p. 149, note 94.— ED.

[24] Thomas Fulton Stephens joined the Oregon caravan from Illinois. The year after his arrival in Oregon he took up donation land near the site of Portland and erected thereon a saw-mill. His death occurred in 1884.— ED.

miles of us; two above and one below; one of fifty-
two wagons, one of thirteen, and one of forty-three
— ours having thirty-seven. We find our cattle growing lame, and most of the company are occupied in
attempting to remedy the lameness. The prairie having been burnt, dry, sharp stubs of clotted grass remain,
which are very hard, and wear and irritate the feet of
the cattle. The foot becomes dry and feverish, and
cracks in the opening of the hoof. In this opening
the rough blades of grass and dirt collect, and the foot
generally festers, and swells very much. Our mode
of treating it was, to wash the foot with strong soap
suds, scrape or cut away all the diseased flesh, and
then pour boiling pitch or tar upon the sore. If applied
early this remedy will cure. Should the heel become
worn out, apply tar or pitch, and singe with a hot iron.
At our encampment to-night we have abundance of
wood for fuel.

[21] *June* 8. We advanced to-day about twelve
miles. The bottom near our camp is narrow, but
abounds in timber, being covered with ash; it, however, affords poor grazing. So far as we have traveled
along the Platte, we find numerous islands in the river,
and some of them quite large. In the evening a young
man, named Foster,[28] was wounded by the accidental
discharge of a gun. The loaded weapon, from which
its owner had neglected to remove the cap, was placed
at the tail of a wagon; as some one was taking out a
tent-cloth, the gun was knocked down, and went off.
The ball passed through a spoke of the wagon-wheel,

[28] John Foster was born in Ohio in 1822, removed to Missouri in early
life, and in 1897 was still residing in Oregon.— ED.

struck the felloe, and glanced. Foster was walking some two rods from the wagon, when the half spent ball struck him in the back, near the spine; and, entering between the skin and the ribs, came out about three inches from where it entered, making merely a flesh wound. A small fragment of the ball had lodged in his arm.

June 9. The morning is rainy. To-day we passed Stephens' company, which passed us on yesterday. Our dissensions are all healed; and they have decided to act upon our plan.

June 10. Yesterday we traveled fifteen miles; to-day the same distance. We find the grazing continues poor. In getting to our encampment, we passed through a large dog town. These singular communities may be seen often, along the banks of the Platte, occupying various areas, from one to five hundred acres. The one in question covered some two hundred or three hundred acres. The prairie-dog is something larger than a common sized gray squirrel, of a dun color; the head resembles that of a bull dog: the tail is about three inches in length. Their food is prairie grass. Like rabbits, they burrow in the ground, throwing out heaps of earth, and often large stones, which remain at the mouth of their holes. The entrance to their burrows is about four inches in diameter, and runs obliquely into the earth about three feet, when the holes ramify in every direction and connect with each other on every side. Some kind of police seems to be observed among them; for at the approach of man, one of the dogs will run to the entrance of a burrow, and, squatting down, utter a shrill bark. At once, the smaller part of the community will retreat to their holes, while numbers of the larger dogs will squat, like the first, at their doors, and unite in the barking. A near approach drives them all under ground. It is singular, [22] but true, that the little screech-owl and the rattlesnake keep them company in their burrows. I have frequently seen the owls, but not the snake, with them. The mountaineers, however, inform me, that they often catch all three in the same hole. The dog is eaten by the Indians, with quite a relish; and often by the mountaineers. I am not prepared to speak of its qualities as an article of food.

During the night, a mule, belonging to a Mr. Risley,[20] of our company, broke from its tether, and in attempting to secure it, its owner was repeatedly shot at by the guard; but, fortunately, was not hit. He had run from his tent without having been perceived by the guard, and was crawling over the ground, endeavoring to seize the trail rope, which was tied to his mule's neck. The guard mistook him for an Indian, trying to steal horses, and called to him several times; but a high wind blowing he did not hear. The guard leveled and fired, but his gun did not go off. Another guard, standing near, presented his piece and fired; the cap burst, without discharging the load. The first guard, by this time prepared, fired a second time, without effect. By this

---

[20] Orville Risley was born in New York state about 1807. In early life he removed to Ohio, where he joined the Oregon emigrants of 1845. Upon reaching the Willamette valley he took up land in Clackamas County, and later was a merchant at Lafayette. In his last years he resided principally at Portland, where he was known as Judge Risley, from having once held the office of justice of the peace. His death occurred at his Clackamas farm in 1884.— ED.

time the camp was roused, and nearly all seized their fire-arms, when we discovered that the supposed Indian was one of our own party. We regarded it as providential that the man escaped, as the guard was a good shot, and his mark was not more than eighty yards distant. This incident made us somewhat more cautious about leaving the camp, without notifying the guard.

June 11. To-day we traveled ten or twelve miles. Six miles brought us to the lower crossing of Platte river, which is five or six miles above the forks, and where the high ground commences between the two streams. There is a trail which turns over the bluff to the left; we however took the right, and crossed the river.[37] The south fork is at this place about one fourth of a mile wide, and from one to three feet deep, with a sandy bottom, which made the fording so heavy that we were compelled to double teams. The water through the day is warm; but as the nights are cool, it is quite cool enough in the morning. On the west bank of the river was encamped Brown's company, which passed us whilst we were organizing at Caw River. We passed them, and proceeded along the west side of the south fork, and encamped on the river bank. At night our hunters brought in some buffalo meat.

June 13. Yesterday we followed the river about thirteen miles, and encamped on its bank, where the road between the [23] two forks strikes across the ridge toward the North fork. To-day we have followed that route: directly across, the distance does not exceed four miles: but the road runs obliquely between the two streams, and reaches the North fork about nine

---

[37] For the fords of the South Platte see our volume xxi, p. 173, note 27.— ED.

miles from our last camp. We found quite a hill to descend, as the road runs up the bottom a half mile and then ascends the bluff. Emigrants should keep the bluff sixteen or seventeen miles. We descended a ravine and rested on the bank of the river.

June 15. Yesterday we advanced eight miles, and halted to wash and rest our teams. We have remained all this day in camp. At daylight a herd of buffalo approached near the camp; they were crossing the river, but as soon as they caught the scent, they retreated to the other side. It was a laughable sight to see them running in the water. Some of our men having been out with their guns, returned at noon overloaded with buffalo meat. We then commenced jerking it. This is a process resorted to for want of time or means to cure meat by salting. The meat is sliced thin, and a scaffold prepared, by setting forks in the ground, about three feet high, and laying small poles or sticks crosswise upon them. The meat is laid upon those pieces, and a slow fire built beneath; the heat and smoke completes the process in half a day; and with an occasional sunning the meat will keep for months.

An unoccupied spectator, who could have beheld our camp to-day, would think it a singular spectacle. The hunters returning with the spoil; some erecting scaffolds, and others drying the meat. Of the women, some were washing, some ironing, some baking. At two of the tents the fiddle was employed in uttering its unaccustomed voice among the solitudes of the Platte; at one tent I heard singing; at others the occupants were engaged in reading, some the Bible, others poring over novels. While all this was going on, that nothing might be wanting to complete the harmony of the scene, a Campbellite preacher, named Foster, was reading a hymn, preparatory to religious worship. The fiddles were silenced, and those who had been occupied with that amusement, betook themselves to cards. Such is but a miniature of the great world we had left behind us, when we crossed the line that separates civilized man from the wilderness. But even here the variety of occupation, the active exercise of body and mind, either in labor or pleasure, the commingling of evil and good, show that the likeness is a true one.

[24] *June* 17. On our travel of eight miles, yesterday, we found the bluffs quite high, often approaching with their rocky fronts to the water's edge, and now and then a cedar nodding at the top. Our camp, last night, was in a cedar and ash grove, with a high, frowning bluff overhanging us; but a wide bottom, with fine grass around us, and near at hand an excellent spring. To-day five miles over the ridge brought us to Ash Hollow. Here the trail, which follows the east side of the South fork of Platte, from where we crossed it, connects with this trail.[34] The road then turns down Ash Hollow to the river; a quarter of a mile from the latter is a fine spring, and around it wood and grass in abundance. Our road, to-day, has been very sandy. The bluffs are generally rocky, at times presenting perpendicular cliffs of three hundred feet high. We passed two companies, both of which we had before passed; but whilst we were lying by on the North fork,

[34] Ash Hollow, called by Frémont Coulée des Frênes, was a well known landmark, where the Oregon Trail crossed the North Platte. It is now known as Ash Creek, in Deuel County, Nebraska.— ED.

they had traveled up the South fork and descended Ash Hollow.

June 18. We met a company of mountaineers from Fort Laramie, who had started for the settlements early in the season, with flat-boats loaded with buffalo robes, and other articles of Indian traffic. The river became so low, that they were obliged to lay by; part of the company had returned to the fort for teams; others were at the boat landing, while fifteen of the party were footing their way to the States. They were a jolly set of fellows. Four wagons joined us from one of the other divisions, and among them was John Nelson, with his family, formerly of Franklin county, Indiana. We traveled fifteen miles, passing Captain Smith's company.

June 19. Five miles, to-day, brought us to Spring creek; eleven miles further to another creek, the name of which I could not ascertain; there we encamped, opposite the Solitary Tower.[19] This singular natural object is a stupendous pile of sand and clay, so cemented as to resemble stone, but which crumbles away at the slightest touch. I conceive it is about seven miles distant from the mouth of the creek; though it appears to be not more than three. The height of this tower is somewhere between six hundred and eight hundred feet from the level of the river. Viewed from the road, the beholder might easily imagine he was gazing upon

[19] Spring Creek was probably the one now known as Rush, formed by springs issuing in Cheyenne County, Nebraska. The second creek was that now entitled Pumpkinseed. In the days of trail-travelling it was called Gonneville, from a trapper who had been killed thereon. The Solitary Tower is on its bank — a huge mass of indurated clay, more frequently known as the Court House or the Castle.— ED.

some ancient structure of the old world. A nearer approach dispels the illusion, and it looks, as it is, rough and unseemly. It can be ascended, at its north side, by clambering up the rock; holes having been cut in its face for that purpose. The second, or [25] main bench, can be ascended with greater ease at an opening on the south side, where the water has washed out a crevice large enough to admit the body; so that by pushing against the sides of the crevice one can force himself upward fifteen or twenty feet, which places the adventurer on the slope of the second bench. Passing round the eastern point of the tower, the ascent may be continued up its north face. A stream of water runs along the north-eastern side, some twenty rods distant from the tower; and deep ravines are cut out by the washing of the water from the tower to the creek. Near by stands another pile of materials, similar to that composing the tower, but neither so large nor so high. The bluffs in this vicinity appear to be of the same material. Between this tower and the river stretches out a rolling plain, barren and desolate enough.

June 20. Traveling fourteen miles, we halted in the neighborhood of the Chimney Rock. This is a sharp-pointed rock, of much the same material as the Solitary Tower, standing at the base of the bluff, and four or five miles from the road. It is visible at a distance of thirty miles, and has the unpoetical appearance of a hay-stack, with a pole running far above its top.[20]

June 24. Since the 20th we have traveled about

---

[20] For a note on Chimney Rock consult De Smet's *Letters* in our volume xxvii, p. 219, note 89. See also engraving in Frémont's "Exploring Tour," *Senate Docs.*, 28 Cong., 2 sess., 174, p. 38.— Ed.

sixty-two miles, and are now at Fort Laramie; making our whole travel from Independence about six hundred and thirty miles. On the 22d we passed over Scott's Bluffs, where we found a good spring, and abundance of wood and grass. A melancholy tradition accounts for the name of this spot. A party who had been trading with the Indians were returning to the States and encountering a band of hostile savages, were robbed of their peltries and food. As they struggled homeward, one of the number, named Scott, fell sick and could not travel. The others remained with him, until the sufferer, despairing of ever beholding his home, prevailed on his companions to abandon him. They left him alone in the wilderness, several miles from this spot. Here human bones were afterwards found; and, supposing he had crawled here and died, the subsequent travelers have given his name to the neighboring bluff.[51]

June 25. Our camp is stationary to-day; part of the emigrants are shoeing their horses and oxen; others are trading at the fort and with the Indians. Flour, sugar, coffee, tea, tobacco, powder and lead, sell readily, at high prices. In the [26] afternoon we gave the Indians a feast, and held a long *talk* with them. Each family, as they could best spare it, contributed a portion of bread, meat, coffee or sugar, which being cooked, a table was set by spreading buffalo skins upon the ground, and arranging the provisions upon them.

[51] This story is told with variations by many writers, notably Washington Irving in his *Rocky Mountains* (Philadelphia, 1837), i, pp. 45, 46. The event appears to have occurred about 1830. The range of bluffs, about nine hundred yards in length, still retains the name. It is situated on the western borders of Nebraska, in a county of the same name.— ED.

Around this attractive board, the Indian chiefs and
their principal men seated themselves, occupying one
fourth of the circle; the remainder of the male Indians
made out the semi-circle; the rest of the circle was
completed by the whites. The squaws and younger
Indians formed an outer semi-circular row immediately
behind their dusky lords and fathers. Two stout young
warriors were now designated as waiters, and all the
preparations being completed, the Indian chiefs and
principal men shook hands, and at a signal the white
chief performed the same ceremony, commencing with
the principal chief, and saluting him and those of his
followers who composed the first division of the circle;
the others being considered inferiors, were not thus noticed.

The talk preceded the dinner. A trader acted as
interpreter. The chief informed us, that "a long while
ago some white chiefs passed up the Missouri, through
his country, saying they were the red man's friends,
and that as the red man found them, so would he find
all the other pale faces. This country belongs to the red
man, but his white brethren travels through, shooting
the game and scaring it away. Thus the Indian loses
all that he depends upon to support his wives and children. The children of the red man cry for food, but
there is no food. But on the other hand, the Indian
profits by the trade with the white man. He was glad
to see us and meet us as friends. It was the custom
when the pale faces passed through his country, to make
presents to the Indians of powder, lead, &c. His
tribe was very numerous, but the most of the people
had gone to the mountains to hunt. Before the white
man came, the game was tame, and easily caught, with

the bow and arrow. Now the white man has frightened
it, and the red man must go to the mountains. The red
man needed long guns." This, with much more of the
like, made up the talk of the chief, when a reply from
our side was expected.

As it devolved on me to play the part of the white
chief, I told my red brethren, that we were journeying
to the great waters of the west. Our great father owned
a large country there, and we were going to settle upon
it. For this purpose we brought with us our wives
and little ones. We were compelled [27] to pass through
the red man's country, but we traveled as friends, and
not as enemies. As friends we feasted them, shook
them by the hand, and smoked with them the pipe of
peace. They must know that we came among them
as friends, for we brought with us our wives and children. The red man does not take his squaws into battle:
neither does the pale face. But friendly as we felt, we
were ready for enemies; and if molested, we should
punish the offenders. Some of us expected to return.
Our fathers, our brothers and our children were coming behind us, and we hoped the red man would treat
them kindly. We did not expect to meet so many of
them; we were glad to see them, and to hear that they
were the white man's friends. We met peacefully —
so let us part. We had set them a feast, and were glad
to hold a talk with them; but we were not traders, and
had no powder or ball to give them. We were going
to plough and to plant the ground, and had nothing
more than we needed for ourselves. We told them to
eat what was before them, and be satisfied; and that
we had nothing more to say.

The two Indian servants began their services by placing a tin cup before each of the guests, always waiting first upon the chiefs; they then distributed the bread and cakes, until each person had as much as it was supposed he would eat; the remainder being delivered to two squaws, who in like manner served the squaws and children. The waiters then distributed the meat and coffee. All was order. No one touched the food before him until all were served, when at a signal from the chief the eating began. Having filled themselves, the Indians retired, taking with them all that they were unable to eat.

This is a branch of the Sioux nation, and those living in this region number near fifteen hundred lodges.[22] They are a healthy, athletic, good-looking set of men, and have according to the Indian code, a respectable sense of honor, but will steal when they can do so without fear of detection. On this occasion, however, we missed nothing but a frying pan, which a squaw slipped under her blanket, and made off with. As it was a trifling loss, we made no complaint to the chief.

Here are two forts. Fort Laramie, situated upon the west side of Laramie's fork, two miles from Platte river, belongs to the North American Fur Company.[23]

---

[22] The usual habitat of the Dakota or Sioux was along the Missouri River or eastward. The Teton Sioux were in the habit of wandering westward for summer hunts, and this was probably a band of the Oglala or Brulé Teton, who frequently were encountered in this region. For the Teton subdivisions see our volume xxii, p. 326, note 287.— ED.

[23] The succession of trading posts on the Laramie branch of Platte River is somewhat confusing, due to differences in nomenclature. Consult our volume xxi, p. 181, note 30. The fort here described appears to be the new Fort Laramie (which must thus have been built in 1845, not 1846). Alexander Culbertson, who was at one time in command for the American Fur

The fort is built of *adobes*. The walls are about two feet thick, and twelve or fourteen feet high, the tops being picketed or spiked. Posts are planted in these walls, and support the timber for the roof. [28] They are then covered with mud. In the centre is an open square, perhaps twenty-five yards each way, along the sides of which are ranged the dwellings, store rooms, smith shop, carpenter's shop, offices, &c., all fronting upon the inner area. There are two principal entrances; one at the north, the other at the south. On the eastern side is an additional wall, connected at its extremities with the first, enclosing ground for stables and *carrell*. This enclosure has a gateway upon its south side, and a passage into the square of the principal enclosure. At a short distance from the fort is a field of about four acres, in which, by way of experiment, corn is planted; but from its present appearance it will probably prove a failure. Fort John stands about a mile below Fort Laramie, and is built of the same material as the latter, but is not so extensive. Its present occupants are a company from St. Louis.[34]

June 26. This day, leaving Fort Laramie behind us, we advanced along the bank of the river, into the vast region that was still between us and our destination. After moving five miles, we found a good spot for a camp, and as our teams still required rest, we

Company, says that this post cost $10,000, and was the best built stronghold in the company's possession. Fort John was the old American Fur Company's post. How a rival company had secured it, seems a mystery; possibly Palmer has confused it with Fort Platte, which Frémont notes in 1842 at the mouth of the Laramie, belonging to Sybille, Adams, and Company. See his "Exploring Tour" (cited in note 30, *ante*), p. 35.— ED.

[34] Since the above was written, the North American Fur Company has purchased Fort John, and demolished it.— PALMER.

halted and encamped, and determined to repose until Saturday the 28th.

June 28. A drive of ten miles brought us to Big Spring, a creek which bursts out at the base of a hill, and runs down a sandy hollow. The spring is one fourth of a mile below the road. We found the water too warm to be palatable.[35] Five miles beyond the creek the road forks; we took the right hand trail, which is the best of the two, and traversed the Black Hills, as they are called. The season has been so dry that vegetation is literally parched up; of course the grazing is miserable. After proceeding eighteen miles we encamped on Bitter Cottonwood.[36]

June 29. To-day we find the country very rough, though our road is not bad. In the morning some of our cattle were missing, and four of the company started back to hunt for them. At the end of fourteen miles we rested at Horse Shoe creek, a beautiful stream of clear water, lined with trees, and with wide bottoms on each side, covered with excellent grass. At this point our road was about three miles from the river.[37]

July 1. As the men who left the company on the 29th, to look for our lost cattle, were not returned, we remained in [29] camp yesterday. Game seemed abundant along the creek, and our efforts to profit by it were

[35] The trail lay back from the river, for some distance above Fort Laramie. Big Spring was frequently known as Warm Spring, and the coulée, in Laramie County, Wyoming, still retains the name of Warm Spring Cañon.— ED.

[36] On the general use of the term Black Hills see our volume xxiii, p. 244, note 204. The stream called Fourche Amère (bitter fork) by Frémont is now known simply as Cottonwood Creek.— ED.

[37] Retaining the same name, Horseshoe Creek is a considerable wooded stream in western Laramie County, Wyoming.— ED.

rewarded with three elk and three deer. To-day our cattle hunters still remain behind. We sent back a reinforcement, and hitching up our teams advanced about sixteen miles. Eight miles brought us to the Dalles of Platte, where the river bursts through a mountain spur. Perpendicular cliffs, rising abruptly from the water, five hundred or six hundred feet high, form the left bank of the river. These cliffs present various strata, some resembling flint, others like marble, lime, &c. The most interesting feature of these magnificent masses, is the variety of colors that are presented; yellow, red, black and white, and all the shades between, as they blend and are lost in each other. On the top nods a tuft of scrubby cedars. Upon the south side, a narrow slope between the bluff and river, affords a pass for a footman along the water's edge, while beyond the bluff rises abruptly. Frequently cedar and wild sage is to be seen. I walked up the river a distance of half a mile, when I reached a spot where the rocks had tumbled down, and found something of a slope, by which I could, with the assistance of a long pole, and another person sometimes pushing and then pulling, ascend; we succeeded in clambering up to the top — which proved to be a naked, rough black rock, with here and there a scrubby cedar and wild sage bush. It appeared to be a place of resort for mountain sheep and bears. We followed this ridge south to where it gradually descended to the road. The river in this *kanyon* is about one hundred and fifty yards wide, and looks deep."[38] At the eastern end of this *kanyon* comes in a stream which,

[38] This is now known as Lower Platte Cañon, and is traversed by the Wyoming branch of the Colorado and Southern Railway.— ED.

from appearance, conveys torrents of water at certain seasons of the year. Here, too, is a very good camp. By going up the right hand branch five or six miles, then turning to the right up one of the ridges, and crossing a small branch (which joins the river six or seven miles above the *kanyon*) and striking the road on the ridge three miles east of the Big Timber creek, a saving might be made of at least ten miles travel. We did not travel this route; but, from the appearance of the country, there would be no difficulty.

July 2. This day we traveled about sixteen miles. The road left the river bottom soon after we started. A trail, however, crosses the bottom for about two miles, and then winds back to the hill. The nearest road is up a small sandy ravine, for two miles, then turn to the right up a ridge, and follow this ridge for eight or ten miles. At the distance of thirteen [30] or fourteen miles, the road which turned to the left near the Big Spring, connects with this. The road then turns down the hill to the right, into a dry branch, which it descends to Big Timber creek, where we encamped."

July 3. This day we traveled about fifteen miles. Six miles brought us to a small branch, where is a good camp. Near this branch there is abundance of marble, variegated with blue and red, but it is full of seams. The hills in this vicinity are of the red shale formation. In the mountain near by is stone coal. The hills were generally covered with grass. The streams are lined

[20] Big Timber Creek was called La Fourche Boisée by Frémont; more frequently it was known by the name it still retains — La Bonté Creek, in Converse County, Wyoming. The cut-off recommended by Palmer would be by way of Elkhorn Creek and an affluent of La Bonté.— ED.

with cotton wood, willow and boxalder. The road was very dusty.

July 4. We traveled about fifteen miles to-day, the road generally good, with a few difficult places. Two wagons upset, but little damage was done. We crossed several beautiful streams flowing from the Black hills; they are lined with timber. To-day, as on yesterday, we found abundance of red, yellow and black currants, with some gooseberries, along the streams.

July 5. We this day traveled about twelve miles. Three miles brought us to Deer creek.⁴⁰ Here is an excellent camp ground. Some very good bottom land. The banks are lined with timber. Stone coal was found near the road. This would be a suitable place for a fort, as the soil and timber is better than is generally found along the upper Platte. Game in abundance, such as elk, buffalo, deer, antelope and bear. The timber is chiefly cotton wood, but there is pine on the mountains within ten or twelve miles. The road was generally along the river bottom, and much of the way extremely barren. We encamped on the bank of the river.

July 6. In traveling through the sand and hot sun, our wagon tires had become loose; and we had wedged until the tire would no longer remain on the wheels. One or two axletrees and tongues had been broken, and we found it necessary to encamp and repair them. For this purpose all hands were busily em-

---

⁴⁰ Deer Creek is the largest southern affluent of the Platte, between the Laramie and the Sweetwater. It is well-timbered, and its mouth was a familiar camping place on the Oregon Trail. It is in the western part of Converse County, Wyoming, about 770 miles from the starting point at Independence.— ED.

ployed. We had neither bellows nor anvil, and of course could not cut and weld tire. But as a substitute, we took off the tire, shaved thin hoops and tacked them on the felloes, heated our tire and replaced it. This we found to answer a good purpose.

July 7. This day we traveled about ten miles. In crossing a small ravine, an axletree of one of the wagons was broken. [31] The road is mostly on the river bottom. Much of the country is barren.

July 8. Six miles travel brought us to the crossing of the north fork of the Platte. At 1 o'clock, P. M. all were safely over, and we proceeded up half a mile to a grove of timber and encamped.[41] Near the crossing was encamped Colonel Kearney's regiment of dragoons, on their return from the South Pass. Many of them were sick.

July 9. We traveled about ten miles this day, and encamped at the Mineral Spring. The road leaves the Platte at the crossing, and passes over the *Red Buttes*.[42] The plains in this region are literally covered with buffalo.

July 10. To-day we traveled about ten miles. The range is very poor, and it has become necessary to divide into small parties, in order to procure forage for our cattle. Out of the company five divisions were formed. In my division we had eleven wagons; and we travel

[41] The best ford in this stretch of the river; it averaged only about three feet in depth at the ordinary stage of water, and its width varied from eight hundred to fifteen hundred feet. It was a little above the present town of Casper, Wyoming.— ED.

[42] The Mineral Spring was usually called Red Spring, near Poison Spider Creek, and shows traces of petroleum. For a description of Red Buttes see our volume xxi, p. 183.— ED.

more expeditiously, with but little difficulty in finding grass for our cattle.

July 11. We this day traveled about twelve miles. Soon after starting we passed an excellent spring: it is to the right of the road, in a thicket of willows. One fourth of a mile further the road ascends a hill, winds round and passes several marshy springs. The grass is very good, but is confined to patches. Our camp was on a small branch running into the Sweet Water.

(*July* 12. This day we arrived at *Independence Rock*. This is a solitary pile of gray granite, standing in an open plain. It is about one-eighth of a mile long and some six or eight rods wide, and is elevated about sixty or seventy feet above the plain. On the north-eastern side the slope is sufficiently gradual to be easily ascended. Portions of it are covered with inscriptions of the names of travelers, with the dates of their arrival — some carved, some in black paint, and others in red.) Sweet Water, a stream heading in the Wind River Mountains, and entering the Platte, runs immediately along its southern side, leaving a strip of some twenty or thirty feet of grassy plain between the base of the rock and the creek. We encamped two miles above the rock, having traveled about thirteen miles.[a]

July 13. We traveled about thirteen miles this day. Three miles brought us to the *Gap*, or *Devil's Gate*, as it is sometimes called. The Sweet Water breaks through a spur of the mountain, which from appearance is four or five hundred feet high. [32] On the south side the rocks project over the stream, but on the north slope

<hr>

[a] For Independence Rock and Sweetwater River see our volume xxi, p. 53, notes 33, 34.— ED.

back a little. The whole mountain is a mass of gray granite rock, destitute of vegetation, save an occasional scrubby cedar or bush of artemisia. From where the creek enters to where it emerges from this *kanyon* is three or four hundred yards. The water rushes through like a torrent. At the distance of one hundred rods south of this is the Gap, where the road passes; but the rock is not so high. South of this again is another gap, perhaps half or three-fourths of a mile wide. The rocks there rise mountain high.⁴⁴ South-west of this is a valley extending as far as the eye can penetrate. As the road passes through this gap, it bears to the right, up the valley of the Sweet Water.

July 14. This day we traveled about twenty-two miles. The road sometimes leaves the creek for several miles, and passes over a barren, sandy plain; no kind of vegetation but the wild sage. We this day met a party of men from California and Oregon. A portion of those from California spoke unfavorably of that country; and those from Oregon spoke highly of the latter country. On this day's march we came in sight of the long-looked-for snow-capped mountains. They were the Wind River Mountains. On our right is a mass of naked rock; on our left and to the distance of ten or twelve miles is a high range of mountains, mostly covered with timber; whilst in the valley there is no timber, and much of the plain entirely destitute of vegetation. We encamped near the Narrows.⁴⁵

⁴⁴ For this gap, or cañon, see De Smet's *Letters* in our volume xxvii, p. 241, note 113.— ED.

⁴⁵ The Wind River Mountains are noted in our volume xxi, p. 184, note 35. The trail along the Sweetwater is for the most part over a rough, undulating prairie, but at times the hills force the road close to the river valley. At one

July 15. We traveled about eleven miles to-day. There are two trails, which diverge below the Narrows. The nearest and best is that to the right up the creek, crossing it several times; they unite again near where we encamped. The road was good, but as usual very dusty. Our hunters wounded a buffalo, and drove him into camp. About twenty men ran to meet him. He gave them battle. They fired a volley that brought him to his knees, and whilst in that position Mr. Creighton (a young man from Ohio) ran across the creek, intending to shoot the animal in the head. When Creighton had approached within ten or twelve feet, the enraged animal sprung to his feet and made at him. Creighton wheeled and "split" for the camp; the buffalo pursuing to near the bank of the creek, where he stopped. By this time others had arrived with guns, and the buffalo was compelled to yield. In the "spree" one of my horses was shot with a ball in the [33] knee; no bones were broken, and he was able to travel, but he was a long time very lame.

July 16. This day we traveled about twenty-six miles. Four miles brought us to a marshy bottom, where was very good grass. In the centre of this quagmire and near where the road crosses the bottom is a spring of good water. Eight miles brought us to a small stream; but little grass. Six miles brought us to Sweet Water; crossed and left it and struck it again in six or eight miles. The grass here is good. Wild sage was our only fuel. This night there was a heavy frost.

---

place, about thirty-six miles above the river's mouth, the route grows rugged and crosses the river three times. This was usually known as the Three Crossings, and is probably the stretch that Palmer calls the Narrows.— ED.

July 17. Our cattle being much fatigued, we drove but five miles. The road is up the creek bottom, which is mostly covered with grass. A heavy frost: ice formed in buckets one-fourth of an inch thick. We here found the celebrated mountaineer Walker, who was traveling to Bridger's fort.[46]

July 18. We traveled about twenty-two miles this day. The road ascends the bluff and winds among rocky hills for six miles, passing over ledges that are entirely naked for rods. The appearance of the country is extremely barren. We passed several rivulets where small parties may obtain grazing for their stock. The day has been quite cold. The Wind River Mountains are on our right, about twenty miles distant. They presented a most grand appearance. Huge masses of ice and snow piled up peak upon peak, with large bodies of timber covering portions of the mountains. We viewed the southern termination of this range;

[46] Joseph R. Walker was born (1798) in Tennessee. In early life he migrated to the Missouri frontier, and for many years was a trapper and trader in the direction of Santa Fé. Once he was captured by the Mexicans, and afterwards participated in a battle between them and the Pawnee Indians. In 1832 Captain Bonneville secured Walker as a member of his trading party, and the following year sent him on an expedition that explored a route from Salt Lake to California, through Walker's Pass, which took its name from this explorer. On this journey he claimed first of any American to have seen the Yosemite. His knowledge of the West brought his services in demand as a guide or pilot. In 1843 he led out a small party of emigrants. From Bridger's Fort, whither he was going when met by Palmer, he joined Frémont's third exploring expedition, and was sent forward with a portion of the party by his former route of 1833. The junction with his chief's party was made after the latter's visit to Monterey. Walker, however, did not remain to take part in the events that led to the American conquest of California, but started back to the states with a drove of California horses for sale, and was again at Fort Bridger in July, 1846. For twenty years longer he continued his vagrant life in the mountains, finally settling (1866-67) in Contra Costa County, California, where he died in 1876.— ED.

but they extend to the north further than the eye can penetrate. The country between us and the mountains is rolling, and much of it apparently barren. Hard frost.

July 19. This morning we ascended the bank on the south side of Sweet Water. Six miles brought us again to the creek, where is good grass in the bottom and willow for fuel. We crossed, went up the bottom two miles, and crossed back and left the Sweet Water. *This day we passed over the dividing ridge which separates the waters flowing into the Atlantic from those which find their way into the Pacific Ocean.* WE HAD REACHED THE SUMMIT OF THE ROCKY MOUNTAINS. Six miles brought us to a spring, the waters of which run into Green river, or the great Colorado of the west.[47]— Here, then, we hailed OREGON. Here we found a bottom covered with good grass, where we halted until four o'clock, P. M., when we again hitched up and took the plain for Little Sandy. Ten miles brought us to a dry branch, where by digging to the [34] depth of one foot we procured water; but it was brackish, and had a very unpleasant taste. A white sediment, such as we had noticed elsewhere on the road, covered the surface of the ground. Ten miles more brought us to Little Sandy, which we reached at one o'clock in the night, having traveled thirty-one miles. The road was over a barren plain of light sand, and was very dusty. From the spring to Little Sandy there is no

---

[47] For South Pass and Green River see our volume xxi, pp. 58-60, notes 37, 38.

The springs were known as Pacific Springs, running into a creek of that name, affluent of the Big Sandy in Fremont County, Wyoming.— ED.

vegetation but the wild sage, and it had a withered
appearance. The night was cold, freezing quite hard.
Little Sandy has its source in the Wind river moun-
tains.⁴⁸ Along this stream is a narrow bottom, covered
with grass and willows. We are now out of the range
of · the buffalo, and although not often mentioned, we
have seen thousands of these huge animals. There
have been so many companies of emigrants in advance
of us, that they have frightened the buffalo from the
road. We daily see hundreds of antelope.

July 20. This day we traveled about thirteen miles,
to Big Sandy. The road was over a level sandy plain,
covered with wild sage. At Little Sandy the road
forks — one taking to the right and striking Big Sandy
in six miles, and thence forty miles to Green river, striking the latter some thirty or forty miles above the lower
ford, and thence to Big Bear river, striking it about
fifteen miles below the old road. By taking this trail
two and a half days' travel may be saved; but in the
forty miles between Big Sandy and Green river there
is no water, and but little grass. Camps may be had
within reasonable distances between Green and Bear
rivers.⁴⁹ The left hand trail, which we took, twelve
miles from Little Sandy strikes the Big Sandy, follows
down it and strikes Green river above the mouth of
Big Sandy.

July 21. We traveled about fourteen miles to-day.
Six miles brought us to Green river, or Colorado. This

⁴⁸ The dry branch is known as Dry Sandy Creek. For the Little Sandy
see our volume xxi, p. 187, note 36.— ED.

⁴⁹ This was known as Sublette's Cut-off; see De Smet's *Letters* in our volume
xxvii, p. 242, note 115.— ED.

is a beautiful clear stream, about one hundred yards
wide, with a rapid current over a gravelly bottom. It
flows through a barren, sandy country; occasionally
the bottoms spread to a mile in width, covered with
grass. There is mostly a belt of timber along the banks
of the stream.— Emigrants had been in the habit of
crossing the river on rafts. We succeeded in finding
a place where, by hoisting up the wagon-beds six inches,
we could ford the river without damaging our goods.
This was done by cutting poles and placing them under
the wagon-beds, and in one hour we were all safely
over. We proceeded down the river eight miles, and
encamped in a grove near some [35] cabins built by a
party of traders. There is an abundance of fish in this
stream, and we had great sport in fishing.

July 23. This day we traveled about fifteen miles.
The road leaves Green river near our camp, and passes
over a high, barren country, to Black's fork; this we
followed up some four miles and encamped.[59] As upon
other streams, there is occasionally a grassy bottom
with a little cotton wood and willow brush. Snowy
mountains to be seen in the south.

July 24. We traveled, to-day, about fourteen miles,
over a barren country, crossing the creek several times.
We noticed a number of piles of stone and earth, some
forty or fifty feet high, scattered in different directions,

---

[59] At this point, Green River bears considerably east of south, the trail
therefore turns southwest, striking Black Fork of Green, not far from the
present Granger, Wyoming, at the junction of the Union Pacific and Oregon
Short Line railways. Black Fork rises in the extreme southeastern corner of
Wyoming, flows northeast, thence east and southeast, entering the Green in
Sweetwater County. It is a shallow, somewhat sluggish stream, passing through
an alkaline country.— ED.

giving the appearance of the general surface having been worn away to that extent by the ravages of time and the elements.

July 25. This day we traveled about sixteen miles, crossed the creek several times, and encamped near Fort Bridger. This is a trading fort owned by Bridger and Bascus. It is built of poles and daubed with mud; it is a shabby concern.[61] Here are about twenty-five lodges of Indians, or rather white trappers' lodges occupied by their Indian wives. They have a good supply of robes, dressed deer, elk and antelope skins, coats, pants, moccasins, and other Indian fixens, which they trade low for flour, pork, powder, lead, blankets, butcher-knives, spirits, hats, ready made clothes, coffee, sugar, &c. They ask for a horse from twenty-five to fifty dollars, in trade. Their wives are mostly of the Pyentes and Snake Indians.[62] They have a herd

[61] The site of Fort Bridger was chosen by its founder as the best station for trade with emigrants following the Oregon Trail. Its building (1843) marked an epoch in Western emigration, showing the importance of trade with the increasing number of travellers. The place was an oasis in the desert-like neighborhood, the stream of Black Fork coming from the Unita Mountains, and in this wooded valley dividing into several branches. In 1854 Bridger sold his post to a Mormon named Lewis Robinson, who maintained it until 1858, when United States troops wintering during the Mormon campaign built at this site a government post, also known as Fort Bridger, which was garrisoned about twenty years longer. For Bridger, the founder, see De Smet's *Letters,* in our volume xxvii, p. 299, note 156. His partner was Louis Vasques (not Bascus), a Mexican who for many years had been a mountain man. For some time he was in partnership with Sublette in a trading post on the South Platte. About 1840 he entered into partnership with Bridger, and is remembered to have lived with some luxury, riding about the country near Fort Bridger in a coach and four. See Wyoming Historical Society *Collections,* i, p. 68.— ED.

[62] For the Snake (Shoshoni) Indians, see our volume v, p. 227, note 123. The Paiute are referred to in our volume xviii, p. 140, note 70; also in De Smet's *Letters,* in our volume xxvii, pp. 165, 167, notes 35, 38.— ED.

of cattle, twenty-five or thirty goats and some sheep. They generally abandon this fort during the winter months. At this place the bottoms are wide, and covered with good grass. Cotton wood timber in plenty. The stream abounds with trout.

July 26. Remained at the fort the whole of this day.

July 27. We traveled about eight miles, to-day, to Little Muddy. The grazing and water bad. Several bad hills.

July 28. To-day we traveled about sixteen miles. Ten miles brought us to the Big Muddy.⁴⁸ Country barren. Our course is up the Big Muddy, and nearly north. Encamped on the creek. Very poor grazing. This is a limestone country.

July 29. This day we traveled about sixteen miles. Our course is still up the Muddy. Emigrants would do well to push on up to near the head of this creek, as the grass is good, [36] and there are excellent springs of water. The country is very rough. We saw a few beaver dams.

July 30. We traveled about twenty-five miles this day. Twelve miles brought us to the dividing ridge between the waters of Green and Bear rivers. The ridge is high, but the ascent is not difficult. From this ridge the scenery is most delightful. In one view is the meanders of Muddy creek. Two companies with large herds of cattle are winding their way up the valley.

---

⁴⁸ By the Little Muddy, Palmer refers to the stream now known as the Muddy, a branch of Black Fork, which would be reached in about eight miles from Fort Bridger, by travelling northwest. Palmer's " Big Muddy " is the stream usually known as Ham's Fork, for which see our volume xxi, p. 197, note 43.— ED.

The bold mountains on either side are very high and rugged. In front and at the distance of twelve miles is the valley of Big Bear river. A ravine at our feet cuts the spur of the mountain, and empties its waters into Bear river. The valley of Bear river is four or five miles wide, with willows along its banks. At a distance beyond the Bear river is a range of high mountains, stretching as far as the eye can reach, their snowy tops glistening in the rays of the sun. The mountains near the trail are rough and have a singular appearance; the earth being of various colors — black, white, red, yellow, and intermediate shades. Occasionally there is a grove of quaking aspen, and a few sour-berry bushes and some cedar. Our camp to-night was on Bear river; the bottom is sandy, and mostly covered with wild sage.[44]

July 31. This day we traveled down Bear river fifteen miles. The bottom is from two to four miles wide, and mostly covered with good grass. The road excellent. We encamped two miles above Smith's fork. The upper road from Green river comes in two miles back.

August 1. We traveled fifteen miles this day. Two miles brought us to Smith's fork. This is a bold, clear, and beautiful stream, coming in from the east. It is about fifteen yards wide, lined with timber and undergrowth.[45] In this stream is an abundance of moun-

[44] The divide between the waters of Green and Bear River may be crossed at several points. Its altitude is about eight thousand feet, and all travellers speak of the wide view. The mountains to the west are those of the Bear River range, running between the arms of the river, for which see our volume xxi, p. 199, note 44.— ED.

[45] The upper road from Green River, usually known as Sublette's road,

tain trout, some of them very large. The road leads
down the bottom of Bear river three miles to Spring
branch, one mile to the Narrows and three miles to the
first crossing of Bear river.⁵⁹ Here are two trails. The
nearest turns to the right up a creek for a mile and a
half, crosses the creek and passes over the hill, and strikes
the other trail at the foot of Big Hill, six miles from
the crossings. The other trail crosses the river, follows
up its bottom round the bend for eight miles, to where
it crosses the river, then follows down the bottom three
miles, and takes up a valley for one mile to the foot
of the Big Hill, where it intersects the other trail. This
is the most level road, but the other is not a bad one.
[37] The hills bordering on Bear river on this day's
travel are very high and rugged; they are covered with
grass. The bottoms are from one to four miles wide.
We saw this day large herds of antelope. We encamped
in the bend of the river, near the second crossings.

August 2. This day we traveled about nineteen
miles. Four or five miles brought us to the big hill or
mountain. It is about half a mile to the top of the first
ridge, and quite steep. The road then turns a few
rods to the right, then to the left down a ravine for three
hundred yards, and then up a ravine for half a mile
to the top of the mountain. We traveled about two

---

comes across by way of Crow Creek, a branch of Ham's Fork, and Sublette
Creek, a tributary of the Bear. Smith's Fork comes almost directly from
the north, its headwaters nearly interlacing with Salt River branch of Lewis
(or Snake) River. It enters Bear River quite near the dividing line between
Wyoming and Idaho.— ED.

⁵⁹ The first crossing of Bear River is just above the mouth of Thomas's
Fork. For a detailed map of this stretch of the road see Frémont's " Exploring Tour " (*op. cit.* in note 30), p. 132.— ED.

miles along the ridge, and then turned to the left down the mountain. It is about one mile to the plain, and generally very steep and stony; but all reached the plain safely, and were truly thankful that they had safely passed one of the most difficult mountains on the road. From the top of this mountain we had a most delightful view of the surrounding country. This is one of the ranges which border this stream. At this place they close in upon both sides so as not to admit of a passage with teams along the river. A road could easily be cut around the point, and save the fatigue of climbing this mountain; the distance would not be materially increased. The valley of Bear river bears off to the north-west, and can be seen a great distance. From the south comes in a broad valley, up which can be seen Bear Lake. A high range of mountains separates it from the river. The outlet of this lake is two or three miles below the narrows made by this mountain.[57] A high range of snow covered mountains can be seen to the south-west. The road strikes the river two miles from the foot of the mountain, at Big Timber. Here is a good camp. Eight miles brought us to a spring branch. The bottom here is wide; a low marsh prevents driving to the river. The grass is good. There is a little timber on the mountains. At Big Timber is a company of trappers and traders attached to Bridger's party.

[57] The big hill is just beyond the bend of the Bear, below Thomas's Fork, and the nearest approach the road makes to the valley of Bear Lake. This lake is evidently the remains of one that occupied a much larger area, as the marshes at its upper end signify. It now measures about nineteen miles in length, with an average width of six, and a depth of from forty to sixty feet. The lower portion of the lake is in Utah and the upper in Idaho. Its waters are noted for their exquisite blue tint.— ED.

August 3. We traveled about fourteen miles, cross-ing a number of spring branches, coming in from the mountains. These branches abound in trout. The ground, for a strip of about four miles, was covered with black crickets of a large size. I saw some that were about three inches in length, and measuring about three-fourths of an inch in diameter; but the common size were two inches in length and one-half or five-eighths of an inch in diameter; their legs were large in pro-portion [38] to the size of their bodies. Some were singing on stalks of wild sage; others crawling in every direction. Our teams made great havoc among them; so numerous were they that we crushed them at every step. As soon as one was killed, others of them would alight upon it and devour it. The bottoms are wide, and covered with grass, and the soil looks well. A few patches of snow were seen upon the mountain some ten miles distant. A portion of the mountain is covered with fine timber. The bottoms are rolling.

August 4. We reached the Soda springs, having traveled about eight miles.[44] The first view we had was of two or three white hillocks or mounds, standing up at different points to the right of the road, and near a grove of cedar and pine timber. One of them is about ten rods long at the base, and three or four rods in width; its elevation is probably twenty-five or thirty feet from the plain in which it is situated. The size of these mounds continually increases, as the water oozes out at different points, and produces a crust which becomes quite hard. The rocks, for miles around, are of the soda formation. Upon these mounds the

[44] For the location of these springs see our volume xxi, p. 200, note 45.—ED.

water is warm. In a small bottom, immediately before reaching the first of these mounds, and about two hundred yards above the road, is a hole about eight feet in diameter; in this is a pool of water, strongly impregnated with soda. I had no means of ascertaining the depth, but believe it to be considerable; at one edge of it the water was boiling and sparkling; it would sometimes swell four inches above the surface. This pool, and others contiguous, affords excellent drinking water; it was cool, and, when sweetened, would compare favourably with any soda water. Just below the mound, and near the grove, is a rapid stream of water, coursing over a rocky bottom, formed by soda. At the crossing of this creek, and below the road, is a morass; and immediately on the bank of the rivulet, is a crevice in the rock, from which a small stream of water issues; this was the best to drink of any I found. After crossing the creek, the distance to the springs generally resorted to is about three-fourths of a mile; they boil up in every direction. Several mounds have been formed, of ten feet in height. The water has found some other passage, and left them to moulder away. The centre or middle of these are concave. The surface of the earth here is some twelve or fifteen feet above the level of the river, the bank of which is of rock, of the soda formation. A grove of cedar and pine timber extends from the river back to [39] the mountain, a distance of two and a half or three miles; the space between the road and the river is covered with grass; but between it and the mountain it is barren of vegetation of any kind. The soda has left a sediment, which is now crumbled and loose, with an occasional mound of ten or twelve feet elevation, but no water running. The river here is about one hundred yards in width, and about eighteen inches in depth, running very rapidly. The soda water is bubbling up in every direction, and sometimes rises six inches above the surface of the river. This bubbling extends for near half a mile. A stream comes in from the north at the western edge of the springs, tumbles over the rocks, and finally into the river. Near where one branch of this falls over the rock (it has several passages where the road crosses it) is a circular basin in the rock, being two feet in diameter at the top, but larger below. It was covered with grass; and, in walking along, I barely avoided stepping into it; whilst at its edge the purling or gurgling of the water, as it boils up, apprized me of its vicinity. The surface of the water is about three feet below the top of the rock. The water is cool, much more so than the water of the springs, and is remarkably clear.

Three hundred yards below the crossing of this branch, and immediately on the bank of the river, is the Steamboat Spring.[10] The water has formed a small cone of about two and a half feet in height, and three feet in diameter, at the base. A hole of six inches in diameter at the top, allows the water to discharge itself. It swells out at intervals of eight or ten seconds, and sometimes flows four or five feet in disjointed fragments. It is lukewarm, and has a milky appearance; but when taken in a vessel becomes as transparent as crystal. It

---

[10] A map of these springs can be found in Frémont's "Exploring Tour" (*op. cit.* in note 30), p. 135. Steamboat Spring is a miniature geyser, an analysis of whose waters is given by Frémont, p. 136.— ED.

produces a sound similar to the puffing of a steamboat, but not quite so deep. It can frequently be heard at the distance of a quarter of a mile. About six feet from this is a small fissure in the rock, which is called the escape-pipe or gas-pipe. It makes a hissing noise, corresponding with the belching of the spring. The gas emitted from this fissure is so strong that it would suffocate a person, holding his head near the ground. To the rear of this, across the road, are mounds fifty or sixty feet in height; these were entirely dry. Up this creek is very good grazing for cattle, but there are found some marshy places contiguous. The bottom upon the opposite side of the river is four or five miles in width, and covered with a good coat of grass. The soil looks good; and if the seasons are not too [40] short, would produce well. The mountain upon the south side is covered with heavy pine timber; on the north side but little timber was observed; what little was noticed consisted principally of scrubby cedars. Antelope found in abundance. The water, in many of the springs, is sufficiently strong to raise bread, equally as well as saleratus or yeast. Were it not for their remote situation, these springs would be much resorted to, especially during the summer months. The country is mountainous, and its altitude so great, that the air is always cool, and consequently must be healthy.

Companies wishing to remain for a length of time at the springs, would pursue a proper course in driving their cattle over the river, as good grazing can thereby be had.

August 5. We traveled about nineteen miles. Five miles brought us to where the road leaves the river,

and bears northward through a valley. The river
bears to the southward and empties its waters into
Big Salt Lake.[60] The range of mountains bounding
the north side of the river here comes to within a half
mile of it, then bears off to the north, leaving a valley
of about seven or eight miles in width between it and
a range coming from Lewis river, and extending south
towards Salt Lake. The range bounding the south
side of the river comes abruptly to the stream at this
point, presenting huge and cumbrous masses of basaltic
rock, but it is generally covered with heavy timber. At
this point two trails are found: one striking west, across
the valley, to the opposite side; the other, which is the
nearest and best, follows around the point, hugging the
base of the mountain for several miles. Two and one
half miles distant, and immediately beneath a cliff of
rocks by the road side, is to be found a soda pool. A
little spring of cool soda water runs out at the base of
the rock, and a basin of eight or ten yards in extent,
and about two and one half feet high has been formed.
Inside of this, is a pool of water; — the material composing the bank around, is of a white color. In a few
miles travel, we crossed several spring branches. We
then directed our course through the plain for some
eight or nine miles, to where we encamped. Our camp
was located near a spring branch; but a small quantity
of wood was found; grazing was excellent. From where
the road leaves the river, the country presents every
appearance of having been volcanic at some period.
Craters are yet standing in the plain, exhibiting positive
evidence of this fact. A large mound has been formed

---

[60] For a brief note on Salt Lake see our volume xxi, p. 199, note 44.— ED.

by the lava ejected from this crater.   In the centre is [41]
a deep cavity; now partially filled, from the falling in
of the masses of bank surrounding it.   In every direction the eye rests upon fragments of rock, which have
been thrown out in a hot and burning condition, many
of them melted and united; pieces resembling broken
junk bottles or black glass lay scattered over the plain.
The valley for ten or twelve miles is covered with stone
of this description.   In many places the rocks have
been lifted or bulged up to an elevation of ten or fifteen
feet, the top has been burst asunder, presenting a cavity
of eight or ten feet in width, caused by the fragments
having been cast out; the depth of the cavity is from
twenty to thirty feet, the sides have a black appearance,
and exhibit indications of having been burned; at other
places the rock had been lifted up, and elevated above
the surface of the earth some five or six feet, and about
the same in width, having numerous small apertures
in it, the centre being concave.   The stone forms a
complete arch.   At other places the rock has been rent,
and a chasm of thirty or forty feet in depth and from
two to ten feet in width, has been the result.   These
chasms are about one quarter of a mile in length.   The
fragments lay in every direction.

The country over this plain is rather barren; but at
certain seasons of the year, is covered with grass, which
during the summer months dies, leaving but little appearance of vegetation.   After we had halted for the night,
three families who had separated from our company at
the Soda Springs, passed us.   A few hours had elapsed,
and we espied one of their number returning post haste
to our camp.   When he arrived, he was so paralysed

with fear, that it was with difficulty we obtained from him the cause of his alarm. It appeared evident, from his statement, that a party of Snake Indians meditated an attack upon their party. We dispatched a company to their relief, but soon had the gratification to witness the return of their wagons to our camp. It appears that one of their number had marched about two miles in advance of the wagons, when he was discovered by a party of Snake Indians, lurking in the vicinity, who immediately gave him chase, at every step uttering the most terrific yells, and endeavoured to surround him; but as he was astride a fleet American courser, he succeeded in outstripping them, and arrived at the wagons in time to prepare for their approach. The wagons were then in a deep ravine, and could not be seen, by the Indians in pursuit, until within seventy-five yards. As soon as the Indians discovered [42] their proximity to the wagons they commenced a precipitate retreat, and the emigrants rejoined our party.

August 6. We traveled this day about fifteen miles. The road for seven miles is up the valley; it then takes over the mountain, to the waters running into Snake or Lewis river. The high range of mountains which bears off towards *Salt Lake*, terminates near the road on the left. The road follows a ravine, and winds about among the hills, and thickets of quaking aspen, until it reaches a spring branch, down which it follows, to near Fort Hall. Over the ridge, and for two miles down the branch, there is but little grass found. At the distance of three miles, on our left up the mountain, were several patches of snow. A few of our party brought some of the snow to our camp.

August 7. This day we made about eighteen miles. For ten miles the road is very good. Along the stream is found willow brush, answering for fuel. The last seven miles is over a sandy plain; it was dry, and very heavy traveling. Our camp was at a large spring of cold water; grazing was very good.

August 8. We traveled but five miles, which brought us to Fort Hall.[61] This is a trading post in the possession of the *Hudson's Bay Company*. Like the forts on the east side of the mountains, it is built of mud or adobes. (This term applies to sun-burnt brick.) They are of a similar construction. At each corner is a bastion, projecting out some eight or ten feet, perforated with holes for fire-arms. Captain Grant is now the officer in command; he has the bearing of a gentleman.[62] The garrison was supplied with flour, which had been procured from the settlements in Oregon, and brought here on pack horses. They sold it to the emigrants for twenty dollars per cwt., taking cattle in exchange; and as many of the emigrants were nearly out of flour, and had a few lame cattle, a brisk trade was carried on between them and the inhabitants of the fort. In the exchange of cattle for flour, an allowance was made of from five to twelve dollars per head. They also had

[61] The entire route from Soda Springs at the bend of Bear River to Fort Hall was about fifty miles in length, crossing the basaltic, volcanic plateau which Palmer describes, to the waters of Portneuf River, down which the trail passed to Fort Hall. For the founding of this post see Townsend's *Narrative*, in our volume xxi, pp. 209-211.— ED.

[62] Captain James Grant was Hudson's Bay factor in charge at Fort Hall for several years during the immigration movement. Most of the travellers speak of his courtesy and readiness to assist. He was at this post in 1842, when Matthieu describes him as a large man, resembling Dr. McLoughlin — *Oregon Historical Quarterly*, i, p. 84. He seems to have later settled in Oregon.— ED.

horses which they readily exchanged for cattle or sold for cash. The price demanded for horses was from fifteen to twenty-five dollars. They could not be prevailed upon to receive anything in exchange for their goods or provisions, excepting cattle or money.

The bottoms here are wide, and covered with grass. There is an abundance of wood for fuel, fencing, and other purposes. [43] No attempt has, as yet, been made to cultivate the soil. I think the drought too great; but if irrigation were resorted to, I doubt not it would produce some kinds of grain, such as wheat, corn, potatoes, &c.

Our camp was located one mile to the south-west of the fort; and as at all the other forts, the Indians swarmed about us. They are of the Snake tribe, and inhabit the country bordering on Lewis and Bear rivers, and their various tributaries. This tribe is said to be numerous; but in consequence of the continual wars which they have engaged in with the Sioux, Crows and Blackfeet, their numbers are rapidly diminishing.

Snake river, which flows within one half mile of the fort, is a clear and beautiful stream of water.[68] It courses over a pebbly bottom. Its width is about one hundred and fifty yards. It abounds in fish of different varieties, which are readily taken with the hook.

While we remained in this place, great efforts were made to induce the emigrants to pursue the route to California. The most extravagant tales were related respecting the dangers that awaited a trip to Oregon, and of the difficulties and trials to be surmounted. The

---

[68] For a brief description of Snake (or Lewis) River, see our volume xxviii, p. 303, note 179.— ED.

perils of the way were so magnified as to make us suppose
the journey to Oregon almost impossible. For instance,
the two crossings of *Snake* river, and the crossing of the
Columbia, and other smaller streams, were represented
as being attended with great danger; also that no company heretofore attempting the passage of these streams,
succeeded, but with the loss of men, from the violence
and rapidity of the current; as also that they had never
succeeded in getting more than fifteen or twenty head
of cattle into the Willamette valley. In addition to the
above, it was asserted that three or four tribes of Indians,
in the middle region, had combined for the purpose
of preventing our passage through their country, and
should we attempt it, we would be compelled to contend
with these hostile tribes. In case we escaped destruc-
tion at the hands of the savages, a more fearful enemy,
that of famine, would attend our march; as the distance
was so great that winter would overtake us before
making the passage of the Cascade Mountains.

On the other hand, as an inducement to pursue the
California route, we were informed of the shortness
of the route, when compared with that to Oregon; as
also of many other superior advantages it possessed.

[44] These tales, told and rehearsed, were likely to produce the effect of turning the tide of emigration thither.
Mr. Greenwood, an old mountaineer, well stocked with
falsehoods, had been dispatched from California to
pilot the emigrants through;" and assisted by a young

" This attempt to deflect Oregon immigrants to California arose from the
unsettled conditions in that Mexican province, and the determination of earlier
American settlers to secure California for the United States. Caleb Greenwood, who was sent to Fort Hall from Sutter's Fort (Sacramento), was an aged
mountaineer and trapper, who reared a half-breed family by a wife of the

man by the name of McDougal, from Indiana, so far succeeded as to induce thirty-five or thirty-six wagons to take that trail.⁶⁵

About fifteen wagons had been fitted out, expressly for California; and, joined by the thirty-five afore-mentioned, completed a train of fifty wagons; what the result of their expedition has been, I have not been able to learn.⁶⁶

August 9. This day we traveled about eight miles; five miles brought us to the crossing of Portneth. This is a stream heading in the mountains near the Soda Springs, receiving numerous branches in this bottom, and is here about eighty yards in width.⁶⁷ From this place, it is one mile to the crossing of a narrow slough, with steep banks. We crossed, and journeyed two

Crow tribe. In 1844 he guided the Stevens party to California, and during the winter of 1844-45 served in Sutter's division of Micheltorena's army against Alvarado and Castro. Sutter wrote in regard to his mission, "I am glad that they meet with some good pilots at Fort Hall who went there from here to pilot emigrants by the new road."— ED.

⁶⁵ George McDougall was a native of Ohio, but started on his journey from Indiana. He conducted the advance party of young men known as the Swasey-Todd party, over the Truckee route to Sutter's, leaving Fort Hall about August 13, and arriving at New Helvetia late in September. McDougall served the next year in the California battalion, and was known to have been at San Francisco in 1847-48. He several times returned East, and after 1853 became a confirmed wanderer, being found in Patagonia in 1867. He is thought to have died at Washington, D. C., in 1872. He was eccentric, but brave, and a favorite with the frontier population. Many of the emigrants who turned off at Fort Hall for California went overland to Oregon the next year. Consult H. H. Bancroft, *History of Oregon* (San Francisco, 1886), i, p. 522.— ED.

⁶⁶ The writer has recently learned that the emigrants alluded to, not finding California equal, in point of soil, to their high wrought anticipations, have made the best of their way to Oregon.— PALMER.

⁶⁷ For another description of Portneuf (not Portneth) River see De Smet's *Letters* in our volume xxvii, p. 249, with accompanying note.— ED.

miles to the bank of Snake river, where we encamped.
Eight wagons joined us at our encampment.

August 10. We remained in camp.

August 11. This day we traveled about eight miles;
which brought us to within one mile of the American
falls.[68] Our camp was at the springs. An island
in the river afforded excellent grazing for cattle. The
country is extremely barren, being sandy sage plains.[69]

August 12. We traveled about fifteen miles, which
brought us to Levy creek, or Beaver-dam creek, as it
is sometimes termed; it is a small stream; its waters
flow down a succession of falls, producing a handsome
cascade: it has the appearance of having been built
up by beaver. The property of the water has turned
the material into stone; the water appears to be impregnated with soda; the rocks along the bank are of that
formation.[70] The best camp is two miles farther on.

August 13. This day we traveled about eight miles,
to Cassia creek; here the California trail turns off. The
road [45] has been very dusty and heavy traveling.
The country presents the same usual barren appearance.[71]

---

[68] These falls derive their name from the following circumstance. A
number of American trappers going down this stream in their canoes, not being
aware of their proximity to the falls, were hurried along by the violence of
the current; and passing over the falls, but one of the number survived.—
PALMER.

[69] The trail from Fort Hall led down the eastern and southern bank of the
Lewis; see our volume xxviii, p. 310, note 190. American Falls is a well-
known landmark, flowing over a rock about forty feet in height; see Frémont's
" Exploring Tour" (*op. cit.* in note 30), p. 164, for an engraving thereof. The
once barren land of this region is now being made fertile by irrigation.— ED.

[70] Fall Creek, in Oneida County, so called by Frémont, and still known
by this name. Its bed is composed of calcareous tufa, chiefly the remains
of reeds and mosses, forming a beautiful succession of cascades.— ED.

[71] Cassia Creek is an important western affluent of Raft River, of Cassia

August 14. This day we traveled about fifteen miles, and reached marshy springs; the road has been stony and dusty; the country mostly destitute of vegetation — nothing growing but the wild sage and wormwood."

August 15. We traveled but eleven miles. The road runs over a sage plain for eight miles, when it crosses the stream from the marsh; no water running, and but little standing in pools. At the distance of three miles the road strikes the river bottom, at the lower end of this, at which place the road leaves it; here was found a good camp.

August 16. We traveled about twenty-three miles. Four miles brought us to Goose creek. We found difficulty in crossing, and no good location for a camp." After seven miles travel we reached the river; but little grass. Twelve miles brought us to Dry Branch; here also was unsuitable ground for encamping, as the water was standing in pools. The road we traveled was very dusty, and portions of it quite stony; here the river runs through a rocky *kanyon*. The cliffs are sometimes of the height of one thousand feet, and nearly

County, Idaho. Upon its banks was the earliest settlement in this region, and the valley is still noted for its farms. The first party to take this route to California was that of J. B. Chiles (1843), guided by Joseph Walker. They struck across from the Snake to Humboldt River, down that stream to its sink, and by the Walker Pass into California. In 1844 the Stevens party followed a similar route; crossing the Sierras, however, by Truckee and Bear River road, the line of the present Central Pacific railway.— ED.

[72] Called by Frémont Swamp Creek, now known as Marsh Creek, a small southern affluent of the Lewis. It forms a circular basin or valley, about six miles in diameter, where there was grass and consequently a good camping place.— ED.

[73] Goose Creek is a deep, rocky stream rising in Goose Creek range, lying on the border between Idaho and Utah. The creek flows north, receiving several branches before entering the Lewis in Cassia County. Placer mines of considerable value have been found on this creek.— ED.

perpendicular.["] Above the *kanyon*, the river is two
or three hundred yards wide; but at this place it is not
more than one hundred and fifty feet; and at one place,
where there is a fall of some twenty feet, its width does
not exceed seventy-five feet. In our march this day
I attempted to get down to the river, to procure a drink
of water, but for six miles was unable to do so, owing
to the steep precipitous banks.

August 17. We traveled but eight miles. The road
lay over a sage plain to the bottom on Rock creek.["]
Here we found a very good camp.

August 18. This day we traveled about twenty
miles. After the distance of eight miles we arrived
at the crossing of Rock creek, (in a *kanyon*,) here we
halted for dinner, and gave our cattle water. We then
took up the bluff, and traveled over sand and sage plains
for about twelve miles. When night overtook us we
drove to the top of the river bluff and encamped. We

[74] Dry Creek is still to be found on the maps of Cassia County. Frémont says
of this portion of the trail: "All the day the course of the river has been
between walls of black volcanic rock, a dark line of the escarpment on the
opposite side pointing out its course, and sweeping along in foam at places
where the mountains which border the valley present always on the left two
ranges, the lower one a spur of the higher; and on the opposite side, the Salmon
River mountains are visible at a great distance." (See *op. cit., ante*, in note 30,
p. 167.) — ED.

[75] The falls mentioned by Palmer are the Great Shoshone Falls of the
Lewis River, where the cañon is over eight hundred feet deep: the first fall
has a plunge of thirty feet, and then a sheer descent of a hundred and ninety.
These are, in the United States, exceeded in grandeur only by Niagara and
the Yosemite. Palmer's failure to appreciate their height and magnificence
was probably due to the depth of the cañon from the top of which he viewed
them; or he may not have seen the lower falls at all, for the trail wound back
from the river in many places.

Rock Creek is a considerable stream, with a swift current, flowing northwest into the Lewis in Cassia County, Idaho.— ED.

drove our cattle one and a half miles down the bluff
to the river for water. Here we found a little grass and
green brush, but it was not sufficient in quantity to
supply our cattle, and we could do no better. We
packed water up the bluff to our camp. The bluffs
at this place exceed one thousand feet in height; they
are of basalt. The road is on a high barren [46]
plain; a range of mountains is on our left hard by,
and at a great distance on our right another range
appears.

August 19. We traveled about twelve miles. Nine
miles brought us to where we pass down to the river
bottom; from this point the distance to the river was
three miles. A warm spring branch empties itself into
the river at this place. Emigrants would pursue a more
proper course by encamping on the bottom, near the
source of Rock creek, then drive down to where the
road crosses in a *kanyon*, then following the road for
eight or nine miles to where the road leaves the bluff
of the creek and encamp, driving their cattle into the
creek bottom. From this place they can drive to Salmon
Fall creek, just four miles below our present encampment, follow down this creek to its mouth, where will
be found an excellent camp.

August 20. We traveled about nine miles, reaching
the Salmon Falls.[70] Here are eighteen or twenty Indian
huts. Salmon come up to these falls: the Indians

[70] Salmon Falls River is the largest southern affluent of the Lewis that has
been crossed since leaving Fort Hall. It rises in many branches on the boundaries of Nevada and flows north through a valley now noted as a hay- and stock-
raising section. Salmon Falls (also called Fishing Falls) is a series of cataracts
with sharply inclined planes, forming a barrier to the ascent of the salmon,
and thus a fishing resort for Indians.— ED.

have an abundance of them, which they very readily dispose of for hooks, powder, balls, clothing, calico and knives, and in fact for almost anything we have at our disposal.

The river at this place is a succession of cataracts for several miles, the highest of which does not exceed twelve feet. The grazing was very poor, and the country barren as usual.

August 21. We traveled about twelve miles; for two miles the road is up a sandy hill, it then strikes a sandy sage plain, over which it takes its course for ten miles. Here night overtook us, as we had commenced our march at a very late hour on account of having lost some horses. Our camp was on the top of the river bluff. It is one mile to water; but little grass was found. This day we found several head of cattle that had given out from fatigue of traveling. Some of the companies had been racing, endeavoring to pass each other, and now they have reached a region where but little grass is found — are beginning to reap the reward of their folly.

August 22. Our cattle were so much scattered that it was late in the day when we prepared to resume our march. We traveled about ten miles. At night we left the road, and directed our course to the right, down a ravine to the river, where we encamped. Our cattle suffered much for want of food.

August 23. This morning we turned up the ravine for one and a half miles, and then struck up the hill to the road. Three and a half miles brought us to where the road crosses [47] the Snake river. In coming down to the river bottom, there is a very steep hill. Along the shore of this river was a little grass; there are two islands covered with grass, so that our cattle were soon repaid for their privations heretofore. The difficulties attending the crossing of this stream had been represented as being almost insurmountable; but upon examination we found it an exaggeration. From the main shore to first island there is no difficulty; from first to second island, turn well up, until nearly across, then bear down to where the road enters it. The water is not deep until nearly across, and not then if you keep well up stream. From second island to main shore is more difficult; it is about three hundred yards wide and the current very rapid. Strike in, heading well up for two rods, then quartering a little down until eight or ten rods from shore: then quartering a little up for fifteen or twenty rods; then strike up for the coming out place; the bottom is gravelly. With the exception of a few holes, the water for the first fifteen rods is the deepest part of the ford. The bottom is very uneven; there are holes found of six or eight feet in width, many of them swimming. Those crossing this stream can escape the deepest of these holes by having horsemen in the van and at each side; it is necessary that there be attached to each wagon four or six yoke of oxen, the current being swift; and in the passage of these holes, previously alluded to, when one yoke is compelled to swim, the others may be in shallow water. Great care must be taken that these teams be not beat down too low and pass over the ripple; and to prevent such a casualty, two drivers must attend each wagon. Before attempting the passage of the river all articles liable to damage, from coming in contact with the water, should be piled on the top of the wagon bed. We commenced crossing at eleven o'clock, A. M., and at one o'clock, P. M., we effected the passage of the stream, and were so fortunate as to land our goods free from all damage. We traveled two miles to a spring branch and pitched our encampment. Good grass, wood and water, were procured in plenty."

August 24. We traveled but six miles. Soon after leaving camp we directed our course up a stony hill; thence over a sage plain to a spring branch."' We pursued our way up this branch for one mile, where we obtained good grazing for our cattle; a high range of hills appearing on our right, at the distance of two miles, an occasional grove of pine timber upon them; but, in general, the mountains here are covered with [48] grass; numerous streams issuing from their sides, and pouring their waters in the plain below. There is no appearance of vegetation until you reach the low bottoms immediately along the water's edge. The road traveled to-day was quite stony.

The Indians along this road are expert in theft and roguery. A young man having a horse which he had taken much pains to get along, when night approached, staked and hobbled him, that he might not stray off; but at night an Indian stole into the camp, unhobbled the horse, cut the rope, and took him off, leaving the young man undisturbed in his sleep. A few days thereafter, this Indian effected a sale of the horse to one of a party of emigrants traveling behind us.

August 25. We remained in camp.

 " For this crossing see our volume xxviii, p. 314, note 193.— ED.

"' The emigrants were in Elmore County, Idaho, where a number of small streams come from the north into Lewis River; one is known as Cold Spring Creek, possibly the branch mentioned by Palmer.— ED.

August 26. We traveled about ten miles; our camp
was located on a small rivulet, at a quarter of a mile's
distance above the road, and near the mouth of the *Hot*
Spring branch. Between the road and the mountain
good grazing was found.   The river is about eight miles
on our left; the space between is a barren, sandy sage
plain.

August 27. We traveled about sixteen miles; one
mile brought us to the Hot Springs, near which the road
passes.[79]   These springs are in a constant state of ebulli-
tion. They number from five to six, extending over a
surface of two to three yards, all uniting and forming
a stream of one yard in width and about three inches
deep, running quite rapid. The water is sufficiently
hot for culinary purposes. About fifteen rods off,
approaching the mountain, which is half a mile distant,
are similar springs, the waters of which flow into a reser-
voir a short distance below. An ox, belonging to our
party, appeared desirous to test the qualities of the water
afforded by these springs. His owners, seeing his incli-
nation, attempted to arrest his steps, but failed; when
he arrived at the brink of one of them, and stuck his
nose in, preparatory to indulging in a draught of the
delicious nectar, he immediately wheeled, and made
the welkin ring by his bellowing; kicking and running,
he showed he was evidently displeased with himself.
Our camp was on Barrel creek bottom, which is very
narrow.

August 28. We traveled about eighteen miles, crossing several running branches. The road is near the base

---

[79] For these springs see Farnham's *Travels* in our volume xxviii, p. 314,
note 194.— ED.

of the mountain; wild sage and grease wood found in plenty. Encamped on Charlotte's fork, a small branch.

August 29. We traveled about eighteen miles, which brought us to Bois river, a stream of forty or fifty yards in [49] width, and abounding in salmon; its banks are lined with Balm of Gilead timber.[60] The bottoms here are two or three miles wide, and covered with grass.

August 30. We traveled about eleven miles. The road is sometimes on bottom, at others, on bluff. The Indians are very numerous along this stream; they have a large number of horses; clothing is in much demand; for articles of clothing costing in the States ten or twelve dollars, a very good horse can be obtained.

August 31. We traveled about 14 miles. The road pursues its course down the valley of the Bois river.

September 1. We traveled about thirteen miles. Two miles from camp we crossed Bois river. Some of the bottoms are covered with grass, others with wild sage and grease wood. The road was very dusty. There is not much timber along the stream, but great quantities of brush.

September 2. We reached Fort Bois. This is a trading post of the Hudson's Bay Company, established upon the northern side of Snake or Lewis river, and one mile below the mouth of Bois river. This fort was erected for the purpose of recruiting, or as an intermediate post, more than as a trading point. It is built of the same materials, and modeled after Fort Hall,

---

[60] For Boise River see our volume xxi, p. 249, note 63. The trail approached this stream near the present site of Boise City, and followed its banks to Lewis River.— Ed.

but is of a smaller compass. Portions of the bottoms around it afford grazing; but, in a general view, the surrounding country is barren.[81]

North of this fort is an extensive plain, which has an extremely unfertile appearance; but, I am informed, that during the winter and spring months it affords good grazing. At this fort they have a quantity of flour in store, brought from OREGON CITY, for which they demanded twenty dollars per cwt., in cash; a few of our company being in extreme want, were obliged to purchase at this exorbitant price. At this place the road crosses the river; the ford is about four hundred yards below the fort, and strikes across to the head of an island, then bears to the left to the southern bank; the water is quite deep, but not rapid; it swam some of our smallest work cattle; the bottom is solid and smooth. We cut poles, and laid them across the top of our wagon-beds, piling our loading on them; answering a twofold purpose — preventing our loading from damage, as also by its weight keeping the wagons steady and guarding them against floating. In about three hours we effected our passage in safety, but few of the goods getting wet. We went up the bottom a half mile, and there encamped; [50] driving our cattle on an island hard by, to graze. Fort Bois is about two hundred and eighty miles below Fort Hall, following the wagon road; but by crossing the river at Fort Hall, and going down on the north side, the distance would be lessened, as the river bears off south, and then north; and judging from the appearance of the country, I think a road

[81] For a brief sketch of Fort Boise see Farnham's *Travels* in our volume xxviii, p. 321, note 199.— ED.

may be found, equal, if not better than the one on the south side; and, I doubt not, the grazing will be found better.⁸²

September 3. We traveled fifteen miles, to Malheur, or Malore, as it is sometimes called: here is a good camp. This is a stream of about ten yards in width, having its source in a range of mountains to the south-west, and pursuing its meanderings through a succession of hills, sage and sand plains, and occasionally a fertile bottom, until it arrives at Snake river, into which it empties. A few miles below Fort Bois, its course from its source is north of east. Along its banks, near to where the road crosses it, are a number of hot springs; they are of the same temperature of those between the two crossings of Snake river.⁸³ Here we met Dr. White, a sub-Indian agent, accompanied by three others, on their way from OREGON to the STATES.⁸⁴ At this place

⁸² This northern and more direct route was followed by Wyeth in 1834 — see Townsend's *Narrative* in our volume xxi, pp. 231-249. He found the difficulties of the passage great, and the longer and more southern route was the one usually followed.— ED.

⁸³ For Malheur River see our volume xxi, p. 264, note 64. The Hot Springs are noted in our volume xxviii, p. 323, note 202.— ED.

⁸⁴ For a brief sketch of the life of Dr. Elijah White see Farnham's *Travels* in our volume xxix, p. 20, note 12. He was at this time returning to Washington to secure the settlement of his accounts as Indian sub-agent, and with the hope of securing further preferment — if possible, the governorship of Oregon. He was the bearer of a memorial from the provisional government of Oregon, requesting Congress to extend the sovereignty and laws of the United States over the Oregon settlements. See *Cong. Globe*, 29 Cong., 1 sess., p. 24. Later advices from Oregon, however, frustrated the plans of Dr. White, who was retired to private life. On his return his companions across the plains (1845) were William Chapman and Orris Brown of the immigration of 1843, and Joseph Charles Saxton of 1844. Only Brown returned to Oregon; he went back in 1846 accompanied by his own family, and that of his mother, Mrs. Tabitha Brown, who was connected with the history of early education

are two trails; the fork is in the bottom above the crossing of the creek, and there is a possibility of emigrants
pursuing the wrong route. I do not deem it amiss
to give some particulars in relation to this road. Mr.
Meek, who had been engaged as our pilot, but had
previously went in advance of the companies who had
employed him, and who had after reaching Fort Hall,
fitted up a party to pilot through to Oregon, informed
the emigrants that he could, by taking up this stream
to near its source, and then striking across the plains,
so as to intersect the old road near to the mouth of
Deshutes or Falls river, save about one hundred and
fifty miles travel; also that he was perfectly familiar
with the country through which the proposed route
lay, as he had traveled it; that no difficulty or danger
attended its travel. He succeeded in inducing about
two hundred families to pursue this route; they accordingly directed their course to the left, up this creek,
about ten days previous to our arrival at the forks.

September 4. We traveled about twenty miles; ten
miles brought us to a sulphur spring, and ten miles
more to Birch creek, where we encamped.[85] The
country is considerably rolling, and much of it barren:
no timber found.

September 5. We traveled about eight miles; three
miles [51] brought us to Snake river, and five more

in Oregon. The Brown family settled at Forest Grove, the immigrant of
1843 finally dying at Salem in 1874. White, in his *Ten Years in Oregon*
(New York, 1859), p. 282, speaks of meeting a party (Palmer's) near Fort
Boise, who brought him important letters, including one from his wife, the
first received in fifteen months.— ED.

   [85] Birch Creek (Rivière aux Bouleaux) rises in Burnt River Mountains
and flows southeast into Lewis River, in Malheur County, Oregon.— ED.

to Burnt river. The road is hilly but good; the country mountainous. Here is a good camp.

September 6. We made about twelve miles. The road is up Burnt river, and the most difficult road we have encountered since we started. The difficulties arise from the frequent crossings of the creek, which is crooked, narrow and stony. We were often compelled to follow the road, in its windings for some distance, over high, sidelong and stony ridges, and frequently through thickets of brush. The stream is about ten or twelve yards in width, and is generally rapid. The hills are high, and covered with grass."

September 7. This day we traveled about twelve miles. The road exceeded in roughness that of yester-day. Sometimes it pursued its course along the bottom of the creek, at other times it wound its way along the sides of the mountains, so sidelong as to require the weight of two or more men on the upper side of the wagons to preserve their equilibrium. The creek and road are so enclosed by the high mountains, as to afford but little room to pass along, rendering it in some places almost impassable. Many of the mountains viewed from here seem almost perpendicular, and of course present a barren surface. The eye is occasion-ally relieved by a few scrubby cedars; but along the creek is found birch, bitter cottonwood, alder, &c., in quantity, and several kinds of brush and briars, so impenetrable as to preclude ingress. The road pursues its course through these thickets, the axe having been employed; but it is so very narrow as almost to prevent

---

" For Burnt River and the course of the trail through its valley see Town-send's description in our volume xxi, pp. 267, 268.— ED.

travel. A little digging, and the use of the axe, united with the erection of bridges, would make this a very good road. At first view this road appeared to us impassable, and so difficult of travel, as almost to deter us from the attempt; but knowing that those who had preceded us had surmounted the difficulties, encouraged us to persevere. It required much carefulness, and the exercise of skill on the part of our drivers to pass along and avoid the dangers of the way. We pursued our route without any loss, with the exception of that attending the breakage of two wagon tongues, done in crossing some deep ravines. We also experienced difficulty in finding our cattle, which had strayed away. Five miles from camp the road turns up a spring branch to the right, which we followed two miles, crossing it very frequently; it then turns up the mountain of the left, until it strikes another ravine. We followed [52] up this for one mile, where water makes its appearance. Here is found a good camp. The road then takes to the left up the hill, and then down to a dry branch: here is a good camp, one mile to running water. This portion of the road is solid and of good travel.

September 8. This day we traveled about fourteen miles. Two miles brought us to the creek again; the bottom here is of some extent. We followed this bottom for the distance of one mile; the road then led up the right hand branch, crossing several small branches, taking up a ravine to the left over a ridge, until it reaches the fork of the river; pursues its route up this river some six or seven miles, crossing it twice, then directs its course to the right, through a narrow ravine over the mountain, then strikes Dry Branch; we followed up this branch to running water, and near to a scrubby pine; here we encamped. The road has been solid and good. The hills and valleys appear well covered with grass.

September 9. This day we traveled about sixteen miles. The road runs up the branch for one mile, then turns to the left over the hill, pursuing a very winding course for some thirteen miles, until it reaches a slough in Powder river bottoms. Powder river is a stream of some eight or ten yards in width, having its source in the high range of mountains on our left, which mountains in many places are covered with snow.[87] An abundance of pine timber is found covering the sides of these mountains, sometimes extending far down into the bottoms, which here are between six and seven miles in width. The soil is fertile and would undoubtedly yield abundantly.

To our right, at the distance of fifteen or twenty miles, is presented a high range of mountains, their base covered with grass, their sides with heavy pine timber. At their summit they are entirely destitute of vegetation: some of these are very lofty, their peaks present a very lustrous appearance, resembling the snow mountains. This shining, dazzling appearance they possess, is derived I think from the material of which they are composed, being a kind of white clay.

The valley between Powder river and this range is very rolling, portions of it covered with wild sage. Wild fowl abound in this valley.

September 10. This day we traveled about ten miles; our course was down the valley of Powder river; eight

---

[87] For Powder River see our volume xxi, p. 268, note 68. The mountains seen were the Blue; see a brief description in *ibid.*, p. 273, note 71.— ED.

miles brought us to the crossing of the same, one
mile to the middle [53] fork, and one to the third fork.
There is good ground for encampments at any point
along these streams.

At our camp we were visited by an Indian chief of
the tribe Caäguas,[99] accompanied by his son. He was
of a friendly disposition; his object in visiting us was
principally to barter for cattle; he had in his possession
thirty or more horses.

September 11. This day we traveled about twelve
miles; for the first five or six miles, the road was quite
level and good, it then follows a ridge dividing Powder
river and Grand Round; this portion of the road is
very uneven and stony. The road leading down into
the valley of Grand Round, is circuitous, and its difficulty of travel enhanced by its roughness; it is about
one and a half miles in length, to where it reaches the
bottom. Grand Round is a valley, whose average
width does not exceed twenty miles, and is about thirty
miles in length; a stream of water of some twenty yards
in width passes through this valley, receiving considerable addition to its volume from the many rivulets that
pour down their waters from the mountains, by which
this valley is enclosed. The bottoms are of rich friable
earth, and afford grass of various kinds, among others
that of red clover. There is a root here found in great
abundance, and known as the *camas*, which is held in
high repute by the Indians for some medicinal qualities
it is thought to possess; wild flax and a variety of other
plants grow in luxuriance, like to those I have observed

---

[99] Pronounced Kiwaw or Kioose.— PALMER.
Comment by Ed.   For the Cayuse see our volume vii, p. 137, note 37.

in the western prairies."⁸ The streams are generally lined with timber, and abound in salmon and other varieties of fish. Upon the sides of the mountains and extending down into the valley are found beautiful groves of yellow pine timber. These mountains are places of resort for bear, deer, and elk.

This bottom affords an excellent situation for a settlement, possessing more advantages in that respect, than any found since our departure from the lower Platte river. North of this and at the distance of about twenty miles, is another valley, similar in appearance to this, but of greater extent.⁹⁰ The streams having their course through this valley empty into Lewis river, which is eighty or ninety miles to the north. Our camp was at the foot of the hill, convenient to a spring branch. At twilight we were visited by four or five of the Caäguas, the tribe alluded to previously.

An incident quite worthy of note, occurred at this place. The [54] chief (Aliquot by name)⁹¹ who had

---

⁸⁹ For the valley of Grande Ronde see our volume xxi, p. 271, note 69. Consult on camas, *ibid.*, p. 247, note 61.— ED.

⁹⁰ This northern valley is the lower portion of the Grande Ronde. Frémont says: "We passed out of the Grand Rond by a fine road along the creek, which, for a short distance, runs in a kind of rocky chasm. Crossing a low point, which was a little rocky, the trail conducted into the open valley of the stream — a handsome place for farms." (*op. cit.* in note 30, p. 179.) This is now the most flourishing settlement in eastern Oregon with a railway running through the valley to Elgin.— ED.

⁹¹ Probably this was the Cayuse chief Tiloukaikt, who had early come under Dr. Whitman's influence, but nevertheless was treacherous, and unstable in his professions of Christianity. In 1841 he had insulted Dr. Whitman because of the punishment of one of his nephews by a missionary teacher. In 1843 he entered into the treaty with some reluctance, and in 1847 was one of the principals concerned in the Whitman massacre. The following year he was one of the five chiefs who gave themselves up to the civil authorities, and he paid the penalty of his murderous instincts upon the scaffold.— ED.

joined us at our other encampment, and had pursued this day's journey in company, had pitched his tent some three hundred yards to the rear of our camp. In the evening, in strolling about the camp, I came near his tent, and entered with the intention of employing his squaw in the soling of my moccasins; while she was engaged in this employment, a conversation had sprung up between the old chief and myself, in which be took occasion to ask me if I were a christian, as also whether there were many upon the road; to which questions I of course answered in the affirmative, supposing that he merely wished to know, whether I classed myself with the heathen or christians. On my return to our camp, some one of our party proposed that we should while away an hour or so, in a game at cards, which was readily assented to. We had but engaged in our amusement, when the old chief Aliquot made his appearance, holding a small stick in his hand; he stood transfixed for a moment, and then advanced to me, raising his hand, which held the stick in the act of chastising me, and gently taking me by the arm, said "Captain — Captain — no good; no good." You may guess my astonishment, at being thus lectured by a "wild and untutored savage," twenty five hundred miles from a civilized land. I inwardly resolved to abandon card playing forever.

September 12. This day we traveled about seven miles; the road runs across the upper end of Grand round, to a small spring branch, when it again ascends the mountains. At this spring branch we pitched our camp, and while here, were visited by great numbers of Indians, including men, squaws, and papooses. These

Indians have decidedly a better appearance than any
I have met; tall and athletic in form, and of great sym-
metry of person; they are generally well clad, and
observe pride in personal cleanliness. They brought
wheat, corn, potatoes, peas, pumpkins, fish, &c. which
they were anxious to dispose of for cloths, calico, nankins
and other articles of wearing apparel; they also had
dressed deer skins and moccasins; they had good horses,
which they offered in exchange for cows and heifers;
they would gladly exchange a horse for a cow, esteem-
ing the cow as of equal value. They remained with
us throughout the day, and when evening approached
returned to their lodges along the river two miles distant.
I noticed a few of the Nez Perces (Pierced Noses) tribe
of Indians among them.[82] Both of these tribes are
under the influence and control of two Presbyterian
missionaries, Dr. [55] Whitman and Mr. Spalding, who
have resided among them for the last ten years; the
former among the Caäguas, which inhabit the country
bordering on Wallawalla river and its tributaries, the
Blue mountains and Grand round: the latter among the
Nez Perces who inhabit the country lying along Lewis
river, and its tributaries, from the eastern base of the
Blue mountains to the Columbia river.[83] These missionary establishments are of a like character to those farther
north. As I shall have occasion to speak of these missionaries, as also the beneficial results which have flowed
from their residence among the savages, I will return
to my travels.

---

[82] For the Nez Percés see Franchère's *Narrative* in our volume vi, p. 340,
note 145.— ED.

[83] For Whitman and Spaulding see our volume xxi, p. 352, note 125.— ED.

Some of our party becoming scant of provision, started for Dr. Whitman's, the missionary establishment referred to above, intending to rejoin us at Umatillo river, my old friend Aliquot generously proffered his services as pilot for them, which were readily accepted.

September 13. This day we traveled about seven miles. From Grand Round the road ascends the Blue mountains, and for two miles is quite steep and precipitous; and to such an extent, as to require six yoke of oxen, or more, to be attached to a wagon; from the summit of these mountains is presented a rolling country for some four miles, alternately prairie and groves of yellow pine timber. In the prairie the grass is quite dry, but among the groves of timber it is green and flourishing. The road is very stony; at the end of four miles it takes down the mountain to Grand Round river, one mile in distance; it then crosses. Here is another bottom covered with grass and bushes, where we pitched our encampment. It is a remarkable circumstance that when individuals are engaged in conversation, their voices can be heard distinctly at a quarter of a mile distance; the discharge of a gun resembles that of a cannon, and is echoed from hill to hill, the reverberations continuing for some length of time.

September 14. This day we traveled about ten miles. The road ascended the mountain for one and a half or two miles, then wound along the ridge crossing many deep ravines, and pursuing its route over high craggy rocks; sometimes directing its course over an open plain, at others through thick groves of timber, winding among fallen trees and logs, by which the road was encumbered. The scenery is grand and beautiful, and cannot be surpassed; the country to a great distance is rough in the extreme. It may strictly be termed a timber country, although many small prairies are dotted over its surface. [56] The valleys are beautiful and the soil presents a very rich appearance. We encamped in an opening, on the south side of a range of mountains running to the north, and found water in plenty in the bottom of the ravine, on our left, about one fourth of a mile from the road. The timber growing in this region is principally yellow pine, spruce, balsam fir, and hemlock; among the bushes I noticed laurel.

September 15. This day we traveled about nine miles, over the main ridge of the Blue Mountains. It is mostly a timbered country through which we passed; the scenery is delightful, resembling in grandeur that presented on yesterday's travel.[54] We had a fine view of the Cascade Mountains to the west. Mount Hood, the loftiest of these, was plain to the view. It was some one hundred and fifty miles distant, and being covered with snow, appeared as a white cloud rising above those surrounding it. To the north of Mount Hood, and north of the Columbia, is seen Mount Saint Helen. We halted for the night at Lee's encampment.[55]

[54] On the crossing of Blue Mountains compare our volume xxviii, p. 328, note 206.— ED.

[55] For the location of these peaks see our volume vi, pp. 246, 248, notes 50 and 54 respectively. Lee's encampment was the place upon which Henry A. G. Lee had waited for the immigrants of 1844. Lee, who was a member of the train of 1843, was commissioned by Dr. Elijah White as Indian sub-agent to encounter the party of 1844 among the Cayuse and assist in the trading between Indians and immigrants, and thus protect both parties. The policy did not prove successful; see Lee's own letter on the subject in *Oregon Historical Quarterly*, v, p. 300. Lee emigrated from the southwestern states, and

September 16. We traveled about sixteen miles this day, which brought us to Umatillo river. Here is an Indian town, the residence of the principal chiefs of the Caäguas.[90] At this time they were mostly in the mountains hunting. The road has been good; the first twelve miles led us through a well timbered country, the last four miles over prairie; the country has a dry appearance; the banks of the streams are lined with cottonwood, balm of gilead, choke cherries and every variety of bushes. The Indians have a few cultivated fields along this stream; they raise wheat, corn, potatoes, peas and a variety of vegetables. After the planting of crops, the labour of tending devolves upon the squaws, or is done by slaves, of which they have a number, being captives taken in their expeditions against other tribes. They brought us the different products of their farms for traffic. As they expressed great eagerness to obtain clothes, and we had a like desire to obtain vegetables, a brisk traffic was continued until dark. On yesterday morning when about ready to start, we discovered that eight or ten of our work cattle were missing. Four of our number, myself included, remained to hunt

immediately became a leader in Oregon politics. He was elected to the legislature of 1845, and was an officer in the Cayuse War of 1847-48, during which he was appointed Indian agent to succeed General Joel Palmer. The following year he resigned his office, and soon thereafter left for the California gold mines. He returned to Oregon to enter the mercantile business; but died on a voyage to New York in 1850.— ED.

[90] For the Umatilla River see our volume vi, p. 338, note 141.

The Indian village was probably that of Five Crows, who in 1843 was elected head-chief of the Cayuse. His baptismal name was Hezekiah, and he took no active part in the Whitman massacre (1847); nevertheless he did nothing to prevent its occurrence and secured the person of some of the prisoners, notably a Miss Bewley, whom he took as a wife. Five Crows afterwards was active in the Cayuse War (1878), in which he was severely wounded.— ED.

them up.   In our search we rambled over the mountains
for several miles, and at night found them about three
miles from camp; we then followed the road and arrived
at Lee's encampment just after dark.   This morning
an ox, a mule and a horse were missing.   Three of us
remained to hunt for them.   We searched the prairies
and [57] thickets for miles around, but were unsuccessful.   We then pursued the road to Umatillo, which we
reached at night.

September 17.   At eight o'clock this morning, the
men who had left us at Grand Round for Dr. Whitman's
station, rejoined us, accompanied by the doctor and his
lady.[97]   They came in a two horse wagon, bringing
with them a plentiful supply of flour, meal and potatoes.
After our party had taken some refreshment, the march
was resumed; our visitors accompanying us to our camp
four miles down the river.   Our present location affords
but little grazing.

The doctor and lady remained with us during the day;
he took occasion to inform us of the many incidents
that marked his ten years' sojourn in this wilderness
region, of a highly interesting character.   Among other
things, he related that during his residence in this country,
he had been reduced to such necessity for want of food,
as to be compelled to slay his horse; stating that within
that period, no less than thirty-two horses had been
served up at his table.   It appears that the soil has
never been cultivated until within a few years back;
but at this time, so much attention is given to the culture
of the soil, which yields abundantly, that the privations
of famine, or even scarcity, will probably not again

[97] For Mrs. Whitman see our volume xxi, p. 355, note 128.— ED.

recur. The condition of the savages has been greatly
ameliorated and their improvement is chiefly attribu-
table to the missionary residents. They have a good
stock of cattle, hogs, sheep, &c., and raise an amount
of grain not only sufficient to supply their own wants,
but affords a surplus. These tribes differ in their appearance and customs from any we have met. They recognise
the change which has taken place, and are not ignorant
that it has been effected by the efforts and labor of the
missionaries. On the other hand, they acknowledge the
benefits derived by yielding to their instructions. They
have embraced the Christian religion, and appear devout
in their espousal of Christian doctrines. The entire
time of the missionaries is devoted to the cause for which
they have forsaken their friends and kindred; they have
left the comforts of home, and those places which have
been endeared by early associations, for the wild wilderness and the habitation of the savage, prompted by those
principles of charity and benevolence which the Christian
religion always inculcates. Their privations and trials
have been great, but they have borne them with humility
and meekness, and the fruits of their devotion are now
manifest; and if any class of people deserve well of their
country, or are entitled to the thanks of [58] a christian
community, it is the missionaries. Having no family
of their own, they generously take families of orphan
children, raise and educate them in a manner that is
worthy of all commendation.**

** Mary Ann Bridger and Helen Mar Meek, half-breed children of James
Bridger and Joseph Meek, were brought to the Whitmans before 1842; also
a half-breed Spanish boy, David Malin. The migration of 1843 left with Mrs.
Whitman two motherless English girls, Ann and Emma Hobson; while in

September 18. This morning, after breakfast, our worthy guests left us and we took up our line of march, traveling down the Umatillo valley for some twelve miles, crossing the *stream* twice. The road then takes up the bluff to the right, over a high grassy plain. Our encampment was pitched on the bluff on the left of the road. The water required at camp, was packed about one and a half miles, being procured at the base of the bluffs, up which we had to climb. The country is very rolling, covered with dry grass; it is mostly prairie. From this point two snowy peaks appear in view, as also the great valley of the Columbia; in truth it may be said that our present location is in that valley, although it is generally termed the middle region.

September 19. This day we traveled about ten miles. Eight miles brought us to the river; we followed the banks of the river for two miles, and encamped; good grazing is found. The stream as usual is lined with timber, but with this exception, it is a rolling prairie as far as can be seen, extending to the north and south, and bounded on the east and west by the Blue and Cascade mountains. Whilst at this camp, we were visited by the Wallawalla Indians; they reside along the lower part of the Wallawalla, the low bottoms of the Umatillo and the Columbia, from the mouth of Lewis river for one hundred miles south. They furnished us with potatoes and venison. In their personal appearance they are

---

1844 seven children of the Sager family, both of whose parents had died en route across the plains, were adopted by the Whitmans. Of these children the two eldest Sager boys were killed during the massacre; the half-breed girls and one of the Sager girls died a few days later, from exposure and fright.— ED.

much inferior to the Caäguas, and want the cleanliness that characterizes that tribe.⁰⁰

September 20. This day we traveled about fifteen miles. For the first eight miles the soil was remarkably rich in appearance, an admixture of sand and loam, and covered with good grass; the stream is lined with timber, in common with many of those that we have passed; the last seven miles was sandy and heavy traveling. The Columbia river presents itself on our right, at the distance of four miles. The river is in view for miles along this road. The prickly pear is found in abundance. It was our intention to have reached the Columbia before encamping, but from the difficult traveling, were compelled to encamp on the sandy plain, deprived of water, wood and grass.

[59] *September* 21. This morning at day-light we started for the Columbia, distance three and a half miles. The river at this place is from a half to three-fourths of a mile in width. It is a beautiful stream; its waters are clear and course gently over a pebbly bottom. Along the Columbia, is a strip of barren country of twelve miles in width; a little dry grass in bunches, prickly pear and grease wood, dot its surface. With this exception, its appearance was wild and solitary to a great degree; but sterile as it is in appearance, the view is relieved by the majesty of the river that flows by it. Immediately along the bank of the Columbia is a narrow bottom, covered with green grass, cucklebur, wild sunflower, pig weed, and several other kinds of weeds, all of which were in full bloom. There was something inspiriting and animating in beholding this. A feeling

⁰⁰ For the Wallawalla Indians see our volume vii, p. 137, note 37.— ED.

of pleasure would animate our breasts akin to that filling the breast of the mariner, when after years of absence, the shores of his native land appear to view. We could scarce persuade ourselves but that our journey had arrived at its termination. We were full of hope, and as it was understood that we had but one more difficult part of the road to surmount, we moved forward with redoubled energy; our horses and cattle were much jaded, but we believed that they could be got through, or at least the greater part of them.

The Indians were constantly paying us visits, furnishing us with vegetables, which, hy the by, were quite welcome; but they would in return · demand wearing apparel, until by traffic, we were left with but one suit. We were compelled to keep a sharp look out over our kitchen furniture, as during these visits it was liable to diminish in quantity by forming an attachment towards these children of the forest, and following them off. Many of these savages were nearly naked; they differ greatly from the Caäguas, being much inferior; they are a greasy, filthy, dirty set of miscreants as ever might be met.

September 22. This day we remained in camp, engaged in traffic with the Indians. Some of our party were in want of horses, and took this occasion to supply themselves.

September 23. This day we traveled about twenty miles. The first eight miles the road is heavy traveling; the remaining portion however is much better, with the exception of the last five miles, which proved to be quite rocky. There is an occasional green spot to be found, but the whole distance we have traveled since we first struck the river cannot be regarded [60] as more than a barren sandy plain. In our route this day we passed several Indian villages; they are but temporary establishments, as their migratory disposition will not justify more permanent structures.

September 24. This day we traveled but sixteen miles. After a march of seven miles, we arrived at a small creek, a good situation for encamping; nine miles more brought us to Dry Branch, from whence we proceeded down the bluff to the river; a great portion of the road traveled was sandy and heavy.[100]

September 25. This day we traveled about fourteen miles. The road was quite hilly; sometimes it followed the bank of the river, at others pursued its course along the high bluff. The river is confined to a very narrow channel; country very barren, and the bluffs of great height.

September 26. This day we traveled about three miles. The road ascends the bluff; is very difficult in ascent from its steepness, requiring twice the force to impel the wagons usually employed; after effecting the ascent, the sinuosity of the road led us among the rocks to the bluff on John Day's river; here we had another obstacle to surmount, that of going down a hill very precipitous in its descent, but we accomplished it without loss or injury to our teams. This stream comes tumbling through kanyons and rolling over rocks at a violent rate. It is very difficult to cross, on account

---

[100] Probably Willow Creek, which drains Morrow County and affords water for stock-raising and sheep-pasturage. Late in the year, when Palmer passed, the stream was dry. The sandy margin along the Columbia from the mouth of Umatilla River to the Dalles, has always been an annoyance to traffic. Sand frequently drifts over the railway track in this region.— ED.

of the stone forming the bed of the creek; its width, however, does not exceed ten yards. The grazing is indifferent, the grass being completely dried.[101]

September 27. This morning we discovered that several of our trail ropes had been stolen. Our horses could not be found until very late; notwithstanding the delay thus occasioned we traveled some twenty miles. The road for the first three miles is up hill; it then pursues its course over a grassy, rolling plain for fifteen or sixteen miles, when it again descends the bluff to the bank of the Columbia, which we followed down for one mile and there encamped. The bluffs are very high and rocky. We suffered great inconvenience from the want of fuel, as there is none to be found along the Columbia; we collected a few dry sticks of driftwood and weeds, which enabled us to partially cook our food. The road we traveled this day was very good.

September 28. This day we traveled about twelve miles. Two miles brought us to the crossing of Deshutes or Falls [61] river; a stream having its source in a marshy plain bordering on the Great Basin, and receives numerous tributaries heading in the Cascade mountains, the eastern base of which it follows and pours its waters into the Columbia. The mouth of De Shutes river is near fifteen miles east of the Dalles or eastern base of these mountains; the river is about one hundred yards wide, and the current very rapid; the stream is enclosed by lofty cliffs of basaltic rock. Four hundred yards from the Columbia is a rapid or cascade. Within the distance of thirty yards its descent is from fifteen to

[101] For a brief note on John Day River see our volume xxi, p. 357, note 129.— ED.

twenty feet.[102] The current of this stream was so rapid and violent, and withal of such depth, as to require us to ferry it. Some of the companies behind us, however, drove over at its mouth by crossing on a bar. Preparatory to ferrying, we unloaded our wagons, and taking them apart, put them aboard some Indian canoes, which were in waiting, and crossed in safety; after putting our wagons in order of travel, and preparing to start, we discovered ourselves minus a quantity of powder and shot, two shirts and two pairs of pantaloons, which the Indians had appropriated to their own use, doubtless to pay the trouble of ferriage.

In the morning a quarrel ensued among the Indians respecting their canoes, closing in a *melee*, and such a fight I never before witnessed; stones and missiles of every description that were at hand were used with freedom. We did not interfere with them, and when they were tired of fighting the effects of the battle were visible in numerous instances, such as bloody noses and battered, bleeding heads.

We ascended the bluff and traveled along the brink for several miles, then crossed over the ridge to a small creek; after crossing it, we took up a dry run for one or two miles, thence over a ridge to a running branch, and there encamped. The country through which we traveled this day was extremely rough; all prairie, and covered with grass, but very dry.

September 29. This day we traveled about five miles, which brought us to the *Dalles*, or Methodist Missions.[103]

[102] For this river see our volume vii, p. 133, note 32; also our volume xxviii, p. 354, note 222.— ED.

[103] For the Dalles and the mission there located, consult our volumes xxi, p. 285, note 77; xxviii, pp. 355, 357, notes 223, 226.— ED.

Here was the end of our road, as no wagons had ever gone below this place. We found some sixty families in waiting for a passage down the river; and as there were but two small boats running to the Cascade falls, our prospect for a speedy passage was not overly flattering.

September 30. This day we intended to make arrangements for our passage down the river, but we found upon inquiry, that the two boats spoken of were engaged for at least [62] ten days, and that their charges were exorbitant, and would probably absorb what little we had left to pay our way to *Oregon City*. We then determined to make a trip over the mountains, and made inquiries respecting its practicability of some Indians, but could learn nothing definite, excepting that grass, timber and water would be found in abundance; we finally ascertained that a Mr. Barlow and Mr. Nighton had, with the same object, penetrated some twenty or twenty-five miles into the interior, and found it impracticable. Nighton had returned, but Barlow was yet in the mountains, endeavoring to force a passage; they had been absent six days, with seven wagons in their train, intending to go as far as they could, and if found to be impracticable, to return and go down the river.[104]

We succeeded in persuading fifteen families to accom-

<hr>

[104] Samuel Kimborough Barlow was of Scotch descent, the son of a Kentucky pioneer. Born (1795) in Nicholas County, in that state, he removed to Indiana (1818), where he married Susanna Lee of South Carolina. A further move to Fulton County, Illinois, paved the way for emigration to Oregon in 1845. Arrived in Oregon City, Christmas of that year, Barlow kept a hotel there until 1848, when he bought land in Clackamas County of Thomas McKay. Later (1852), he removed to Canemah, just above Oregon City, where he died in 1867. He was public-spirited and active in the affairs of the new commonwealth. For an account of the road constructed over the trail made

pany us in our trip over the mountains, and immediately made preparations for our march. On the afternoon of the first of October, our preparations were announced as complete, and we took up our line of march; others in the mean time had joined us, and should we fall in with Barlow, our train would consist of some thirty wagons.

But before proceeding with a description of this route, I will enter into a detail of the difficulties undergone by the company of two hundred wagons, which had separated from us at Malheur creek, under the pilotage of Mr. Meek.

It will be remembered that S. L. Meek had induced about two hundred families, with their wagons and stock, to turn off at Malheur, with the view of saving thereby some one hundred and fifty miles travel; and they had started about the last of August. They followed up Malheur creek, keeping up the southern branch, and pursuing a southern course. For a long time they found a very good road, plenty of grass, fuel and water; they left these waters, and directed their course over a rough mountainous country, almost entirely bereft of vegetation, were for many days destitute of water, and when they were so fortunate as to procure this indispensable element, it was found stagnant in pools, unfit even for the use of cattle; but necessity compelled them to the use of it. The result was, that it made many of them sick; many

in 1845, see Mary S. Barlow, "History of the Barlow Road," in *Oregon Historical Quarterly*, iii, pp. 71-81.

H. M. Knighton was second marshal of Oregon under the provisional government, and sergeant-at-arms of the house of representatives of 1846. He lived at Oregon City, where he kept an inn. In 1848 he was settled at St. Helena.— ED.

of the cattle died, and the majority were unfit for labor. A disease termed camp-fever, broke out among the different companies, of which many became the victims.

[63] They at length arrived at a marshy lake, which they attempted to cross, but found it impracticable; and as the marsh appeared to bear south, and many of them were nearly out of provisions, they came to a determination to pursue a northern course, and strike the Columbia. Meek, however, wished to go south of the lake, but they would not follow him. They turned north, and after a few days' travel arrived at Deshutes or Falls river. They traveled up and down this river, endeavoring to find a passage, but as it ran through rocky *kanyons*, it was impossible to cross.

Their sufferings were daily increasing, their stock of provisions was rapidly wasting away, their cattle were becoming exhausted, and many attached to the company were laboring under severe attacks of sickness; — at length Meek informed them that they were not more than two days' ride from the Dalles. Ten men started on horseback for the Methodist stations, with the view of procuring provisions; they took with them a scanty supply of provisions, intended for the two days' journey. After riding faithfully for ten days, they at last arrived at the Dalles. On their way they encountered an Indian, who furnished them with a fish and a rabbit; this with the provision they had started with, was their only food for the ten days' travel. Upon their arrival at the Dalles they were so exhausted in strength, and the rigidity of their limbs, from riding, was so great, as to render them unable to dismount without assistance. They reached the Dalles the day previous to our arrival.

At this place they met an old mountaineer, usually called Black Harris, who volunteered his services as a pilot.[188] He in company with several others, started in search of the lost company, whom they found reduced to great extremities; their provisions nearly exhausted, and the company weakened by exertion, and despairing of ever reaching the settlements. They succeeded in finding a place where their cattle could be driven down to the river, and made to swim across; after crossing, the bluff had to be ascended. Great difficulty arose in the attempt to effect a passage with the wagons. The means finally resorted to for the transportation of the families and wagons were novel in the extreme. A large rope was swung across the stream and attached to the rocks on either side; a light wagon bed was suspended from this rope with pulleys, to which ropes were attached; this bed served to convey the families and loading in safety across; the wagons [64] were then drawn over the bed of the river by ropes. The passage of this river occupied some two weeks. The distance was thirty-five miles to the Dalles, at which place they arrived about the 13th, or 14th of October. Some twenty of their number had perished by disease, previous to their arrival at the Dalles, and a like number were lost, after their arrival, from the same cause. This company has been

[188] Moses Harris, usually called Black Harris, was a well-known scout and trapper who came to Oregon with the emigrant train of 1844. See an amusing story concerning Harris, related by Peter H. Burnett in his "Recollections," in *Oregon Historical Quarterly*, iii, p. 152. While in Oregon Harris joined several exploring expeditions, notably that of Dr. Elijah White (1845) and that of Levi Scott (1846) in the attempt to find a shorter route from Lewis River to the Willamette valley. In 1846 Harris again went to the rescue of the emigrants who were trying a new route into Oregon; the following year, however, he returned to the states, dying at Independence, Missouri.— ED.

known by the name of the St. Joseph company; but there were persons from every state of the Union within its ranks. Illinois and Missouri, however, had the largest representation.

The statements I have given are as correct as I could arrive at, from consultation with many of the members. This expedition was unfortunate in the extreme. Although commenced under favorable auspices, its termination assumed a gloomy character.[100]

It has been stated that some members of the Hudson's Bay Company were instrumental in this expedition, but such is not the fact. Whilst I was at Fort Hall, I conversed with Captain Grant respecting the practicability of this same route, and was advised of the fact, that the teams would be unable to get through. The individual in charge at Fort Bois also advised me to the same purport. The censure rests, in the origin of the expedition, upon Meek; but I have not the least doubt but he supposed they could get through in safety. I have understood that a few of the members controlled Meek, and caused him to depart from his original plan. It was his design to have conducted the party to the *Willamette Valley*, instead of going to the Dalles; and the direction he first traveled induced this belief. Meek is yet of the opinion that had he gone round the marshy lake to the south, he would have struck the settlement on the Willamette, within the time required to travel to

[100] For other brief descriptions of the experiences of Meek's party, see H. H. Bancroft, *History of Oregon*, i, pp. 512-516, this latter being founded upon manuscript accounts, notably that of Samuel Hancock, a transcript of which is in the possession of Professor Joseph Schafer of the University of Oregon, – who has kindly loaned it to the present Editor. Consult also Oregon Pioneer Association *Transactions*, 1877, pp. 50-53; 1895, p. 101.— ED.

the Dalles. Had he discovered this route, it would have proved a great saving in the distance. I do not question but that there may be a route found to the south of this, opening into the valley of the Willamette.[107] But I must again return to the subject of my travels.

October 1. At four o'clock, P. M., every thing was ready for our departure, and we pursued our way over the ridge, in a southern course. The country was very rolling, and principally prairie. We found excellent grazing. Our camp was pitched on a small spring branch.

October 2. This day we made about ten miles, crossing several ravines, many of which had running water in them; [65] the country, like that of yesterday's travel, proved to be very rolling; our camp was situated on a small spring branch, having its source in the mountain.

October 3. This morning I started on horseback in advance of the company, accompanied by one of its members. Our course led us south over a rolling, grassy plain; portions of the road were very stony. After a travel of fourteen miles, we arrived at a long and steep declivity, which we descended, and after crossing the creek at its base, ascended a bluff; in the bottom are seen several small enclosures, where the

---

[107] There had been an Indian trail through the Cascades up the fork of the Santiam River, and over what is now known as the Minto Pass. Stephen Meek, who had trapped on the headwaters of John Day River, and there met Indians from the Willamette, thought that he could find this trail; but as a matter of fact it was not discovered by whites until 1873. Dr. White (1845) and Cornelius Gilliam (1846) made essays to open a road through the eastern barrier of the valley. See John Minto, "History of the Minto Pass," in *Oregon Historical Quarterly*, iv, pp. 241-250.— ED.

Indians have cultivated the soil; a few Indian huts may be seen along this stream.

Meek's company crossed Deshute's river near the mouth of this stream, which is five miles distant.[100] After ascending, we turned to the right, directing our course over a level grassy plain for some five miles or more, when we crossed a running branch; five miles brought us to Stony Branch, and to scattering yellow pine timber. Here we found Barlow's company of seven wagons. Barlow was absent at the time, having with three others started into the mountain two days before. We remained with them all night.

October 4. This morning myself and companion, with a scanty supply of provisions for a two days' journey, started on a westerly course into the mountains. From the open ground we could see Mount Hood. Our object was to go south and near to this peak. For five miles the country was alternately prairie and yellow pine; we then ascended a ridge, which ascended gradually to the west. This we followed for ten miles. After the crossing of a little brushy bottom, we took over another ridge for four or five miles, very heavily timbered and densely covered with undergrowth. We descended the ridge for a short distance, and traveled a level bench for four miles; this is covered with very large and tall fir timber; we then descended the mountain, traveling westward for one and a half miles; we then came to a small branch, which we named Rock creek.[100] After crossing the

---

[100] This was Tygh Creek, a western affluent of Deschutes River, about thirty-five miles above its mouth.— Ed.

[100] Marked on the United States land commissioner's map of Oregon (1897) as an affluent of White River, a branch of the Tygh.— Ed.

creek, we ascended a hill for one fourth of a mile, then bore to the left around the hill, through a dense forest of spruce pine.   After five miles travel from Rock creek we came to a marshy cedar swamp; we turned to the left, and there found a suitable place for crossing.   Here is a stream of from five to six yards in width, when confined to one channel; but in many places it runs over a bottom of two rods in width, strewed with old moss [66] covered logs and roots.   The water was extremely clear and cold.   Four miles brought us to the top of the bluff of a deep gulf; we turned our course northward for two miles, when darkness overtook us, forcing us to encamp. A little grass was discernible on the mountain sides, which afforded our jaded horses a scanty supply.

October 5.   At an early hour this morning, I proceeded down the mountain to the stream at its base.   I found the descent very abrupt and difficult; the distance was one half mile.   The water was running very rapid; it had the same appearance as the water of the *Missouri*, being filled with white sand.   I followed this stream up for some distance, and ascertained that its source was in Mount Hood; and from the appearance of the banks, it seems that its waters swell during the night, overflowing its banks, and subside again by day; it empties into Deshute's river, having a sandy bottom of from two rods to half a mile wide, covered with scrubby pines, and sometimes a slough of alder bushes, with a little grass and rushes.   We then ascended the mountain, and as our stock of provisions was barely sufficient to last us through the day, it was found necessary to return to camp.   We retraced our steps to where we had struck the bluff, and followed down a short distance where we found the mountain of sufficiently gradual descent to admit of the passage of teams; we could then follow up the bottom towards *Mount Hood*, and as we supposed that this peak was the dividing ridge, we had reasonable grounds to hope that we could get through. We then took our trail in the direction of the camp; and late in the evening, tired and hungry, we arrived at Rock creek, where we found our company encamped. Barlow had not yet returned, but we resolved to push forward.

October 6. We remained in camp. As the grazing was poor in the timber, and our loose cattle much trouble to us, we determined to send a party with them to the settlement. The Indians had informed us that there was a trail to the north, which ran over Mount Hood, and thence to Oregon city. This party was to proceed up one of the ridges until they struck this trail, and then follow it to the settlement. Two families decided upon going with this party, and as I expected to have no further use for my horse, I sent him with them. They were to procure provisions and assistance, and meet us on the way. We had forwarded, by a company of cattle-drivers from the Dalles, which started for the settlement on the first of the [67] month, a request that they would send us provisions and assistance; but as we knew nothing of their whereabouts, we had little hope of being benefited by them.[110] The day was spent in making the necessary arrangements for the cattle-drivers, and for working the road. In the afternoon, Barlow and his

---

[110] See an account of this party of cattle drivers and their adventures in "Occasional Address," by Hon. Stephen Staats, in Oregon Pioneer Association *Transactions*, 1877, pp. 51, 52. Staats was one of the party who reached Oregon City in thirteen days from the Dalles.— ED.

party returned. They had taken nearly the same route that we had; they had followed up the bluff of this branch of the De Shutes, to within twelve or fifteen miles of Mount Hood, where they supposed they had seen Willamette valley. They had then taken the Indian trail spoken of, and followed it to one of the ridges leading down to the river De Shutes; this they followed, and came out near our camp. We now jointly adopted measures for the prosecution of the work before us.

October 7. Early in the morning, the party designated to drive our loose cattle made their arrangements, and left us. And as we supposed our stock of provisions was insufficient to supply us until these men returned, we dispatched a few men to the Dalles for a beef and some wheat; after which, we divided our company so as that a portion were to remain and take charge of the camp. A sufficient number were to pack provisions, and the remainder were to be engaged in opening the road. All being ready, each one entered upon the duty assigned him with an alacrity and willingness that showed a full determination to prosecute it to completion, if possible. On the evening of the 10th, we had opened a road to the top of the mountain, which we were to descend to the branch of the De Shutes.[111] The side of the mountain was covered with a species of laurel bush, and so thick, that it was almost impossible to pass through it, and as it was very dry we set it on fire. We passed down and encamped on the creek, and during the night

[111] The Little Deschutes, rising on the slopes of Mount Hood. See reminiscences of William Barlow, son of the leader of this party, in *Oregon Historical Quarterly*, iii, pp. 71-81. He speaks of the lack of good tools for opening the road, rusty saws and axes being the only implements available to the builders. They frequently reverted to firing the underbrush ahead of them.— ED.

the fire had nearly cleared the road on the side of the mountain.

On the morning of October 11th, a consultation was had, when it was determined that Mr. Barlow, Mr. Lock, and myself, should go in advance, and ascertain whether we could find a passage over the main dividing ridge. In the mean time, the remainder of the party were to open the road up the creek bottom as far as they could, or until our return. We took some provision in our pockets, an axe, and one rifle, and started. We followed up this branch about fifteen miles, when we reached a creek, coming in from the left. We followed up this for a short distance, and then struck across to [68] the main fork; and in doing so, we came into a cedar swamp, so covered with heavy timber and brush that it was almost impossible to get through it. We were at least one hour in traveling half a mile. We struck the opening along the other fork, traveled up this about eight miles, and struck the Indian trail spoken of before, near where it comes down the mountain. The last eight miles of our course had been nearly north — a high mountain putting down between the branch and main fork. Where we struck the trail, it turned west into a wide, sandy and stony plain, of several miles in width, extending up to *Mount Hood*, about seven or eight miles distant, and in plain view.

I had never before looked upon a sight so nobly grand. We had previously seen only the top of it, but now we had a view of the whole mountain. No pen can give an adequate description of this scene. The bottom which we were ascending, had a rise of about three feet to the rod. A perfect mass of rock and gravel had been washed down from the mountain. In one part of the bottom was standing a grove of dead trees, the top of which could be seen; from appearance, the surface had been filled up seventy-five or eighty feet about them. The water came tumbling down, through a little channel, in torrents. Near the upper end of the bottom, the mountains upon either side narrowed in until they left a deep chasm or gulf, where it emerged from the rocky cliffs above.

Stretching away to the south, was a range of mountain, which from the bottom appeared to be connected with the mountain on our left. It appeared to be covered with timber far up; then a space of over two miles covered with grass; then a space of more than a mile destitute of vegetation; then commenced the snow, and continued rising until the eye was pained in looking to the top. To our right was a high range, which connected with Mount Hood, covered with timber. The timber near the snow was dead.

We followed this trail for five or six miles, when it wound up a grassy ridge to the left — followed it up to where it connected with the main ridge; this we followed up for a mile, when the grass disappeared, and we came to a ridge entirely destitute of vegetation. It appeared to be sand and gravel, or rather, decomposed material from sandstone crumbled to pieces. Before reaching this barren ridge, we met a party of those who had started with the loose cattle, hunting for some which had strayed off. They informed us that they had lost about [69] one-third of their cattle, and were then encamped on the west side of Mount Hood. We determined to lodge with them, and took the trail over the mountain. In the mean time, the cattle-drovers had found a few head, and traveled with us to their camp.

Soon after ascending and winding round this barren

ridge, we crossed a ravine, one or two rods in width, upon the snow, which terminated a short distance below the trail, and extended up to the top of Mount Hood. We then went around the mountain for about two miles, crossing several strips of snow, until we came to a deep kanyon or gulf, cut out by the wash from the mountain above us. A precipitate cliff of rocks, at the head, prevented a passage around it. The hills were of the same material as that we had been traveling over, and were very steep.

I judged the ravine to be three thousand feet deep. The manner of descending is to turn directly to the right, go zigzag for about one hundred yards, then turn short round, and go zigzag until you come under the place where you started from; then to the right, and so on, until you reach the base. In the bottom is a rapid stream, filled with sand. After crossing, we ascended in the same manner, went round the point of a ridge, where we struck another ravine; the sides of this were covered with grass and whortleberry bushes. In this ravine we found the camp of our friends. We reached them about dark; the wind blew a gale, and it was quite cold.

October 12. After taking some refreshment, we ascended the mountain, intending to head the deep ravine, in order to ascertain whether there was any gap in the mountain south of us, which would admit of a pass. From this peak, we overlooked the whole of the mountains. We followed up the grassy ridge for one mile and a half, when it became barren. My two friends began to lag behind, and show signs of fatigue; they finally stopped, and contended that we could not get round the head of the ravine, and that it was useless to attempt an ascent. But I was of a different opinion, and wished to go on. They consented, and followed for half a mile, when they sat down, and requested me to go up to the ledge, and, if we could effect a passage up and get round it, to give them a signal. I did so, and found that by climbing up a cliff of snow and ice, for about forty feet, but not so steep but that by getting upon one cliff, and cutting holes to stand in and hold on by, it could be ascended. I gave the signal, and they came up. In the [70] mean time, I had cut and carved my way up the cliff, and when up to the top was forced to admit that it was something of an undertaking; but as I had arrived safely at the top of the cliff, I doubted not but they could accomplish the same task, and as my moccasins were worn out, and the soles of my feet exposed to the snow, I was disposed to be traveling, and so left them to get up the best way they could. After proceeding about one mile upon the snow, continually winding up, I began to despair of seeing my companions. I came to where a few detached pieces of rock had fallen from the ledge above and rolled down upon the ice and snow, (for the whole mass is more like ice than snow;) I clambered upon one of these, and waited half an hour. I then rolled stones down the mountain for half an hour; but as I could see nothing of my two friends, I began to suspect that they had gone back, and crossed in the trail. I then went round to the south-east side, continually ascending, and taking an observation of the country south, and was fully of the opinion that we could find a passage through.[112]

---

[112] The opinion heretofore entertained, that this peak could not be ascended to its summit, I found to be erroneous. I, however, did not arrive at the highest

The waters of this deep ravine, and of numerous ravines to the north-west, as well as the south-west, form the heads of Big Sandy and Quicksand rivers, which empty into the Columbia, about twenty-five or thirty miles below the Cascade Falls.[113] I could see down this stream some twelve or fifteen miles, where the view was obstructed by a high range coming round from the north-west side, connecting by a low gap with some of the spurs from this peak. All these streams were running through such deep chasms, that it was impossible to pass them with teams. To the south, were two ranges of mountains, connecting by a low gap with this peak, and winding round until they terminated near Big Sandy. I observed that a stream, heading near the base of this peak and running south-east [71] for several miles, there appeared to turn to the west. This I judged to be the head waters of Clackamis, which empties into the Willamette, near Oregon city; but the view was hid by a high range of mountains putting down in that direction.[114] A low gap seemed to connect this stream, or

peak, but went sufficiently near to prove its practicability. I judge the diameter of this peak, at the point where the snow remains the year round, to be about three miles. At the head of many of the ravines, are perpendicular cliffs of rocks, apparently several thousand feet high; and in some places those cliffs rise so precipitately to the summit, that a passage around is impracticable. I think the southern side affords the easiest ascent. The dark strips observable from a distance, are occasioned by blackish rock, so precipitous as not to admit of the snow lying upon it. The upper strata are of gray sandstone, and seem to be of original formation. There is no doubt, but any of the snow peaks upon this range can be ascended to the summit.— PALMER.

[113] This should read Big Sandy or Quicksand River. Lewis and Clark gave it the latter name. It is usually known as the Sandy, and in many branches drains the western slope of Mount Hood, flowing northwest into the Columbia, in Multnomah County.— ED.

[114] For Clackamas River see our volume xxi, p. 320, note 105.— ED.

some other, heading in this high range, with the low bottoms immediately under the base of this peak. I was of the opinion that a pass might be found between this peak and the first range of mountains, by digging down some of the gravel hills; and if not, there would be a chance of passing between the first and second ranges, through this gap to the branch of Clackamis; or, by taking some of the ranges of mountains and following them down, could reach the open ground near the Willamette, as there appeared to be spurs extending in that direction. I could also see a low gap in the direction from where we crossed the small branch, coming up the creek on the 11th, towards several small prairies south of us. It appeared, that if we could get a road opened to that place, our cattle could range about these prairies until we could find a passage for the remainder of the way.

The day was getting far advanced, and we had no provisions, save each of us a small biscuit; and knowing that we had at least twenty-five miles to travel, before reaching those working on the road, I hastened down the mountain. I had no difficulty in finding a passage down; but I saw some deep ravines and crevices in the ice which alarmed me, as I was compelled to travel over them. The snow and ice had melted underneath, and in many places had left but a thin shell upon the surface; some of them had fallen in and presented hideous looking caverns. I was soon out of danger, and upon the east side of the deep ravine I saw my two friends slowly winding their way up the mountain. They had gone to the foot of the ledge, and as they wore boots, and were much fatigued, they abandoned the trip, and returned down the mountain to the trail, where I joined them. We there rested awhile, and struck our course for one of the prairies which we had seen from the mountain. On our way we came to a beautiful spring of water, surrounded with fine timber; the ground was covered with whortle berry bushes, and many of them hanging full of fruit, we halted, ate our biscuit, gathered berries, and then proceeded down the mountain.

After traveling about ten miles, we reached the prairie. It was covered with grass, and was very wet. A red sediment [72] of about two inches in depth covered the surface of the ground in the grass, such as is found around mineral springs. A beautiful clear stream of water was running through the prairie, in a south-east direction. We had seen a prairie about two miles further south, much larger than this, which we supposed to be dry. We now took our course for camp, intending to strike through the gap to the mouth of the small branch; but we failed in finding the right *shute*, and came out into the bottom, three miles above where we had first struck the cattle or Indian trail. We then took down the bottom, and arrived in camp about eleven o'clock at night; and although not often tired, I was willing to acknowledge that I was near being so. I certainly was hungry, but my condition was so much better than that of my two friends, that I could not murmur. Our party had worked the road up to the small branch, where they were encamped.

On the morning of the 13th of October we held a consultation, and determined upon the future movements of the company. The party designated to bring us provisions had performed that service; but the amount of our provisions was nearly exhausted, and many of the party had no means of procuring more. Some of them began to despair of getting through this season. Those left with the camp were unable to keep the cattle together, and a number of them had been lost. The Indians had stolen several horses, and a variety of mishaps occurred, such as would necessarily follow from a company so long remaining in one position. They were now on a small creek, five miles from Stony hill, which we called Camp creek, and near the timber. It was impossible to keep more than one third of the men working at the road; the remainder were needed to attend the camp and pack provisions. It was determined to send a party and view out the road, through to the open country, near the mouth of Clackamis, whilst the others were to open the road as far as the big prairie; a number sufficient to bring up the teams and loose cattle, (for a number of families with their cattle had joined since ours left, and portions of our company did not send their loose cattle,) to a grassy prairie in this bottom, and near the mouth of this creek, as the time required to pack provisions to those working on the road would be saved. All being arranged, the next thing was to designate the persons to go ahead of the party, and if found practicable to return with pro-visions and help; or at all events to ascertain whether the route were practicable.

[73] It was determined that I should undertake this trip. I asked only one man to accompany me. We took our blankets, a limited supply of provisions, and one light axe, and at eight o'clock in the morning set out. I was satisfied that the creek which we were then on, headed in the low gap, seen from Mount Hood; and the

party were to open the road up this branch. But as I was to precede them, I passed up this creek for about eight or ten miles, when I discovered the low gap, went through it, and at noon arrived at the wet prairie, which we had visited the day before. The route was practicable, but would require great labor to remove the timber, and cut out the underbrush.

We halted at the creek and took some refreshment; we then struck for the low gap between the first range of mountains running west, and the base of Mount Hood, and traveled through swamps, small prairies, brush, and heavy timber for about twelve miles, when we found the labor necessary to open a wagon road in this direction, to be greater than we could possibly bestow upon it before the rainy season. We determined to try some other route, retraced our steps six or seven miles, and then bore to the right, around the base of the mountain, when we struck into an old Indian trail. This we followed for seven or eight miles, through the gap I had seen from Mount Hood. It is a rolling bottom of about four or five miles in width, and extending from the base of Mount Hood south for ten or twelve miles. The trail wound around the mountain, but as its course was about that we wished to travel, we followed it until it ran out at the top of the mountain. We then took the ridge west, and traveled until dark; but as the moon shone bright, and the timber was not very thick, we turned an angle down the mountain to the left, to procure water. We traveled about three miles, and struck upon a small running branch; this we followed, until owing to the darkness, we were compelled to encamp, much fatigued, and somewhat disheartened.

October 14. At daylight we were on the way. My moccasins, which the night before had received a pair of soles, in yesterday's tramp had given way, and in traveling after night my feet had been badly snagged, so that I was in poor plight for walking; but as there was no alternative, we started down the mountain, and after traveling a few miles I felt quite well and was able to take the lead. We traveled about three miles, when we struck a large creek which had a very rapid current, over a stony bottom. I had hoped to find a bottom of sufficient [74] width to admit of a wagon road, but after following down this stream six miles, I was satisfied that it would not do to attempt it this season.

The weather, which had been entirely clear for months, had through the night began to cloud up; and in the morning the birds, squirrels, and every thing around, seemed to indicate the approach of a storm. I began for the first time to falter, and was at a stand to know what course to pursue. I had understood that the rainy season commenced in October, and that the streams rose to an alarming height, and I was sensible that if we crossed the branch of the Deshutes, which headed in Mount Hood, and the rainy season set in, we could not get back, and to get forward would be equally impossible; so that in either event starvation would be the result. And as I had been very active in inducing others to embark in the enterprise, my conscience would not allow me to go on and thus endanger so many families. But to go back, and state to them the difficulties to be encountered, and the necessity of taking some other course, seemed to be my duty. I therefore resolved to return, and recommend selecting some suitable place

for a permanent camp, build a cabin, put in such effects
as we could not pack out, and leave our wagons and
effects in the charge of some persons until we could
return the next season, unincumbered with our families
and cattle, and finish the road; — or otherwise to return
to the Dalles with our teams, where we could leave our
baggage in charge of the missionaries, and then descend
the Columbia. And when my mind was fully made
up, we were not long in carrying it into execution.

We accordingly ascended the mountain, as it was
better traveling than in the bottom. The distance to
the summit was about four miles, and the way was
sometimes so steep as to render it necessary to pull up
by the bushes. We then traveled east until we reached
the eastern point of this mountain, and descended to
the bottom, the base of which we had traversed the day
before. We then struck for the trail, soon found it, and
followed it until it led us to the southern end of the wet
prairie. We then struck for the lower gap in the direction of the camp, crossed over and descended the branch
to near its mouth, where we found four of our company
clearing the road, the remainder having returned to
Camp creek for teams. But as we had traveled about
fifty miles this day, I was unable to reach the camp.

October 15. This morning we all started for camp,
carrying [75] with us our tools and provisions. We
reached camp about two P. M. Many of our cattle
could not be found, but before night nearly all were
brought into camp. The whole matter was then laid
before the company, when it was agreed that we should
remove over to the bottom, near the small creek, and
if the weather was unfavorable, leave our baggage and

wagons, and pack out the families as soon as possible.
But as some were out of provisions, it was important
that a messenger should be sent on ahead for provisions, and horses to assist in packing out.   Mr. Buffum,
and lady, concluded to pack out what articles they
could, and leave a man to take charge of the teams and
cattle, until he returned with other horses.   He kindly
furnished me with one of his horses to ride to the settlement.   He also supplied the wife of Mr. Thompson
with a horse.   Mr. Barlow and Mr. Rector made a
proposition to continue working the road until the party
could go to and return from the valley; they agreeing
to insure the safety of the wagons, if compelled to remain
through the winter, by being paid a certain per cent.
upon the valuation.   This proposition was thought
reasonable by some, and it was partially agreed to.
And as there were some who had no horses with which
to pack out their families, they started on foot for the
valley, designing to look out a road as they passed along.
Some men in the mean time were to remain with the
camp, which as above stated was to be removed to the
small branch on Shutes' fork; and those who intended
pushing out at once, could follow up it to the Indian
trail.   This all being agreed upon, arrangements were
made accordingly.

October 16.   The morning was lowering, with every
indication of rain.   Messrs. Barlow and Rector started
on the trip.[115]   All hands were making arrangements

---

[115] William H. Rector settled at Champoeg, which district he represented
in the legislature of 1847.   During the gold excitement the following year, he
went to California, but returned to Oregon, where in 1857 he was instrumental
in starting the pioneer woolen mill at Salem, of which for some time he was
superintendent.   In 1861 he was commissioner of Indian affairs, with head-

for moving the camp. In the mean time Mr. Buffum and his lady, and Mrs. Thompson, were ready to start.[110] I joined them, and we again set out for the settlement. We had traveled about two miles when it commenced raining, and continued raining slightly all day. We encamped on the bottom of Shutes' fork, near the small branch. It rained nearly all night.

On the morning of the 17th October after our horses had filled themselves, we packed up and started. It was still raining. We followed up this bottom to the trail, and then pursued the trail over Mount Hood. Whilst going over this mountain the rain poured down in torrents, it was foggy, and very cold. We arrived at the deep ravine at about four P. M., [76] and before we ascended the opposite bank it was dark; but we felt our way over the ridge, and round the point to the grassy run. Here was grazing for our tired horses,

quarters at Portland. In later life, Rector was interested in railway enterprises. Popular with Oregon settlers, he was quite commonly known as " Uncle Billy."— ED.

[110] William Gilbert Buffum was born in Vermont in 1804. When eleven years of age his family removed to Ashtabula County, Ohio. In 1825 Buffum went to Illinois to work in the mines, later settling in Fulton County, and removing to Missouri in 1841. His wife, Caroline Thurman, was born in Ohio in 1814. After their long journey to Oregon, the Buffums settled in Yamhill County, near Amity, where they afterwards resided, with the exception of a year spent in the California gold fields. Buffum was still living in Amity in 1898. See his reminiscences in Oregon Pioneer Association *Transactions*, 1889, pp. 42-44.

Mrs. Miriam A. Thompson (*née* Robinson) was born in Illinois (1826) and married the year before the migration to Oregon. After reaching the Willamette she settled in Yamhill County, thence removing to Clatsop Plains, where in 1848 her husband left her for California. There he was murdered, and in 1850 his widow married Jeremiah H. Tuller, after 1880 living in Douglas County. For her own account of her adventures, and especially this trip across the Cascade Mountains, see Oregon Pioneer Association *Transactions*, 1895, pp. 87-90.— ED.

and we dismounted. Upon the side of the mountain, where were a few scattering trees, we found some limbs and sticks, with which we succeeded in getting a little fire. We then found a few sticks and constructed a tent, covering it with blankets, which protected our baggage and the two women. Mr. Buffum and myself stood shivering in the rain around the fire, and when daylight appeared, it gave us an opportunity to look at each others' lank visages. Our horses were shivering with the cold, the rain had put out our fire, and it seemed as though every thing had combined to render us miserable. After driving our horses round awhile, they commenced eating; but we had very little to eat, and were not troubled much in cooking it.

October 18. As soon as our horses had satisfied themselves we packed up and ascended the mountain over the ridge, and for two miles winding around up and down over a rough surface covered with grass. The rain was falling in torrents, and it was so foggy that we could barely see the trail. We at length went down a ridge two miles, when we became bewildered in the thick bushes. The trail had entirely disappeared. We could go no farther. The two women sat upon their horses in the rain, whilst I went back to search for the right trail; Buffum endeavoring to make his way down the mountain. I rambled about two miles up the mountain, where I found the right trail, and immediately returned to inform them of it. Buffum had returned, and of course had not found the trail. We then ascended the mountain to the trail, when a breeze sprung up and cleared away the fog. We could then follow the trail.

We soon saw a large band of cattle coming up the
mountain, and in a short time met a party of men following them. They had started from the Dalles about
eight days before, and encamped that night four or five
miles below, and as it was a barren spot, their cattle
had strayed to the mountain to get grass. But what
was very gratifying, they informed us that a party of
men from Oregon city, with provisions for our company
had encamped with them, and were then at their camp.
We hastened down the mountain, and in a few hours
arrived at the camp. But imagine our feelings when
we learned that those having provisions for us, had
despaired of finding us, and [77] having already been
out longer than was expected, had returned to the settlement, carrying with them all the provisions, save what
they had distributed to these men. We were wet, cold,
and hungry, and would not be likely to overtake them.
We prevailed upon one of the men whom we found
at the camp, to mount one of our horses, and follow
them. He was absent about ten minutes, when he
returned and informed us that they were coming. They
soon made their appearance. This revived us, and
for awhile we forgot that we were wet and cold. They
had gone about six miles back, when some good spirit
induced them to return to camp, and make one more
effort to find us. The camp was half a mile from the
creek, and we had nothing but two small coffee-pots,
and a few tin cups, to carry water in; but this was
trifling, as the rain was still pouring down upon us.
We speedily made a good fire, and set to work making
a tent, which we soon accomplished, and the two women
prepared us a good supper of bread and coffee. It was

a rainy night, but we were as comfortable as the circumstances would admit.

October 19. After breakfast, the drovers left us; and
as the party which had brought us provisions had been
longer out than had been contemplated, Mr. Stewart
and Mr. Gilmore wished to return. It was determined
that Mr. Buffum, the two females, Mr. Stewart, and Mr.
N. Gilmore, should go on to the settlement, and that
Mr. C. Gilmore, and the Indian who had been sent
along to assist in driving the horses, and myself, should
hasten on with the provisions to the camp. We were
soon on the way, and climbing up the mountain. The
horses were heavily loaded, and in many places the
mountain was very slippery, and of course we had great
difficulty in getting along. It was still raining heavily,
and the fog so thick that a person could not see more
than fifteen feet around. We traveled about two miles
up the mountain, when we found that whilst it had been
raining in the valley it had been snowing on the mountain.
The trail was so covered with snow that it was difficult
to find it, and, to increase our difficulty, the Indian
refused to go any farther. We showed him the whip,
which increased his speed a little, but he soon forgot
it, was very sulky, and would not assist in driving. We
at length arrived at the deep ravine; here there was no
snow, and we passed it without serious difficulty. Two
of our packs coming off, and rolling down the hill, was
the only serious trouble that we had. When we ascended
the hill to [78] the eastern side of the gulf, we found
the snow much deeper than upon the western side;
besides, it had drifted, and rendered the passage over
the strip of the old snow somewhat dangerous, as in

many places the action of the water had melted the snow upon the under side, and left a thin shell over the surface, and in some places holes had melted through. We were in danger of falling into one of these pits. Coming to one of these ravines where the snow had drifted very much, I dismounted in order to pick a trail through, but before this was completed, our horses started down the bank. I had discovered two of these pits, and ran to head the horses and turn them; but my riding horse started to run, and went directly between the two pits; his weight jarred the crust loose, and it fell in, presenting a chasm of some twenty-five or thirty feet in depth, but the horse, being upon the run, made his way across the pit. The other horses, hearing the noise and seeing the pits before them, turned higher up, where the snow and ice were thicker, and all reached the opposite side in safety.

Our Indian friend now stopped, and endeavored to turn the horses back, but two to one was an uneven game, and it was played to his disadvantage. He wanted an additional blanket; this I promised him, and he consented to go on. We soon met two Indians, on their way from the Dalles to Oregon city; our Indian conversed with them awhile, and then informed us of his intention to return with them. Whilst parleying with him, a party of men from our camp came up the mountain with their cattle; they had driven their teams to the small branch of the De Shutes, twelve miles below the mountain, where they had left the families, and started out with their cattle before the stream should get too high to cross. Whilst we were conversing with these men, our Indian had succeeded in getting one loose horse, and the one which he was riding, so far from the band of pack-horses that, in the fog, we could not see him, and he returned to the settlement with the two Indians we had just met.

Our horses were very troublesome to drive, as they had ate nothing for thirty-six hours; but we succeeded in getting them over the snow, and down to the grassy ridge, where we stopped for the night. My friend Gilmore shouldered a bag of flour, carried it half a mile down the mountain to a running branch, opened the sack, poured in water, and mixed up bread. In the mean time, I had built a fire. We wrapped the dough around sticks and baked it before the fire, heated water in our [79] tin cups and made a good dish of tea, and passed a very comfortable night. It had ceased raining before sunset, and the morning was clear and pleasant; we forgot the past, and looked forward to a bright future.

October 20. At 8 o'clock we packed up, took the trail down the mountain to the gravelly bottom, and then down the creek to the wagon-camp, which we reached at 3 P. M.; and if we had not before forgotten our troubles, we certainly should have done so upon arriving at camp. Several families were entirely out of provisions, others were nearly so, and all were expecting to rely upon their poor famished cattle. True, this would have prevented starvation; but it would have been meagre diet, and there was no certainty of having cattle long, as there was but little grass. A happier set of beings I never saw, and the thanks bestowed upon us by these families would have compensated for no little toil and hardship. They were supplied with an amount of provisions sufficient to last them until they could reach the settlements. After waiting one day, Mr. Gilmore left the camp for the settlement, taking with him three families; others started about the same time, and in a few days all but three families had departed. These were Mr. Barlow's, Mr. Rector's, and Mr. Caplinger's,[117] all of whom had gone on to the settlement for horses. Ten men yet remained at camp, and, after selecting a suitable place for our wagon-yard, we erected a cabin for the use of those who were to remain through the winter, and to stow away such of our effects as we could not pack out. This being done, nothing remained but to await the return of those who had gone for pack horses. We improved the time in hunting and gathering berries, until the 25th, when four of us, loaded with heavy packs, started on foot for the valley of the Willamette.

But before entering upon this trip, I will state by what means the timely assistance afforded us in the way of provisions was effected. The first party starting for the settlement from the Dalles, after we had determined to take the mountain route, carried the news to Oregon city that we were attempting a passage across the Cascade mountains, and that we should need provisions. The good people of that place immediately raised by donation about eleven hundred pounds of flour, over one hundred pounds of sugar, some tea, &c., hired horses, and the Messrs. Gilmore and Mr.

---

[117] Jacob C. Caplinger was born in Virginia in 1815, of German descent. In 1837 he removed to Illinois, in 1841 marrying Jane Woodsides. After reaching the settlements, the Caplingers remained at Oregon City until 1847, when they purchased a farm near Salem, where they were living in 1892.— ED.

Stewart volunteered to bring these articles to us.[118]   The only expense we were asked to defray was the hire of the horses.   They [80] belonged to an Indian chief, and of course he had to be paid.   The hire was about forty dollars, which brought the flour to about four dollars per hundred, as there were about one thousand pounds when they arrived.   Those who had the means paid at once, and those who were unable to pay gave their due bills.   Many of the families constructed pack-saddles and put them on oxen, and, in one instance, a feather bed was rolled up and put upon an ox; but the animal did not seem to like his load, and ran into the woods, scattering the feathers in every direction: he was finally secured, but not until the bed was ruined. In most cases, the oxen performed well.

In the afternoon of the 25th October, accompanied by Messrs. Creighton, Farwell, and Buckley, I again started to the valley.   We had traveled but a short distance when we met Barlow and Rector, who had been to the settlement.   They had some horses, and expected others in a short time.   They had induced a few families whom they met near Mount Hood to return with them, and try their chance back to the Dalles;   but, after waiting one day, they concluded to try the mountain trip again.   We traveled up the bottom to the trail, where we encamped; about this

[118] Matthew (not N.) Gilmore came out in 1843, settling on the Tualatin Plains, where he was chosen delegate to the provisional legislature of 1844. Gilmore was a farmer, not prominent in public life.

Charles Gilmore appears to have been of the migration of 1844.

Peter G. Stewart came with the Applegate party of 1843, and was one of the executive committee of three, chosen in 1844.   He was a man of calm, dispassionate temper, who had been a jeweler in the states.   In 1853 he was port surveyor at Pacific City.— Ed.

time, it commenced raining, which continued through the night.

October 26. This morning at eight o'clock, we were on the way. It was rainy, and disagreeable traveling. We followed the trail over the main part of the mountain, when we overtook several families, who had left us on the twenty-second. Two of the families had encamped the night before in the bottom of the deep ravine; night overtook them, and they were compelled to camp, without fuel, or grass for cattle or horses. Water they had in plenty, for it was pouring down upon them all the night. One of their horses broke loose, and getting to the provision sack, destroyed the whole contents. There were nine persons in the two families, four of them small children, and it was about eighty miles to the nearest settlement. The children, as well as the grown people, were nearly barefoot, and poorly clad. Their names were Powell and Senters. Another family by the name of Hood, had succeeded in getting [110] up the gravelly hill, and finding grass for their animals, and a little fuel, had shared their scanty supply with these two families, and when we overtook them they were all encamped near each other. We gave them about half of our provisions, and encamped near them. Mr. Hood kindly furnished us with a [81] wagon cover, with which we constructed a tent, under which we rested for the night.

October 27. The two families who had lost their

[110] According to H. H. Bancroft, *History of Oregon*, i, pp. 525, 526, these were the families of Andrew Hood and Sharp C. Senters. Rev. Theophilus Powell was born in Kentucky, left for Oregon from Missouri, and died in Marion County, Oregon, in 1861.— ED.

provisions succeeded in finding a heifer that belonged to one of the companies traveling in advance of us. In rambling upon the rocky cliffs above the trail for grass, it had fallen down the ledge, and was so crippled as not to be able to travel. The owners had left it, and as the animal was in good condition, it was slaughtered and the meat cured.

After traveling four miles through the fresh snow, (which had fallen about four inches deep during the night,) we came to where the trail turned down to the Sandy. We were glad to get out of the snow, as we wore moccasins, and the bottoms being worn off, our feet were exposed. Two miles brought us to where we left the Sandy, and near the place where we met the party with provisions; here we met Mr. Buffum, Mr. Lock, and a Mr. Smith,[120] with fourteen pack-horses, going for effects to Fort Deposit — the name which we had given our wagon camp.

The numerous herds of cattle which had passed along had so ate up the grass and bushes, that it was with great difficulty the horses could procure a sufficiency to sustain life. Among the rest, was a horse for me; and as I had a few articles at the fort, Mr. Buffum was to take the horse along and pack them out. Two of his horses were so starved as to be unable to climb the mountains, and we took them back with us. The weather by this time had cleared up; we separated, and each party took its way.

---

[120] Several members of the party of 1845 bore the name of Smith; probably this was Simeon, born in Ohio in 1823, removed to Missouri in 1838, and settled in Marion County, finally making his home in Salem, where he died in 1878. See reference in Stephen Staats's address, in Oregon Pioneer Association *Transactions*, 1877, p. 55; also *ibid.*, 1878, pp. 92, 93.— ED.

A short distance below this, our trail united with one which starting from the Dalles, runs north of Mount Hood, and until this season was the only trail traveled by the whites. We proceeded down the Sandy, crossing it several times, through thickets of spruce and alder, until we arrived at the forks, which were about fifteen miles from the base of Mount Hood. The bottom of the Sandy is similar to the branch of De Shutes which we ascended; but in most cases the gravel and stones are covered with moss; portions of it are entirely destitute of vegetation. The mountains are very high, and are mostly covered with timber. At a few points are ledges of grayish rock, but the greater part of the mountain is composed of sand and gravel; it is much cut up by deep ravines, or kanyons. The trail is sometimes very difficult to follow, on account of the brush and logs; about our camp are a few bunches of [82] brakes, which the horses eat greedily. The stream coming in from the south-east is the one which I followed down on the 14th, and from appearance I came within five miles of the forks. The bottom in this vicinity is more than a mile wide, and is covered with spruce, hemlock and alder, with a variety of small bushes.

October 28. We started early, and after having traveled several miles, found a patch of good grass, where we halted our horses for an hour. We then traveled on, crossing the Sandy three times. This is a rapid stream; the water is cold, and the bottom very stony. We made about fifteen or sixteen miles only, as we could not get our horses along faster. We struck into a road recently opened for the passage of wagons. Mr. Taylor, from Ohio, who had left our company with his family and cattle on the 7th, had arrived safely in the valley, and had procured a party of men and had sent them into the mountains to meet us at the crossing of Sandy.[121]   They had come up this far, and commenced cutting the road toward the settlements.   After traveling this road five or six miles we came upon their camp, where we again found something to eat; our provisions having been all consumed.   The road here runs through a flat or bottom of several miles in width, and extending ten or twelve miles down the Sandy; it bears towards the north, whilst the creek forms an elbow to the south. The soil is good, and is covered with a very heavy growth of pine and white cedar timber.   I saw some trees of white cedar that were seven feet in diameter, and at least one hundred and fifty feet high.   I measured several old trees that had fallen, which were one hundred and eighty feet in length, and about six feet in diameter at the root.   We passed some small prairies and several beautiful streams, which meandered through the timber. The ground lies sloping to the south, as it is on the north side of the creek.   In the evening it commenced raining a little.   We remained at this camp all night.

October 29.   This morning, after breakfast, we parted

---

[121] Colonel James Taylor was born in Pennsylvania (1809), of Scotch-Irish ancestry.   In 1823 he removed to Ohio, where he was active in the state militia and connected with the Indian trade.   His wife was Esther d'Armon, who came with him to Oregon.   See her biography in Oregon Pioneer Association *Transactions*, 1897, pp. 103-105, wherein is recounted her experience in crossing the Cascades.   Colonel Taylor removed in 1846 to Clatsop Plains, but at the outbreak of the Cayuse War (1847) carried his family back to Oregon City, while he served in the extempore army as assistant commissary to General Palmer.   In 1849-51 Taylor was chosen first territorial treasurer.   About 1850 the Taylors returned to Clatsop, removing to Astoria about 1855, where they passed the remainder of their lives, both dying in 1893.— ED.

with our friends and pursued our way. We soon ascended a ridge which we followed for seven or eight miles, alternately prairie and fern openings. In these openings the timber is not large, but grows rather scrubby. There are numerous groves of beautiful pine timber, tall and straight. The soil is of a reddish cast, and very mellow, and I think would produce well. We came to the termination of this ridge and descended to the bottom, which has been covered with heavy timber, but which [83] has been killed by fire. From this ridge we could see several others, of a similar appearance, descending gradually towards the west.

We here crossed the creek or river, which was deep and rapid; and as our horses were barely able to carry themselves, we were compelled to wade the stream. Buckly had been sick for several days, and not able to carry his pack; and if at other times I regretted the necessity of being compelled to carry his pack, I now found it of some advantage in crossing the stream, as it assisted in keeping me erect. Buckly in attempting to wade across, had so far succeeded as to reach the middle of the stream, where he stopped, and was about giving way when he was relieved by Farwell, a strong athletic yankee from the state of Maine. In crossing a small bottom, one of the horses fell; we were unable to raise him to his feet, and were compelled to leave him. The other we succeeded in getting to the top of the hill, where we were also compelled to leave him. The former died, but the latter was taken in a few days after by those who were opening the road. After being relieved of the burthen of the two horses, we pushed forward on foot, as fast as Buckly's strength and our

heavy packs would allow; and as it had been raining all
day, our packs were of double their former weight. At
dark we met a party of men who had been through with
a drove of cattle, and were returning with pack horses
for the three families who were yet at Fort Deposit. We
encamped with them. After crossing the Sandy our
course was south-west, over a rolling and prairie country.
The prairie, as well as the timber land, was covered
with fern. The soil was of a reddish cast, and very
mellow, as are all the ridges leading from the mountain to the Willamette or Columbia river. We traveled
this day sixteen or seventeen miles.

October 30. This morning was rainy as usual. Four
miles brought us to the valley of the Clackamis, which
was here five or six miles wide. The road was over a
rolling country similar to that we passed over on yesterday. To the left of the trail we saw a house at the foot
of the hill; we made for it, and found some of our friends
who had started from camp with C. Gilmore. The
claim was held by a man named McSwain.[122] We tarried
here until the morning of the 31st, when we again started
for Oregon city. Our trail ran for five or six miles along
the foot of the hill, through prairie and timber land. The
soil looks good, but is rather inclined to gravel; [84]
numerous streams flow down from the high ground,
which rises gradually to a rolling fern plain, such as we
traveled over on the 28th, and 29th. We then continued
upon the high ground seven or eight miles, alternately
through timber and fern prairies. We then turned
down to Clackamis bottom, which is here about one
mile wide; this we followed down for three miles, when

[122] Samuel McSwain, of the emigration of 1844.— ED.

night overtook us, and we put up at Mr. Hatche's, having spent just one month in the Cascade mountains.[123]

November 1. This morning we left Hatche's, and in two miles travel we reached the crossings of the Clackamis river. At this point it is one hundred and fifty yards wide, the banks of gentle descent, the water wending its way for the noble Columbia over a pebbly bottom. Here is a village of about twenty families, inhabited by the Clackamis Indians, who are few in number, apparently harmless, and caring for nothing more than a few fish, a little game, or such subsistence as is barely sufficient to support life. There are but two or three houses in the village; they are made by setting up side and centre posts in the ground, the latter being the highest, to receive a long pole to uphold puncheons split out of cedar, which form the covering; the sides are enclosed with the same material, in an upright position. These puncheons are held to their places by leather thongs, fastened around them to the poles that lay upon the posts. After examining this little community, the remains of a once powerful and warlike people,[124] we obtained the

---

[123] Peter H. Hatch, who came to Oregon by sea in 1843.— ED.

[124] The Clackamas Indians were a branch of the Upper Chinook, which had long inhabited the river valley called by their name. Lewis and Clark reported (1806) that there were eleven villages of this tribe, with a population of eight hundred. See Thwaites, *Original Journals of the Lewis and Clark Expedition* (New York, 1905), iv, p. 255; vi, p. 118. The Indian agent for 1851 estimated their number at eighty-eight. The village where Palmer tarried was the one visited in 1841 by members of the Wilkes exploring expedition. A conflict for influence over this tribe was in progress at the time, between the Catholic and Methodist missionaries stationed at the Falls of the Willamette. Captain William Clark thus describes their huts: "they build their houses in the same form with those of the Columbian vally of wide split boa[r]ds and covered with the bark of the white cedar which is the entire length of one side of the roof and jut over at the eve about 18 inches."— ED.

use of their canoes, crossed over the river, and after two miles further travel we reached a point that had long been a desired object; where we were to have rest and refreshment.

We were now at the place destined at no distant period to be an important point in the commercial history of the Union — Oregon City.[128] Passing through the timber that lies to the east of the city, we beheld Oregon and the Falls of the Willamette at the same moment. We were so filled with gratitude that we had reached the settlements of the white man, and with admiration at the appearance of the large sheet of water rolling over the Falls, that we stopped, and in this moment of happiness recounted our toils, in thought, with more rapidity than tongue can express or pen write. Here we hastily scanned over the distance traveled, from point to point, which we computed to be in miles as follows, viz: From Independence to Fort Laramie, 629 miles; from Fort Laramie [85] to Fort Hall, 585 miles; from Fort Hall to Fort Bois, 281 miles; from Fort Bois to the Dalles, 305 miles; from the Dalles to Oregon City, (by the wagon route south of Mount Hood,) 160 miles, making the total distance from Independence to Oregon city, 1960 miles. Actual measurement will vary these distances, most probably lessen them; and it is very certain, that by bridging the streams, the travel will be much shortened, by giving to it a more direct course, and upon ground equally favorable for a good road.

OREGON CITY. Now at rest, having arrived at this

---

[128] For the founding of Oregon City see De Smet's *Oregon Missions*, in our volume xxix, p. 180, note 76.— ED.

place, before entering upon a general description of the country, I will give a short account of Oregon city, as it appeared to me. This town is located upon the east side of the Willamette river, and at the Falls. It is about thirty miles above the junction of the Willamette with the Columbia, following the meanders of the river; but, directly from the Columbia at Vancouver, it is only about twenty miles. It was laid out by Dr. M'Laughlin, in 1842, who holds a claim of six hundred and forty acres upon the east side of the river. From the river, upon this side, immediately at the Falls, there rises a rocky bluff of about eighty feet in height, which bears off to the north-east. Passing down the river, the land lies about ten feet lower than the surface of the water above the Falls. This plateau extends for about one-fourth of a mile, when there is a further descent of about fifteen feet, from which a level and fertile bottom skirts the Willamette for a mile and a half, to where the waters of the Clackamis are united with those of the Willamette. Upon the plateau, immediately below, and a small portion of the higher ground above the Falls, is the portion of his grant, that Dr. M'Laughlin has laid off in town lots.[130] Three years ago, this land was covered with a dense forest, which is now cleared off, to make room for the erection of houses to accommodate the inhabitants of the town.

There were already erected, when I left there, about one hundred houses, most of them not only commodious, but neat. Among the public buildings, the most conspicuous were the neat Methodist church, which is

[130] For a sketch of Dr. John McLoughlin see our volume xxi, p. 296, note 81.— ED.

located near the upper part of the town, and a splendid
Catholic chapel, which stands near the river and the
bluff bank at the lower part of the town site.[127] There
are two grist mills; one owned by M'Laughlin, having
three sets of buhr runners, and will compare well with
most of the mills in the States; the other is a smaller mill,
[86] owned by Governor Abernethy and Mr. Beers.[128]
At each of these grist-mills there are also saw-mills,
which cut a great deal of plank for the use of emigrants.
There are four stores, two taverns, one hatter, one
tannery, three tailor shops, two cabinet-makers, two
silversmiths, one cooper, two blacksmiths, one physician,
three lawyers, one printing office, (at which the Oregon
Spectator is printed, semi-monthly, at five dollars per
annum,)[129] one lath machine, and a good brick yard in

[127] De Smet describes the building of the Catholic church in his *Oregon
Missions*, our volume xxix, p. 167.— ED.

[128] In 1842 the Wallamet Milling Company was organized and proceeded
to erect both flour and grist mills on an island near the falls, in order to accommodate the settlers, who before their erection had been dependent upon the
Hudson's Bay Company's mills near Vancouver. The founders of this enterprise were members of the Methodist mission.

Governor George Abernethy of New York (born in 1807) came to Oregon
as steward of the party of re-inforcement arriving in the "Lausanne" (1840).
His business capacity was appreciated by the members of the mission, and
he was soon established as a merchant at Oregon City. Here he took prominent part in the organization of the provisional government, of which he was
elected governor in 1845. Re-elected the following year, Abernethy continued
in this office until the arrival of Governor Joseph Lane (1849), sent out as
first territorial governor by the United States. During the troubles incident
to the Whitman massacre, Governor Abernethy acted with discretion and
promptness, and retained the good will of Oregonians during his entire term
of office. After retiring from public service he continued in mercantile pur-
suits, dying at Portland in 1877. See his portrait in H. S. Lyman, *History
of Oregon*, iii, p. 286. For Alanson Beers see Farnham's *Travels* in our volume
xxix, p. 21, note 14.— ED.

[129] In 1844 the Oregon Printing Association was formed, and George Abernethy sent to New York for a press upon which was printed the first number

active operation. There are also quite a number of
carpenters, masons, &c., in constant employment, at good
wages, in and about this village. The population is
computed at about six hundred white inhabitants, exclu-
sive of a few lodges of Indians.

The Indians spend most of their nights in gambling.
They have a game peculiar to the tribes of the lower
Columbia, and as I have not seen it described, I will
mention it here. Six men meet in their lodge, when they
divide among themselves into partners of three on each
side, then seat themselves, with a pole between the parties;
the middle man on one of the sides has a small bone
or stick which he holds in his hand; his partners upon
the left and right keep up a regular knocking upon the
pole with sticks, and singing of songs. The man with
the bone keeps shifting it as quickly as possible from
hand to hand, to deceive the middle man of the opposite
side, as to which hand holds the bone; after he is satisfied,
he stops and inquires of his opponent in which hand he
holds it. If the opponent guesses rightly, he throws
the bone, with a small pointed stick, to the winner, who
goes through the same ceremony as the loser had done;
but if the man guesses wrongly as to the hand that holds
the bone, he hands over a little pointed stick. Thus
they keep it up until one or the other has won a certain
number of pointed sticks, which they have agreed shall
constitute the game, when the stakes are delivered over

of the *Oregon Spectator*, February 6, 1846. Its first editor was Colonel William G. T'Vault, a pioneer of 1845; he was succeeded by Henry A. G. Lee,
George L. Curry, Aaron E. Wait, and Rev. Wilson Blain, successively.
Although several times suspended for brief periods, the *Spectator* was published
until 1855. For an account see George H. Himes, " The History of the Press
of Oregon, 1839-1850," in *Oregon Historical Quarterly*, iii, pp. 327-370.— ED.

to the winning party. So desperately attached to this game are these savages, that they will gamble away every species of clothing or property they may possess; after this their wives, and they have been known to stake their own services, for a certain number of moons, and sometimes even to become the slaves for life of the more fortunate gamesters.[120]

The stores have but a very limited supply of such articles as emigrants need; but the present merchants, or others that will soon locate there, will find it to their interest to take out such commodities as will be required. Mr. Engle, who went out [87] with the late emigrants, had erected a small foundry, with the intention of casting some old cannon that lay about the fort, and other broken utensils, into those most needed for culinary purposes; but he had not commenced business when I left.[121]

Unimproved lots sell at from one to five hundred dollars each, (the price varying with their location,) in the currency of the country.

The ground back of the town on the bluff, is rather rocky for half a mile, to the foot of the hill; upon ascending the hill, the country consists of fern openings and

[120] See descriptions of this game in *Original Journals of the Lewis and Clark Expedition*, iv, p. 37; and in Ross's *Oregon Settlers*, our volume vii, pp. 291-293.— ED.

[121] William Engle, of German descent, was born near Harper's Ferry, Virginia, in 1789, and served as a volunteer in the War of 1812-15. Having lived for some years in St. Clair County, Illinois, he went out with the train of 1845 for Oregon, settling first at Oregon City. The following year he took up donation land in Clackamas County, where he resided until 1866, being chosen member of the legislature of 1847, and for two years serving as county judge. Having sold his farm in Clackamas, he removed to Marion County, where he died in 1868. Engle was by trade a carpenter; his experiment as a foundryman does not appear to have been successful.— ED.

timber groves alternately, for a distance of about thirty-five miles, to the Cascade mountains. Upon this bluff, which is covered with timber, there is a small but beautiful lake, supplied with springs, which has an outlet by a rivulet that passes through the town into the river.

The river below the Falls, for several miles, is about two hundred and fifty yards wide, and opposite the town it is very deep. The bank on the east side, with the exception of a few hundred yards, is a cliff of about twenty feet in height, for the first half mile, of a firm basaltic rock; from thence down to the Clackamis the bank is a sandy loam.

Upon the west side of the Willamette, and opposite to Oregon city, are laid out two villages; the upper one is called Linn city, in honor of the late senator from Missouri, whose memory, for his patriotic services in the cause of the Oregon emigrant, is held in high esteem by every true friend of his country and of humanity. When Dr. Linn died, the friends of Oregon lost a champion who would not have shamelessly deserted them in the hour of need.[182] Mr. Moore, late of Missouri, is the proprietor;[183] his claim commences one-fourth

[182] Lewis F. Linn was born in 1796 near Louisville, where he studied medicine and afterwards volunteered for the War of 1812-15. At its close he removed to Ste. Geneviève, Missouri, where he began active practice. In 1827 he was elected to the state senate, and in 1833 was appointed to the United States senate to fill out the term of a deceased senator. Thrice elected thereto by the Missouri legislature, he served until his own death in 1843, being known in the senate as a champion of Oregon interests.

The town opposite Oregon City was known as Linn City. It consisted in December, 1844, of two log buildings and many tents, wherein the emigrants of 1844 made their headquarters. In 1861 all the buildings were swept away by a flood. It has now no separate existence.— ED.

[183] Robert Moore was born in Pennsylvania in 1781, served in the War of 1812-15, and in 1822 emigrated to Ste. Geneviève, Missouri, whence he was

of a mile below the Falls, extends above the Falls one and three-fourths of a mile, and back from the river one half of a mile. When I left, there were about fifteen buildings in this village, inhabited mostly by mechanics. The proprietor had refused to sell water power, which was doubtless one of the reasons why more emigrants did not settle in it.

Next, lower down, is the claim of Mr. Hugh Burns, a native of Ireland, but lately an emigrant from Missouri; he is the proprietor of Multinoma city, which is so called from the Indian name for the Willamette river, and a tribe of Indians of this name that once inhabited that country.[184] This tribe is now nearly extinct. At their burial places, near this, there are hundreds of skulls yet lying over the ground. When I left, [88] there were but few buildings, and some few mechanics settled in it. There are two ferries established over the river, from the villages on the west side, to Oregon city.[186] Upon the west side, the bank of the river is similar to that on the east, quite high, leaving but a small semi-

---

sent to the state legislature. In 1835 he removed to Illinois, where in 1839 he joined the Peoria party for emigration to Oregon. See preface to Farnham's *Travels*, in our volume xxviii. Moore was one of the seceders who went off from Bent's Fort to Fort St. Vrain, where he spent the winter of 1839-40. Arrived in Oregon he purchased land of the Indians on the west side of the Willamette, naming his place the "Robin's Nest," being visited there by Commodore Wilkes in 1841. Moore served on a committee of the provisional government, and held a commission as justice of the peace. He died in Oregon September 1, 1857.— ED.

[184] Hugh Burns was a blacksmith who came to Oregon in 1842, in the party of Medorem Crawford. The same year he was made a magistrate, and concerned himself with public affairs until his return to Missouri in 1846.

For the Multnomah Indians see our volume vi, p. 247, note 53.— ED.

[186] The right to establish public ferries was granted by the provisional legislature of 1844 to Robert Moore and Hugh Burns.— ED.

circular level for the first bottom; and upon a farther ascent of about twenty feet, there is a larger plain at the lower end of this bluff. The bottom corresponds well with that above the Clackamis on the opposite side, and is covered with a dense growth of fir; the trees are tall and straight.

———

DESCRIPTION OF THE COUNTRY. The journey to Oregon city accomplished, and an examination of the immediate vicinity completed, I set about an inquiry as to the features of the country — its fertility, its general susceptibility of improvement, and its capability for the support of a large and industrious population. In so doing, in addition to what I could see for myself, I applied for information to all whose opportunities had been favorable for obtaining a knowledge of any particular section. In this work I was an inquirer after facts, in order to decide the question as to the propriety of taking my family there for a permanent home; and when I noted these facts, no attention was paid to the classification and arrangement of the various subjects, as is generally done by those travelers and geographers whose business is book-making. Necessarily, therefore, my Journal presents facts, just in the order in which they came to me, and as I received them they are placed before the reader.

The landscape immediately adjacent to the villages of Linn city and Multinoma present several abrupt precipices of various heights, upon each of which is a small level, of lesser and greater widths, clothed with fine grass and studded over with oak timber, until the highest ascent is reached, when it spreads out into an

extensive fern opening. From these cliffs there gush
out fine streams of pure spring water; and they will
afford most beautiful country seats for the erection of
residences convenient to the towns, when their improvement shall render such sites desirable. From these
heights, (which are easily ascended,) there is a fine view
of the falls of the river for several miles, and of Mount
Hood. From the heights to Quality Plains, a distance
of twenty-five miles, the country presents rolling plains,
with small groves of oak and fir, and it is well watered
by springs and small rivulets.

[89] From the description given of the towns, the
reader may have already inferred, that the Falls of the
Willamette combine all that is necessary to constitute
great water privileges for propelling machinery; but
before leaving this point, we will take a more particular
view of them.

These falls are occasioned by the descent of the whole
volume of the river over a ledge of basaltic rock that
crosses the entire channel. The greatest fall at any
point is twenty-eight feet, but the whole descent here
is about forty feet. The water is so divided in the
channels at the Falls, and the islands are so situated,
that nearly all of the water may be rendered available,
at a very small expense, when it shall be needed. Nature
rarely at any one point concentrates so many advantages
for the erection and support of a great commercial and
manufacturing city, as are to be found here. There is
an abundance of water to propel the machinery, stone
and timber convenient to erect the necessary buildings,
an extensive country of the best farming lands in the
world to support the towns by their trade, and a fine

navigable river to bring the raw material to the manu-
factories, and when manufactured to carry the surplus
to the Pacific, whence it can easily be taken to the best
markets the world affords. At this place, the business
of the upper Willamette will concentrate, for many years
at least. Tide water reaches to the mouth of the Clackamis, which is within two miles of the Falls. Here there
is a considerable ripple in the river, which can easily
be removed by confining the Clackamis to its original
bed upon the eastern side of the island. As it is, there
are four feet of water over the bar, and not so rapid as to
prevent the ascent of steamboats to the Falls. Vessels
of two hundred and fifty tons burthen have ascended
within two miles of the rapids; but, from the crooked-
ness of the stream and the difficulty in tacking so frequently, they generally receive and discharge their cargoes
at Portland, twelve miles below.[116]

Traveling up the river, five miles from the Falls,
brings us to Rock Island. Here is said to be a serious
obstruction to the navigation of the river. The difficulty
consists in there being several peaks of rocks so elevated,
as to be near the surface of the water in a low stage;
and as the channels between them are very narrow, and

---

[116] The site of Portland was unoccupied until November, 1843, when William
Overton, from Tennessee, and Asa L. Lovejoy staked off claims of three hundred and twenty acres each. In 1844 Overton sold out to F. W. Pettygrove
of Maine for $50, and the first log cabin was built. In 1845 the place was
named and a town platted; the growth was slow, however, and by 1849 there
were only about a hundred inhabitants. Two years later the town was incorporated, at that time claiming a population of a thousand. After that the
growth became more rapid. In 1873 Portland suffered a disastrous confla-
gration. The city's success is due to its position at the head of tidewater
navigation for the Columbia and Willamette valleys, and as being the terminus
of eastern and southern trunk railways.— ED.

the water quite rapid, boats are liable to run on to them. But the rock can be removed at an inconsiderable expense. It is fifteen miles above the Falls to the [90] first gravel bar, at which place, in low water, there is but three feet in the channel.[137]

In traveling up the river about fifty miles, I found, in addition to the obstructions named, four other gravel bars, over some of which there were only thirty inches of water. In going the next seventy-five miles, I approached the river several times, and found it to have a deep channel and smooth current. Persons who had navigated the river considerably further up, in their traffic with the Indians, informed me that it continued equally favourable for navigation. From what I saw and learned of intelligent persons, I think the smaller class of steamboats could for most part of the year ascend two hundred miles above the Falls.

From the Columbia to Upper California, is a mountainous belt, known as the Coast range.[138] Spurs of this range approach nearly to the mouth of the Willamette. Between these spurs and the river, there is but a small portion of the soil well adapted to agriculture. The higher range to the west of the Falls affords a scope of fifty miles, that with the exception of a few openings, and Quality Plains, is tolerably broken, generally well

---

[137] The Willamette is navigable in high water for small steamers as far as Eugene, a hundred and thirty-eight miles above Portland. The first steamers on the upper Willamette were the "Hoosier" and "Yamhill," built in 1851. Since railways have followed both banks of the stream, river navigation has been of minor importance.— ED.

[138] The mountains of the Coast range extend at the highest from four thousand to five thousand feet above sea level, with lower levels half as great. Several passes run through from the Pacific, notably that afforded by the Yaquina and Mary's rivers, through which runs the Oregon Central Railway.— ED.

timbered, finely watered, with many excellent situations for farms; but not so well calculated, as some other parts, for dense settlements.

Quality Plains are distant twenty-five miles west from Oregon city; they are about twenty-five miles in length, are alternately rolling prairie and timber, surrounded by heavy growths of firs, many of which rise to the height of two hundred and fifty feet. These plains are all claimed, settled, and mostly improved.[189] They are well watered by many small streams that constitute the two forks of Quality river, which unite near the south-east part of the plains, and runs an easterly course, through narrow bottoms, well supplied with timber for more than twenty miles, where it discharges its waters into the Willamette, two miles above Oregon city. The principal part of the water that flows in Quality river descends from the Coast Range. This stream, like most others in that region, has several falls and rapids, that furnish very desirable sites for the propelling of machinery; but if ever profitable for navigation, will have to be improved by canals and

---

[189] By this paragraph, Palmer intends to describe Tualatin River and plains. The name is derived from a local Indian word said to signify "smooth and slowly-flowing stream." The land known to the early settlers as Tualatin Plains is now embraced in Washington County — a famous fruit- and wheat-raising region. The plains are encircled by hills, giving the appearance of a large amphitheatre. The earliest settlers in this region were three independent missionaries, Harvey Clark, Alvin T. Smith, and P. B. Littlejohn, who crossed the continent in 1840, and the following spring settled at Tualatin. About the same time, several mountain men, such as Joseph L. Meek and Robert Newell, made their homes in the region. The Red River settlers who had come under the auspices of the Puget Sound Agricultural Association in 1841, being dissatisfied with lands north of the Columbia, gradually drifted south, a number settling at Dairy Creek, in the Tualatin country.

For the Tualatin River see Farnham's *Travels* in our volume xxix, p. 16, note 5.— ED.

lockage around its falls; which can easily be done, when the commerce of the country will justify the expense.

From this stream, and between the Coast Range and Willamette, and to the south, to the Shahalam valley, which commences [91] at the low pass of Quality Plains, is a tract of about twenty by thirty miles in extent, of rolling fertile lands, alternately fern openings and timber groves.

From the Coast Range to the Willamette there is a belt of five or six miles in width, which near the river is covered thinly with yellow pines; but nearer the mountain it is better timbered, and well watered from mountain rivulets; mostly a rich and loose soil, composed chiefly of yellow sand, loam and clay. But little of this tract is claimed by the emigrants, as they usually prefer the prairie country above.

The Shahalam is a small stream, which has its origin in the Coast Range, runs eastwardly and empties into the Willamette, twenty miles above Oregon city. This is skirted with good prairies of five or six miles in width, near the mountains; but towards its mouth the valley is covered with timber and fern. The best portion is claimed.[140]

Eleven miles further up, the Willamette receives the waters of the Yam-hill. At the mouth it is about twenty-five yards in width, quite deep, and will bear upon its bosom crafts of large burthen for ten miles, to the falls.

---

[140] This stream is usually known as the Chehalem, the significance of the name being unknown. Among the earliest settlers in this fertile valley were Ewing Young (see our volume xx, p. 23, note 2), and Sidney Smith (for whom see our volume xxviii, p. 91, note 41). Several mountain men also had farms in the region, as well as Archibald McKinley, a member of the Hudson's Bay Company.— ED.

This stream has two principal branches; the one rising in the Coast Range, runs for twenty miles in a south-easterly direction, through a beautiful and fertile valley of twelve miles in width, handsomely covered with groves of white oak, and other timber; which is intersected with numerous spring branches, the banks of which are lined with timber, leaving in some places fine bottom prairies, covered with a rich sward of grass. Between this fork and the Shahalam is a range of hills averaging about two miles in width, extending from a part of the Coast Range, to within three miles of the Willamette. They are of steep ascent, some of them rising to five or six hundred feet in height, well covered with grass, and from their sides issue numerous spring rivulets, which near their origin are lined with fir trees; thence passing through groves of white oak, alder and willow, to the bottom lands, which in crossing some of them disappear, and others after joining together, continue their courses until they unite with the Shahalam and Yam-hill. The grasses on these hills are a species of red clover, that grows in the summer season about one foot high, and a fine grass, which after the clover disappears, keep them clad in green during the winter. Thus they furnish a perpetual supply of food for cattle the whole year. The soil upon these hills is a mixture of clay and loam, of a reddish color, and in the bottoms it is a rich [92] mixture of loam and muck. However, there are some of the hills somewhat sandy, and occasionally interspersed with stony places.

From the source of this branch of the Yam-hill, (which in the country is called the North Fork,) passes the trace, along which the people on Clatsop plains drive their cattle a distance of about forty miles, when they reach the coast, fifteen miles south of Cape Lookout.

The south fork of Yam-hill has its source in the Coast Range; where it emerges from the mountains, for the first ten miles, its banks are well supplied with large fir trees, as are its several tributaries; its banks are generally steep, bearing the appearance of having washed out a channel from fifteen to twenty feet in depth. It runs an eastern course for about ten miles, then north-east for some miles, and finally takes a northern direction, until it connects with the North fork, near the Falls, after having flowed a distance of about twenty-five miles.

The valley watered by this stream is about fifteen miles wide, after the stream emerges from the heavy growth of firs already noticed; for there are firs, more or less, its whole length. From the water courses, upon an average of a little over one fourth of a mile, the valley is fine prairie land, soil light and rich, occasionally interspersed with fine groves, and well adapted to agricultural purposes. It is well covered with grass, as is every portion of the country that has oaken groves, and the lower bottoms yield an abundant supply of the *Camas*, a tuberous rooted plant, shaped something like an onion, which it resembles in appearance. It is devoured greedily by hogs, and affords very good nutriment. The Indians make much use of it as an article of food. Between these streams and within six miles of their junction, commences the high lands of the Coast Range; the first plateau is about ten miles wide, and well covered with grass. The second plateau, for a few miles is fern openings, with an occasional grove of timber; after this westward to the coast the country is heavily timbered with firs, pine, and occasionally cedar, hemlock, balsam, and nearly all species of the evergreen timber. The streams last described furnish good sites for hydraulic purposes, near the mountains. A considerable portion of the valley of the Yam-hill is not only claimed, but settled, and finely improved.[141]

Leaving the Yam-hill and ascending the Willamette twenty-five miles, we reach the mouth of the Rickerall, a stream [93] which has its source in the same range as the Yam-hill; for the first ten miles it runs rapidly over a pebbly bed, and from thence to the mouth has a deep channel, worn in a rich soil, with timbered banks. It flows in an easterly course from the mountains eighteen miles, and unites with the Willamette. The valley through which this stream flows resembles that described as watered by the Yam-hill; perhaps the soil is a little richer. It is nearly all claimed, and will soon be well settled. Upon this stream there is erected a grist mill, and there was a saw mill, but the freshets washed it away last spring.[142] Five miles above Yam-hill commence a range of hills that extend south to the Rickerall, similar to those between Shahalam and Yam-hill. These hills vary from one to four miles in width, leaving a bottom about six miles wide to skirt the Willamette, which is of good soil, well watered and timbered. Upon the slopes of

[141] Yamhill is said to be a corruption of Cheamhill, a name signifying "bald hills." Among the earliest settlers were Francis Fletcher and Amos Cook, of the Peoria party of 1839. Medorem Crawford (1842) settled near what is now Dayton for the first years of his Oregon life. General Palmer himself chose this valley for his future home, and in 1850 founded therein the town of Dayton. See preface to the present volume.— ED.

[142] Rickerall (commonly Rickreall) is a corruption of La Creole, the name now usually applied to this stream, which drains Polk County and though not navigable has many mill sites and waters a fertile region.— ED.

these hills are several thousands of acres of white oak, from six to twenty feet in height, some of them of large diameter and all with large and bushy tops; the ground being covered with grass, at a distance they look like old orchards. The timber of these trees is very solid, and promises great durability.[143] The valley between the Yam-hill and Rickerall is called the Applegate settlement; there are three brothers of the Applegates, they have fine farms, with good herds of fat and thrifty cattle.[144] The Yam-hill plains is called the Hemerey settlement, from a family of this name there settled.[145]

[143] Known as Polk County Hills, forming a charming background for the western view from Salem.— ED.

[144] Jesse, Charles, and Lindsey Applegate were natives of Kentucky who emigrated to Oregon in 1843, and became leaders in its development. The eldest, Jesse, was a man of marked peculiarities, but accredited with much wisdom and indomitable perseverance, and a natural leader of men. His influence was considerable in forming the provisional government. In 1846 he explored for a southern route into Willamette valley, and thence led emigrants south of Klamath Lake. About 1849 he settled in the Umpqua country, near the site whence he obtained his title as "sage of Yoncalla." A disastrous business venture sent him for a time to the mountains of northern California. During the Rogue River and Modoc Indian wars his knowledge of the character of the aborigines was valuable, and several times he served as special Indian agent, dying in Douglas County in 1888.

Charles Applegate was born in 1806, removed to St. Louis about 1820, migrated to Oregon in 1843, and accompanied his brother Jesse to Douglas County, where he died in 1879.

Lindsey Applegate accompanied General W. H. Ashley on his Arikara campaign of 1823 (see our volume xxiii, p. 224, note 177), wherein he was taken ill. After returning to St. Louis he worked in the Illinois lead mines, and saw service in the Black Hawk War (1832). After his migration to Oregon (1843), he became only second to his eldest brother in services to the young commonwealth. He made his home in the southern part of the state, near Ashland, in Jackson County, where he was living in 1885.— ED.

[145] This name should be Hembree, that of a pioneer family from Tennessee, who came out in 1843. Absalom J. Hembree was a member of the legislature from 1846 to 1855. In the latter year he raised a company for the Yakima

Upon the Rickerall are the Gillams, Fords and Shaws, all doing well.[146] The Gays and Matheneys are settled upon the bottom of the Willamette, between Yam-hill and Rickerall.[147]

Twelve miles above the Rickerall, empties the Lucky-

War, in which he was killed. Many descendants of this family live near Lafayette and other Yamhill County towns.— ED.

[146] These were members of the immigration of 1844, of which Cornelius Gilliam was chosen leader. He had served in both the Black Hawk and Seminole wars, and had been sheriff and member of the legislature in Missouri. His command of the emigrant train did not last through the entire trip, the party breaking into smaller companies, two of which were commanded by William Shaw and Nathaniel Ford. Gilliam was colonel of the regiment raised to avenge the Whitman massacre, and was killed by the accidental discharge of a gun.

William Shaw was born (1795) near Raleigh, North Carolina. When a boy he emigrated to Tennessee and took part in Jackson's campaign before New Orleans (1814-15). About 1819 he removed to Missouri, where he married a sister of Colonel Gilliam. He was captain in the Cayuse War of 1848, and member of the territorial legislature from Marion County, ten miles above Salem, where he made his permanent home.

Nathaniel Ford was a native of Virginia (1795), but was reared in Kentucky, and after coming out to Oregon settled in Polk County, where he died in 1870.— ED.

[147] George Gay was an English sailor. Born in Gloucestershire (1810), he served as ship's apprentice when eleven years of age. In 1832 he reached California on the "Kitty," and there joined Ewing Young's trapping party to the mountains of northern California, returning without entering Oregon. In 1835 he formed one of a party of eight men under the leadership of John Turner, who coming overland to Oregon were attacked by the Rogue River Indians, all being wounded and two killed. Gay reached the settlements after a trip filled with great hardships, and thenceforth made Oregon his home, taking an Indian wife and settling high up on the Willamette, near the southern boundary of Yamhill County. Here he built the first brick house in the territory, and with unbounded hospitality opened it to new emigrants. Wilkes (1841) describes him as a dashing, gay "vaquero," half-Indian in his characteristics, but very useful to the new community. At one time he had considerable wealth in horses and cattle, but died poor in 1882.

Daniel Matheny, of the emigration of 1843, was born in Virginia in 1793. Successive removals carried him to Kentucky, Indiana, and Illinois, where he served in the War of 1812-15, and that of Black Hawk (1832). Having settled near Gay in 1844, he afterwards kept a public ferry, dying on his farm in 1872. Several of his family accompanied him to Oregon.— ED.

muke into the Willamette; it heads in the same range
as the Yam-hill, and, like it, has two principal branches,
of about the same length, depth and width, and passes
through an excellent valley of land, with the same
diversities and excellent qualities for farming which are
attributed to the Yam-hill valley — the timber being
more of oak and less of fir.   Upon this stream several
claims are entered, and there is a fine opening for others
who may desire to settle there.

Mouse river joins the Willamette about thirty-five
miles above the Lucky-muke.[148]   It has its origin in the
Coast range, has two principal branches, which unite
near the mountains, passes ten miles over a pebbly
bottom, and then becomes more sluggish to its mouth.
This, like the other streams described, [94] has timber
upon its borders, but less than some; good country,
fine prospects, and but few claims made.

Between the Lucky-muke and Mouse river there is a
range of hills, as between other streams; but at one
place a spur of the Coast range approaches within ten
miles of the Willamette; from this issue many small
streams which run down it, and through the fine plains
to the Lucky-muke upon the one side, and into Mouse
river on the other.   This is a beautiful region; from the
bottom can be seen, at different points, seven snow-
covered peaks of the Cascade range.[149]   The Cascade
is within view for a great distance, to the north and

[148] Luckiamute is the modern spelling of this name of Indian origin, derived
from a branch of the Kalapuya tribe that formerly inhabited this valley.   In
1851, federal commissioners made a treaty with this tribe whereby they ceded
their lands, and retired soon afterwards to the Grande Ronde reservation.   By
Mouse River Palmer means the stream now known as Mary's River — a name
given by J. C. Avery, the founder of Corvallis, in honor of his wife.— ED.

[149] Mount Jefferson, Hayrick Mountain, Mount Washington, and the Three
Sisters with nei ' ' ' eaks.— ED.

south; which, together with the beautiful scenery in the valley, renders it a picturesque place. Thrifty groves of fir and oak are to be seen in every direction; the earth is carpeted with a covering of luxuriant grass, and fertilized by streams of clear running rivulets, some of which sink down and others pursue their course above ground to the river. Between the forks of Mouse river approaches a part of the Cascade,[160] but it leaves a valley up each branch about one mile in width, the soil of which is rich and good prairie for several miles above the junction. The moun-tain sides are covered very heavily with fir timber. Thus these beautiful valleys offer great inducements to those who wish to have claims of good land, with fine grounds for pasturage and timber close at hand. There are no claims made as yet above the forks. These streams furnish good mill sites for each of the first six miles, and are well filled with trout.

From the forks of this stream starts a trail, (or half-made road,) which leads to the falls of the Alsa, a stream that heads twenty miles to the south of these forks; the trail leads a westerly course for fifteen miles to the Falls; from thence to the coast it is twenty-one miles. From the Falls the river runs in a westerly direction. An old Indian told me that there was some excellent land in this valley, and that there would be but little difficulty in constructing a good road down it. Salmon and other fish are in great abundance in this stream, up to the Falls.[161]

Six miles above Mouse river is the mouth of Long

[160] Our author here intends the Coast (not the Cascade) range, of which Mary's Peak, between the two forks of Mary's (Mouse) River is the highest, rising about five thousand feet above sea level.— ED.

[161] The Alsea, in Lincoln County, flows into a bay of that name, where

Tom Bath;[152] this, like all other streams that enter the Willamette upon the western side, heads in the coast range, and after breaking its way through the spurs to the plains below, passes through a valley of good soil. It has deep banks, is more sluggish in its movements than those that join it lower down, [95] is filled with dirty water, has a miry bottom, shaded upon its margin with timber, and in size is something larger than the Yam-hill.

So far, I have described the valley from personal observation in that direction; but I was informed by those who had good opportunities for obtaining correct information, that it bore off more easterly, and that it was for eighty miles further up as well watered, timbered, and of as luxuriant soil, as that which I have described. It may be proper here to remark, that the further the valley is ascended the oak timber becomes more abundant, and the fir in a corresponding ratio decreases.

Having described the country for more than one hundred miles upon the western side of the Willamette, we will return to the Falls and mention a few facts respecting the eastern bank. Upon this bank, for ten miles to the south of Oregon city, continue fern openings, to a small stream called Pole Alley,[153] which is skirted with beautiful prairie bottoms of from two to eight miles in

small coasting steamers enter and ascend the stream some eighteen or twenty miles. The name is derived from an Indian tribe — one of the Kalapuya stock.— ED.

[152] In the early days of Oregon settlement more frequently spelled Long-tonguebuff (properly Lungtumler), from a branch of the Kalapuya tribe that inhabited its banks. The stream is now known simply as Long Tom River, rising in Lane County and flowing nearly north into Benton County, entering the Willamette not far above Peoria.— ED.

[153] Palmer here refers to Molalla River, a stream of southwestern Clacka-

length and from one to two miles wide; these, with alternate groves of fir, constitute the principal characteristics of Pole Alley valley.   It is not more than half a mile from the mouth of Pole Alley, farther to the south, where Pudding river embogues into the Willamette; it is twenty-five yards in width at the mouth.   The valley up this river to the Cascade mountains, where it rises, is alternately fine prairie and timber lands, with occasional fern openings.   Some of the prairies are claimed by the recent emigrants.   It is finely clothed in grass, and up the river some distance there are valuable mill sites; the water is clear, and well stocked with fish.[184]   From Pudding river further south, there are fern openings, which are succeeded by grassy prairies, which give place to fine groves of fir, but sparsely intermingled with cedar.

Eight miles from Pudding river is a village called Butes.   It was laid out by Messrs. Abernathy and Beers.

mas County, that took its name from a tribe of Indians once roaming upon its banks.   Governor Lane in 1850 refers to this tribe as Mole Alley; and the liquid letters "m" and "p" being nearly interchangeable in the Indian dialect, Palmer gave it the form Pole Alley.   The Molala tribe was an offshoot of the Cayuse, that had its home west of the Cascades.   The early settlers testified to their superior physique and stronger qualities, compared with the degraded Chinook by whom they were surrounded.   In 1851 their tribal lands were purchased, when their number was reported at 123.   The remnant removed to Douglas County, and in 1888 a few calling themselves Molala were found on the Grande Ronde reservation.— ED.

[184] The aboriginal name of this stream was Hanteuc.   Two differing accounts are given of the origin of the present name.   Elijah White (*Ten Years in Oregon*, p. 70) says a party of Hudson's Bay trappers lost their way upon this stream and were forced to kill their horses for sustenance, making pudding of the blood.   Others give the derivation as "Put in"— the stream that puts in just below the early French settlement, thence degenerated to Pudding.   The river rises in the foothills near the centre of Marion County, and flows nearly north, a sluggish, crooked stream from eighty to a hundred feet in width.— ED.

There were but a few cabins in it when I left. The pro-
prietors had erected a warehouse to store the wheat
they might purchase of the settlers back, who should
find it convenient to sell their crops at this point. At
this place are some conical hills, called Butes, which
rise to a considerable height; the sides and tops of them
are clothed with tall fir trees, which can be seen from
the valley above for sixty miles. Immediately at this
village is a fern opening, covered with an undergrowth
of hazle, for three-fourths of a mile back, when it merges
into an extensive and fertile prairie.[155]

[96] South of Butes three miles is the village of Shampoic. It was laid out by a mountaineer, of the name of
Newell, formerly a clerk of the Hudson's Bay Company.[156]

[155] The Butte was a landmark on the upper Willamette, a high escarpment
prominent from the river. Here was formerly a landing for the settlers of
French Prairie, whose farms lay south and east of this point. The town of
Butteville was laid out by merchants of Oregon City — Abernethy and Beers
— to facilitate the commerce in wheat. F. X. Matthieu took up land here as
early as 1846, and in 1850 kept a store. He still lives at Butteville, which in
1900 had a population of 483.— ED.

[156] For Champoeg see De Smet's *Oregon Missions* in our volume xxix,
p. 179, note 75. The early meetings of the provisional government were held
at this place, which was the centre for the old Canadian-French inhabitants
of the country.

Dr. Robert Newell was born in 1807 at Zanesville, Ohio. His fur-trap-
ping experiences were under the auspices of the American Fur Company (not
the Hudson's Bay Company), as companion of Joseph L. Meek. See F. T.
Victor, *River of the West* (Hartford, 1870). His first settlement (1840) after
the migration to Oregon, was at Tualatin Plains; but before 1842 he removed
to Champoeg, where by his influence over the settlers he became the political
as well as social leader. Possibly also Newell laid out a town at this place,
but he was by no means the founder of the village. Newell represented Champoeg in the provisional government for several years, and in 1846 was speaker
of the lower house of the state legislature. After the Whitman massacre (1847)
he was chosen one of the commissioners, with Palmer, to treat with the Indians.
He also raised a company for the Indian war of 1856. In later life he was
connected with railway projects and died at Lewiston, Idaho, in 1869.— ED.

It contains a few old shabby buildings, and a warehouse
owned by the company, where they receive the wheat
of the settlers of the country from thence to the Cascade
mountains.   This is an extensive plain, extending from
Pudding river up the Willamette to the old Methodist
mission ground, which is distant thirty miles from the
mouth of Pudding river.   The soil for this distance, and
for two miles in width, is similar to that described immediately at Butes.   Back of this for twenty-five or thirty
miles is a very handsome country, mostly prairie, and
fine timber, well watered, with occasionally a hill —
the whole covered with a soil quite inviting to the agri-
culturist, with an abundance of pasturage for cattle.
This is called the French settlement, and is one of the
oldest in the valley.   The Catholics have here a mission,
schools, a grist and saw mill, and several mechanics;
they have also several teachers among the Indians, and
it is said that they have done much for the improvement
of these aborigines.   The inhabitants are mostly of
what are called French Canadians, and were formerly
engaged in the service of the Hudson Bay Company,
but have now quit it, made claims, and gone to farming.
They have very pretty orchards of apple trees, and some
peach trees.   Their wives are natives of the country.
Many of them are raising families that, when educated,
will be sprightly, as they are naturally active and hardy,
and appear very friendly and hospitable.   But few of
them speak the English language fluently; they mostly
talk French and Chinook jargon.[187]   They cultivate but

[187] For the early settlement of French Prairie, see De Smet's *Letters* in our
volume xxvii, p. 386, note 203; also our volume vii, p. 231, note 83.   For the
Chinook jargon see our volume vi, p. 240, note 40; also pp. 264-270 of the
present volume.— ED.

little land, but that little is well done, and the rich soil well repays them for the labor expended upon it. I could not satisfactorily ascertain the population of the settlement, which I much regretted.

The old Methodist mission is nearly opposite to what is now called Matheny's Ferry. It was reported to me to have been one of the first missions occupied in the valley, but has been abandoned on account of the overflowing of the river. It consists of only several dilapidated buildings.[148] The soil is gravelly, inclined to barren, with a grove of pines near by.

This place for a number of years was under the superintendance of the Rev. Jason Lee. It is here that the remains of his wife are interred; a tombstone marks her resting place, which informs the passer by that she was the first white woman [97] that was buried in Oregon Territory,— together with the place of her nativity, marriage, &c.[149]

The unfortunate location of the mission, and the circumstances under which Mrs. Lee died, no doubt have had great influence in creating that unfavorable impression of the country in the mind of Mr. Lee, which he has expressed in some of his letters. The country

---

[148] For the earliest site of the Methodist mission see our volume xxi, p. 299, note 84. Matheny's Ferry is mentioned in note 147, *ante*, p. 174.— ED.

[149] For Jason Lee see our volume xxi, p. 138, note 13. His first wife was Anna Maria Pitman, who came out from New York in 1837, the marriage taking place soon after her arrival in May of that year. The following spring Lee returned to the United States. Upon his journey a messenger overtook him, announcing the death of Mrs. Lee on June 26, 1838. The first interment was at the old mission, as here stated. Later the grave was removed to Salem. H. H. Bancroft, *History of Oregon*, i, p. 170, gives the inscription on the tombstone.— ED.

surrounding the mission is covered mostly with scrubby oak and pine trees.

From the mission the road proceeds up the valley, alternately through groves of oak and pine, fern plains, and grassy prairies, in which are several farms, with convenient buildings. After pursuing this route about ten miles, we come to an improvement of several hundred acres, surrounded with small groves of oak. Here the soil is quite gravelly, and not very rich.

Nearly opposite the mouth of the Rickerall is the Methodist Institute, which was located at this place when it was ascertained that the Willamette would overflow its bank at the old mission. My opinion is, that the location is a good one, being in a high and healthy neighborhood, and nearly central of what will be the principal population of the valley for long years to come.

The course of instruction there given is quite respectable, and would compare well with many of those located in the old and populous settlements of the States. This school is unconnected with any mission. When the missionary board concluded to abandon that field of labor, the Institute was bought by the Methodists of Oregon; hence it continued under its old name. The price of tuition is low, and the means of receiving an education at this place is within the power of those who have but a small amount to expend in its attainment.[100]

For the first five miles from the river towards the Cascade range, the soil is gravelly; it is then a sandy loam to the foot of the mountain, and is generally an open plain. The valley upon the east side of the river at this

[100] For the origin of the Willamette Institute see De Smet's *Oregon Missions* in our volume xxix, p. 165, note 62.— ED.

place, is about twenty-five miles in width. It is proper, however, to remark, that there are occasional groves of timber interspersing the prairie, and in some places they reach within a short distance of the river. In this last described tract, there are several varieties of soil, with prairie, timber, upland, bottom, and hill side; the whole is well watered. At the Institute there reside about fifteen families, and near by several claims are taken, and improvements commenced. The Methodist missionaries [98] have erected a saw and grist mill; these mills were sold, as was all the property of the missions in the valley, by Mr. Gerry, who was sent out to close the missionary matters in that region; they are now owned by resident citizens, and in successful operation. At this place a town is laid out.[101]

Six miles above the Institute commences a range of oak hills, which continue about twelve miles in a southeastern direction along the river, where they connect by a low pass with the Cascade Range. From this place, at the lower bench of the Cascade, commences another range of hills, running south-westwardly, which con-

----

[101] In 1843 the Missionary Society of the Methodist Episcopal church decided that the Oregon mission, being no longer useful for the conversion of Indians, should be closed, and the charges organized into a mission conference for whites. In pursuance of this resolve, Rev. George Gary of Black River Conference, New York, was appointed to supersede Jason Lee as superintendent. Early in June, 1844, Gary settled the affairs of the mission, dismissing the lay members, who immediately bought in the mills and other property of the mission. Gary remained in Oregon until 1847, making his headquarters at Oregon City.

The native name of the site at Salem — Chemeketa — was interpreted by Rev. David Leslie as having the same significance as the term Salem — *i. e.*, rest, or peace. The site was chosen in 1840 for the erection of mills on Mill Creek. The trustees of Oregon Institute laid out the town, which grew slowly until in 1851 it became the territorial capital. By the terms of the state constitution the capital was located by popular vote, which resulted in favor of Salem. Its population in 1900 was 4,258.— ED.

tinue about twenty miles in length, to the mouth of the Santaam river, which joins the Willamette twenty miles by land above the Institute. This is a bold and rapid stream, of about one hundred and fifty yards in width; for a considerable portion of its length, it has a pebbly bottom, and banks covered with fir and white cedar trees of the best quality.[162]

The Santa Anna has four principal branches, with several small tributaries, all lined with timber, leaving a strip of beautiful prairie land between each, of from one-half to four miles in width. The two northern branches rise in Mount Jefferson, the first running nearly west from its origin to where it leaves the mountain, when it inclines to the south for a few miles, where it receives another branch; from this junction about eight miles, it is joined by a stream that rises in the Cascade Range, south of Mount Jefferson. Ten miles below this point, the other principal branch, which rises still further to the south, unites with the others, when the river inclines to the west, until it joins the Willamette. From its origin in Mount Jefferson to its termination, is about forty miles; from the Oak hills above named is twenty-five miles.

---

[162] The Santiam River takes its name from the head chief (Sandeam) of the Kalapuya Indians, who dwelt upon its banks. April 16, 1851, the federal commissioners made a treaty with the Santiam branch of the tribe, whereby the latter ceded to the whites a large portion of their lands. Their number at this time was a hundred and fifty-five. Santiam River drains a considerable portion of Marion and Linn counties, its North Fork forming the boundary between the two. The road up this fork leads to Minto Pass; the South Fork formed the line for the Willamette and Cascade Military Road. Palmer's use of the term "Santa Anna" for this stream, in the two following paragraphs, would seem to indicate his ignorance of the Indian origin of the term, and an idea that it had been named for the Mexican general of that period.— Ed.

A considerable portion of the soil in this valley is quite gravelly, but a great portion is rich, and the prairies are well clothed with luxuriant grass. Among the plants, herbs, &c., common to this part of the country, is wild flax.

A few claims have been made along the north-east side of the Oak hills, and improvements commenced. The soil yields a good crop of the agricultural products suited to the climate.

Above the Santa Anna, upon the eastern side of the Willamette, the valley is about twenty miles in average width for ninety miles, to the three forks. In this distance there are many small mountain streams, crossing the valley to the river, all of which are lined with timber, and several of them affording [99] valuable water privileges for such machinery as may be erected, when yankee enterprise shall have settled and improved this desirable portion of our great republic.

After leaving the Santaam, a prairie commences, of from four to twelve miles in width, which continues up the valley for a day's travel, which I suppose to be about forty miles. The mountains upon the east side of the Willamette are covered with timber of quite large growth. In this last prairie has been found some stone coal, near the base of the mountain spurs; but as to quantity or quality I am uninformed. The specimen tried by a blacksmith was by him pronounced to be good.

The Willamette valley, including the first plateaus of the Cascade and Coast ranges of mountains, may be said to average a width of about sixty, and a length of about two hundred miles. It is beautifully diversified with timber and prairie. Unlike our great prairies

east of the Rocky Mountains, those upon the waters
of the Pacific are quite small; instead of dull and sluggish
streams, to engender miasma to disgust and disease man,
those of this valley generally run quite rapidly, freeing
the country of such vegetable matter as may fall into
them, and are capable of being made subservient to the
will and comfort of the human family in propelling
machinery. Their banks are generally lined with fine
groves of timber for purposes of utility, and adding much
to please the eye.

The Willamette itself, throughout its length, has
generally a growth of fir and white cedar, averaging
from one-fourth to three miles in width, which are valuable both for agricultural and commercial purposes. Its
banks are generally about twenty feet above the mid-
dling stages, yet there are some low ravines, (in the country called *slues*,) which are filled with water during
freshets, and at these points the bottoms are overflowed;
but not more so than those upon the rivers east of the
Mississippi. It has been already observed that the soil
in these bottoms and in the prairies is very rich; it is
a black alluvial deposite of muck and loam; in the
timbered portions it is more inclined to be sandy, and
the higher ground is of a reddish colored clay and
loam.

The whole seems to be very productive, especially
of wheat, for which it can be safely said, that it is not
excelled by any portion of the continent. The yield
of this article has frequently been fifty bushels per acre,
and in one case Dr. White harvested from ten acres an
average of over fifty-four [100] bushels to the acre; but
the most common crop is from thirty to forty bushels per

acre, of fall sowing; and of from twenty to twenty-five bushels, from spring sowing.

There is one peculiarity about the wheat, and whether it arises from the climate or variety, I am unable to determine. The straw, instead of being hollow as in the Atlantic states, is filled with a medullary substance, (commonly called pith,) which gives it firmness and strength; hence it is rarely that the wheat from wind or rain lodges or falls before harvesting. The straw is about the height of that grown in the states, always bright, the heads upon it are much longer, and filled with large grains, more rounded in their form, than those harvested in the eastern part of the Union. I have seen around fields, where a single grain has grown to maturity, forty-two stalks, each of which appeared to have borne a well filled head; for the grains were either removed by birds, or some other cause. As it was November when I arrived in the country, I saw wheat only in its grassy state, except what had escaped the late harvest.

The farmers have a white bald wheat, the white bearded, and the red bearded, either of which can be sown in fall or spring, as best suits their convenience, or their necessities demand. That sown in September, October or November, yields the most abundantly; but if sown any time before the middle of May, it will ripen. The time of harvesting is proportioned to the seed time. That which is early sown is ready for the cradle or sickle by the last of June, or the first of July, and the latest about the first of September. In the Oregon valley, there are but few rains in the summer months, and as the wheat stands up very well, farmers are generally but little hurried with their harvesting.

˙ The emigrants usually arrive in the latter part of the summer or fall, and necessarily first provide a shelter for their families, and then turn their attention to putting in a field of wheat. In doing this, they frequently turn under the sod with the plough one day, the next harrow the ground once, then sow their seed, and after going over it again with a harrow, await the harvest, and not unfrequently gather forty bushels from the acre thus sown. In several instances the second crop has been garnered from the one sowing. When the wheat has stood for cutting until very ripe, and shattered considerably in the gathering, the seed thus scattered over the field has been harrowed under, and yielded twenty bushels to the acre, of [101] good merchantable grain. I was told of an instance where a third crop was aimed at in this way; it yielded but about twelve bushels to an acre, and was of a poor quality.

The rust and smut which so often blast the hopes of the farmer, in the old states, are unknown in Oregon, and so far there is but very little cheat.

Harvesting is generally done with cradles, and the grain threshed out with horses, there being no machines for this latter purpose in the territory.

The grain of the wheat, though much larger than in the states, has a very thin husk or bran, and in its manufacture in that country during the winter months requires a coarser bolting cloth than in the Atlantic states, owing to the dampness of the atmosphere at this season.

The farmers already raise a surplus of this commodity, over and above the consumption of the country: but owing to the scarcity of mills to manufacture it, they cannot at all times have it in readiness to supply vessels when they visit the settlements. At the time I left, wheat was worth eighty cents per bushel, and flour three dollars and fifty cents per hundred pounds. The mills above the Falls grind for a toll of one-eighth, but at the Falls they will exchange for wheat, giving thirty-six pounds of fine flour for an American bushel, and forty pounds for a royal bushel. The weight of a bushel of wheat, (according to quality,) is from sixty to seventy pounds.

Oats yield an abundant crop, but this grain is seldom sown, as the stock is generally suffered to gather its support by grazing over the plains.

Peas do well, and are much used in feeding hogs, at the close of their fattening, when taken off of their range of camas and other roots; and it is remarked that this vegetable there is free from the bug or wevil that infests it in the western states.

Barley is very prolific, and of a large and sound growth; but there is as yet little raised, as the demand for it is quite limited.

I saw no rye in the country. Buckwheat grew very well, though not much raised.

For potatoes Oregon is as unequalled, by the states, as it is for wheat. I doubt whether there is any portion of the globe superior to it for the cultivation of this almost indispensable vegetable. I heard of no sweet potatoes, and think there are none in the territory.

Indian corn is raised to some extent upon the lower bottoms [102] in the valleys, but it is not considered a good corn country. It had yielded forty bushels to the acre; they mostly plant the small eight-rowed yankee corn. The summers are too cool for corn. Tobacco has been tried; and although it may be raised to some extent, it is lighter than in Kentucky, and more southern latitudes. The climate and soil are admirably adapted to the culture of flax and hemp, and to all other vegetables, which grow with ordinary care, in any of the northern, eastern and middle states.

During my travels through the valley, I spent some time with Mr. Joel Walker, a gentleman who had resided several years in California, had made several trips from Oregon to the bay of San Francisco, and had spent some time in trapping and trading between the Willamette valley and the 42d degree of north latitude.[106] From this gentleman, as well as from several others, I learned that the trail near two hundred miles south of Oregon city arrives at the California mountains, which is a ridge running from the Cascade to the Coast range of mountains. With the exception of a few peaks, this ridge is susceptible of easy cultivation, being partly prairie and partly covered with timber. Mr. Walker

[106] Joel P. Walker was a brother of Joseph R. Walker (see note 46, *ante*, p. 70). Of Virginian birth he removed at an early age to Tennessee, whence he went out under Andrew Jackson against the Alabama Indians (1814), and later against the Florida Seminole. Some time before 1822, he removed to Missouri, where he married, and engaged in the early Santa Fé trade with Stephen Cooper (see our volume xix, p. 178, note 16). Walker removed with his family to Oregon in 1840 — one of the first families of settlers who came independent of the missionary movement. Wilkes met him on the Willamette in 1841, when he expressed his dissatisfaction with the climate and the conditions. See Wilkes's *Exploring Expedition*, iv, p. 388. That same year he went overland to California, where he worked for Captain Sutter, coming back to Oregon some time before Palmer's visit, with a herd of cattle for sale. This time he remained in Oregon several years, being chosen justice of the peace for Yamhill County (about 1845). In 1848 he returned to California, where he was a member from Napa of the constitutional convention of 1849. In 1853 he removed to Sonoma County where he spent the remainder of his life, dying sometime after 1878.— ED.

doubts not that a good wagon road can be made over this ridge; to cross which requires but a few hours, and brings us into the beautiful country bounded on the east and west by the Cascade and Coast ranges, the California mountains on the north, and the Rogue's River mountains on the south.

This district of country, which is only about forty miles wide from east to west, is drained by the Umpquah river, and its tributaries, which as in the Willamette valley, are skirted with timber; but back from the streams is a prairie country, beautifully alternated with groves of timber.

At the mouth of the Umpquah, which empties into the Pacific about thirty miles from where it leaves this beautiful district of country, the Hudson's Bay Company have a trading post.[164]   If we except this, there is no settlement nor claim made on this river or its tributaries. Passing Rogue's River mountains, the trail enters the valley of the river of that name.   This valley is quite similar to that of the Umpquah, but perhaps not quite so large.[165]   This valley is bounded on the south by the Klamet mountain, which is a spur of the Cascade and Coast mountains.   It is high and somewhat difficult to pass over; but it is believed a route may be found that will admit of an easy passage over.   It is heavily timbered; and as in [103] the Coast range, the timber in

---

[164] For the Umpqua River see our volume vii, p. 231, note 82; the fort is noted in Farnham's *Travels*, our volume xxix, p. 59, note 79.— Ed.

[165] For Rogue River see *ibid.*, p. 82, note 104.   The mountains lie directly north of the river valley in Coos and Curry counties, Oregon.   The first settlers in this valley came there in 1851.   See William V. Colvig, "Indian Wars of Southern Oregon," in *Oregon Historical Quarterly*, iv, pp. 237-240.— Ed.

many places has died, and a thick growth of underbrush sprung up.

South of the Klamet mountains spreads out the beautiful valley watered by the Klamet river. This valley, although not so well known as that of the Willamette, is supposed to be more extensive, and equally susceptible of a high state of cultivation. It is esteemed one of the best portions of Oregon.[166] The land is mostly prairie, but is well diversified with timber, and bountifully supplied with spring branches. The Indians are more numerous here than in the valley further north, and as in the Umpquah and Rogue's river valleys, more hostile. There has been very little trading with them; but they not unfrequently attack persons driving cattle through from California to the settlements in Oregon; and although none of the drivers have been killed for several years, they have lost numbers of their cattle. Before these valleys can be safely settled, posts must be established to protect the inhabitants from the depredations of these merciless savages.[167]

A settlement of about a dozen families has been made

---

[166] By the "Klamet" Mountains, Palmer refers to the chain lying north of Klamath River valley, now usually spoken of as the Siskiyou range. Klamath River is described in Farnham's *Travels*, our volume xxix, p. 46, note 56. The trail into this region followed nearly the route of the Southern Pacific Railway.— Ed.

[167] The Indians of Southern Oregon had always been disposed to molest white wayfarers. Witness the troubles of Jedediah H. Smith in 1828, the massacre of the Turner family in 1835, and the attack on a cattle train in 1837. After 1848, the passage of gold-seekers to and from California intensified the difficulty, whereupon a long series of contests ensued, resulting in open wars, in which Palmer bore an important part. The war of 1853 was terminated by a treaty (September 10) secured by Generals Lane and Palmer; that of 1855 was more serious, being participated in by regular troops as well as Oregon militia. For Palmer's relation to these wars see preface to this volume.— Ed.

upon Clatsop plains. This is a strip of open land, about a mile in width, extending from the south end of Point Adams, or Clatsop Point, at the mouth of the Columbia river, about twenty miles along the margin of the ocean, in the direction of Cape Lookout.[100]   It appears to have been formed by the washing of the waters. Ridges resembling the waves of the ocean extend from north to south throughout the entire length of the plains. These ridges are from twelve to twenty-five feet high, and in some places not more than fifty feet, but at other points as much as three hundred yards asunder. That along the coast is the highest and least fertile, as it seems to be of more recent formation. The soil is composed of vegetable matter and sand, and produces grass more abundantly than the valleys above; the spray and dampness of the ocean keeping the grass green all the year. The land is not so good for fall wheat as in the upper country, but the settlers raise twenty-five bushels of

[100] For Point Adams see our volume vi, p. 233, note 37. The term Clatsop was given for an Indian tribe — *ibid.*, p. 239, note 39. Clatsop Plains were first visited in the winter of 1805-06 by members of the Lewis and Clark expedition, who erected a cairn for the making of salt, in the neighborhood of the present resort known as Seaside. The settlement of this region was begun in 1840 by members of the Methodist mission, reinforced by Solomon H. Smith and Calvin Tibbitts of the Wyeth party, who had married daughters of the Clatsop chief Cobaway (Lewis and Clark spelled it Comowool). J. W. Perry took up a farm in 1842, and several members of the immigration of 1843 settled on the Clatsop Plains. See "Pioneer Women of Clatsop County," in Oregon Pioneer Association *Transactions*, 1897, pp. 77-84. These plains are composed of a sandy loam well adapted for fruit and vegetables, but especially suited to grazing, so that dairying is a leading industry of this region.

Cape Lookout, in Tillamook County, is a conspicuous headland. It was first sighted by Heceta in 1775, and named by Captain Meares in 1789. See our volume xxviii, p. 32, note 9; also our volume vii, p. 112, note 17. The point, however, which Palmer designates as Cape Lookout, is in reality that called by the Lewis and Clark expedition "Clark's Point of View," but now known as Tillamook Head.— ED.

spring wheat to the acre. I think it better for root crops than the valleys above. In the rear of the plains, or about a mile from the shore, is a body of land heavily timbered with hemlock and spruce, which is tall and straight, and splits freely. Near the timber a marsh of some two hundred yards in width extends nearly the entire length of the plains. This marsh is covered with the low kind of cranberries.

A stream some ten or twelve yards in width [100] enters the plains [104] at the south end, runs ten or twelve miles north, when it turns to the west, and after passing through two of the ridges, takes a southerly direction and enters the bay that sets up between the Plains and Cape Lookout, not more than ten rods from its entrance into the Plains. Here a dam is built across the stream, and the claimant is erecting a flouring mill.

On these plains the claims are taken half a mile in width on the coast, and extending back two miles; each claimant therefore having a fair proportion of prairie and timber land, besides a glorious cranberry patch.

Some fifteen miles south-east of Cape Lookout, stands a peak of the Coast range, called Saddle Mountain; and the cape is a spur or ridge extending from this mountain some two or three miles out into the ocean.[170] Around the head of the bay, immediately north of Cape Lookout, is a body of several thousand acres of timber land.

[100] The Necanicum River, called by Lewis and Clark the Clatsop, has a roundabout course, as indicated by Palmer, and drains the southern end of Clatsop Plains.— ED.

[170] Saddle Mountain, the highest point in Clatsop County, shows three peaks as viewed from the Columbia, and takes this name from its form. The aboriginal name was Swollalahost. Lewis and Clark found it covered with snow during most of the winter season of 1805-06.— ED.

The soil is good, but most of it so heavily timbered that it would require much labour to prepare it for farming. But as the streams from the mountain afford an abundance of water power, it would be an easy matter to manufacture the timber into lumber, for which there is a good market for shipping, and thus make the clearing of the land for cultivation a profitable business.

Along the coast from Cape Lookout to the 42d parallel there is much land that can be cultivated; and even the mountains, when cleared of the heavy bodies of timber with which they are clothed, will be good farming land. There is so much pitch in the timber that it burns very freely; sometimes a green standing tree set on fire will all be consumed; so that it is altogether a mistaken idea that the timber lands of the country can never be cultivated. I am fully of the opinion that two-thirds of the country between the Willamette valley and the coast, and extending from the Columbia river to the forty-second parallel, which includes the Coast range of mountains, can be successfully cultivated. This region abounds in valuable cedar, hemlock and fir timber, is well watered, possesses a fertile soil, and being on the coast, it will always have the advantage of a good market; for the statements that soundings cannot be had along the coast, between Puget Sound and the Bay of San Francisco, are altogether erroneous. No place along the range would be more than thirty miles from market; and the difficulty of constructing roads over and through this range would be trifling, compared with that of constructing similar works over the Alleghanies.

[105] The country about Cape Lookout is inhabited

by a tribe of Indians called the Kilamooks. They are a lazy and filthy set of beings, who live chiefly on fish and berries, of which there is here a great abundance. They have a tradition among them that a long time ago the Great Spirit became angry with them, set the mountain on fire, destroyed their towns, turned their *tiye* (chief) and *tilicums* (people) into stone, and cast them in the ocean outside of Cape Lookout; that the Great Spirit becoming appeased, removed the fire to Saddle Mountain, and subsequently to the *Sawhle Illahe* (high mountain,) or Mount Regnier, as it is called by the whites, on the north side of the Columbia river.[171]

In the ocean about a mile west of Cape Lookout, is to be seen at high water a solitary rock, which they call Kilamook's Head, after the chief of the tribe. Around this rock for half a mile in every direction may be seen at low water divers other rocks, which are called the *tilicums*, (people) of the tribe. At low water is to be seen a cavity passing quite through Kilamook's Head, giving the rock the appearance of a solid stone arch.[172]

In support of this tradition, the appearance of the promontory of Cape Lookout indicates that it may be the remains of an extinct volcano; and on Saddle Mountain there is an ancient crater, several hundred feet deep; while Mount Regnier is still a volcano. Those who have visited the rocky cliffs of Cape Lookout, report that there is some singular carving upon the ledges,

[171] For the Tillamook (Kilamook) Indians see our volume vi, p. 258, note 67. Mount Rainier is noted in Farnham's *Travels*, our volume xxix, p. 33, note 30.— ED.

[172] On Tillamook Rock, a large boulder in the ocean, opposite Tillamook Head, a lighthouse was erected in 1879-81. It was a work of much difficulty, the engineers narrowly escaping being washed into the sea.— ED.

resembling more the hieroglyphics of the Chinese, than any thing they have seen elsewhere.

These Indians have another tradition, that five white men, or, as they call them, pale faces, came ashore on this point of rock, and buried something in the cliffs, which have since fallen down and buried the article deep in the rocks; that these pale faces took off the Indian women, and raised a nation of people, who still inhabit the region to the south. And I have met with travelers who say they have seen a race of people in that region, whose appearance would seem to indicate that they may have some European blood in their veins. A reasonable conjecture is, that a vessel may have been cast away upon the coast, and that these five men escaped to Cape Lookout. Another circumstance renders it probable that such might have been the case. Frequently, after a long and heavy south westerly storm, large cakes of bees-wax, from two to four inches thick and from twelve to eighteen inches in diameter, [106] are found along the beach, near the south end of Clatsop Plains. The cakes when found are covered with a kind of sea-moss, and small shells adhere to them, indicating that they have been a long time under water.[173]

In or about Saddle Mountain rises a stream called Skipenoin's river, which, though extremely crooked, runs

---

[173] Palmer probably obtained his information of these Indian traditions from Celiast (or Helen) Smith, daughter of the Clatsop chief, whose son Silas B. Smith has furnished much material for recent historical works. This story of the wreck of the ship carrying beeswax, differs slightly from the version given in Lyman, *History of Oregon*, i, pp. 167-169. Lyman conjectures that it may have been the Spanish ship "San Jose," carrying stores (1769) to San Diego, California, which was never after heard from. Some of the cakes of w ax found bore the letters I. H. S.— ED.

nearly north, and empties into the western side of Young's bay, which, it will be remembered, is a large body of water extending south from the Columbia river between Point Adams and Astoria. Between this river and Clatsop plains is a strip of thick spruce and hemlock, with several low marshes. The landing for Clatsop plains is about two miles up the river; which it is rather difficult to follow, as there are many *slues* putting in from either side, of equal width with the main stream. From the bay a low marshy bottom extends up to the landing, covered with rushes and sea-grass. This bottom is overflowed opposite the landing at high water. Between the landing and Clatsop plains is a lake one or two miles in length, which has its outlet into the bay. Its banks are high, and covered with spruce. Near this is a stream, from the mouth of which it is about two or three miles along the bay to the creek upon which Lewis and Clark wintered; and thence about three and a half miles to the head of the bay where Young's river enters.[174]

Young's river is a stream about one hundred and fifty yards in width, and is navigable for steamboats and small sloops to the forks, six or seven miles up. About seven miles further up are the "Falls," where the water pitches over a ledge of rocks, making a fall of about sixty

---

[174] For Young's Bay see our volume vi, p. 259, note 69. Skipanon is a small creek, a branch of which Clark crossed on a log during his trip from Fort Clatsop to the seacoast. The site of Fort Clatsop was definitely determined by Olin D. Wheeler in 1899 (see his *Trail of Lewis and Clark*, ii, pp. 195, 198), and the Oregon Historical Society in 1900 (see *Proceedings* for 1900). The plan of the fort was discovered by the present Editor among the Clark papers in 1904. See *Original Journals of the Lewis and Clark Expedition*, iii, pp. 268, 298. The river upon which the fort was located was known by the native name of Netul, now called Lewis and Clark River, a tributary of Young's Bay west of Young's River.— ED.

feet. Around the falls the mountains are covered with heavy timber. Near the forks the river receives from the east a small stream, upon which a machine for making shingles has been erected; and as the timber in the vicinity is good for shingles, which can be readily sold for the Sandwich Islands market, the owners expect to do a profitable business. Young's river rises in or near Saddle mountain.[176] From the mouth of this river it is about eight or ten miles, around the point which forms on the east Young's Bay, to Astoria, or Fort George, as it is called by the Hudson's Bay Company. This stands on the south side of the Columbia river, about sixteen miles from its mouth.[176]

The Columbia river and its location have been so often described, that it is hardly necessary for me to go into details. But as this work is designed to be afforded so low as to place [107] it within the reach of every one, and may fall into the hands of many whose means will not enable them to procure expensive works on Oregon, it may not be amiss to say something about that noble stream, which discharges its waters into the ocean between cape Disappointment on the north, and point Adams or Clatsop point on the south, and in latitude about 46° 15′ north.

At its mouth the Columbia is narrowed to about six

[176] Young's River was called by Lewis and Clark Kilhawánackkle, and is the largest stream in Clatsop County. The falls are at the head of tidewater and flow over a black basalt cliff. The eastern tributary is the Klaskanine River. See *Original Journals of the Lewis and Clark Expedition*, iv, p. 137.— ED.

[176] For the history of this place see Franchère's *Narrative* in our volume vi, and Ross's *Oregon Settlers* in our volume vii. The later history of Fort George is sketched in Farnham's *Travels*, our volume xxix, p. 57, note 74.— ED.

miles in width by cape Disappointment extending in a
south west direction far out into the stream, the cape
being washed on the west side by the ocean. Cape
Disappointment and Chinook point, a few miles above
it, form Baker's bay, which affords good anchorage for
vessels as soon as they round the point.[177] This cape
presents a rocky shore, is quite high, and covered
with timber. An American had taken it as his land
claim, according to the laws of the territory; but during
the last winter, he sold his right to Mr. Ogden, then one
of the principal factors, but now Governor of the Hudson's Bay Company in Oregon, for one thousand dollars.
A fortification on this cape would command the entrance
of the river by the northern channel, which is immediately
around the point, and as it is said, not more than half a
mile in width.[178]

Point Adams, the southern cape of the Columbia,
is a little above cape Disappointment. It is low and
sandy, and continues a sand ridge four miles to Clatsop
plains. This point, and the high ground at Astoria,
as before stated, form Young's bay, near which the
ridge is covered with timber. Near point Adams is the
southern channel or entrance into the Columbia, which
is thought to be preferable to the northern channel; and
I think either of them much better than heretofore

[177] For Cape Disappointment and Baker's Bay see our volume vi, pp. 233,
234, notes 36, 38. Chinook Point was the site of a populous village of that
tribe just west of Point Ellice, which is the southernmost promontory between
Gray's and Baker's Bay. Lewis and Clark found the village deserted, but
in early Astorian times it was populated — see our volumes vi, p. 240; vii,
p. 87.— ED.

[178] For Peter Skeen Ogden see our volume xxi, p. 314, note 99. The United
States government has recently chosen this site for a fort now (1906) in process
of erection, to be known as Fort Columbia.— ED.

represented. In each there is a sufficiency of water to float any sized vessel. With the advantages of light houses, buoys, and skillful pilots, which the increasing commerce of the country must soon secure, the harbor at the mouth of the Columbia would compare well with those on the Atlantic coast; and I may say that it would be superior to many of them.

As we ascend, Astoria occupies probably the first suitable site for a town. It stands upon a gradual slope, which extends from the bank of the river up to the mountain. The timber was once taken off of some forty or fifty acres here, which, except about twenty acres, has since been suffered to grow up again, and it is now a thicket of spruce and briars. Five or six old dilapidated buildings, which are occupied by the Hudson's Bay Company, who have a small stock of goods for trading [108] with the natives, and a few old looking lodges upon the bank of the river, filled with greasy, filthy Indians, constitute Astoria.[179]

The person in charge of this establishment, whose name is Birney, seems to be a distant, haughty, sulky fellow, whose demeanor and looks belie the character generally given to a mountaineer or backwoodsman.[180] As evidence of his real character, I will state one circumstance as it was related to me by persons residing in the vicinity of the place. During the summer or fall, while

---

[179] Astoria, as an American town, began in 1846 with the settlement of James Welch, who defied the Hudson's Bay Company officers to drive him from the site. The post-office was begun in 1847, and a custom house two years later. In 1856 a town government was established, while twenty years later Astoria was incorporated as a city. Its population is now about ten thousand, with good prospects for a large growth in the near future.— ED.

[180] For James Birnie see our volume xxi, p. 361, note 130.— ED.

the British war vessel Modesté was lying at Astoria, one
of the sailors fell overboard and was drowned. Search
was made, but his body could not be found. Several
weeks afterwards the body of a man was found upon
the shore, a short distance above Astoria. Information
was immediately communicated to Birney, who promised
to give the body a decent burial. About two weeks after
this, some Indians travelling along the shore, attracted
to the place by a disagreeable scent and the number of
buzzards collected together, discovered the body of a
man much mangled, and in a state of putrefaction.
They informed two white men, Trask, and Duncan,[181]
who immediately made enquiry as to whether the body
found on the beach previously had been buried, and
received for answer from Birney, *that it was no country-
man of his, but it was likely one of the late emigrants from
the States that had been drowned at the Cascade Falls.*
Trask and Duncan proceeded to bury the body, and
found it to be in the garb of a British sailor or marine.
This, to say the least, was carrying national prejudice
a little too far.

Near Astoria, and along the river, several claims
have been taken, and commencements made at improv-
ing. Anchorage may be had near the shore. Three
miles above Astoria is Tongue point,[182] a narrow rocky
ridge some three hundred feet high, putting out about

[181] Elbridge Trask came to Oregon in 1842, apparently a sailor on an
American vessel. He lived for a time at Clatsop Plains. Probably his companion was Captain Alexander Duncan, commander of the "Dryad," and a
friend of James Birnie.— ED.

[182] For Tongue Point, which takes its name from its peculiar shape, see
our volume vi, p. 242, note 44. Gray's Bay is noted in volume vii, p. 116,
note 20.— ED.

a mile into the river; but at the neck it is low and not more than two hundred yards across. The two channels of the river unite below this point. Opposite is Gray's bay, a large, beautiful sheet of water, of sufficient depth to float ships. Above and on the south side of the river is Swan bay, a large sheet of water, though shallow, presenting numerous bars at low tides. A deep channel has been cut through this bay, which affords an entrance into a stream that comes in from the south, about two hundred yards wide, and from appearance is navigable some distance up.[183] In this vicinity the whole country is covered with heavy timber. In [109] the indentation in the mountain range south of the river, there seems to be large scopes of good rich land, which would produce well if cleared of timber. From Tongue point across Gray's bay to Catalamet point is about sixteen miles. Small craft are frequently compelled to run the southern channel, inside of a cluster of islands called Catalamet Islands, which passes "old Catalamet town," as it is called, a point where once stood an Indian village. Four or five claims have been taken here, but none of them have been improved. A short distance from the river are several beautiful prairies, surrounded with heavy timber. A small stream enters here, which affords water power a short distance up.[184]

[183] By Swan Bay, Palmer intends that stretch of the river lying between Tongue and Cathlamet points, which is more usually known as Cathlamet Bay. The river is the John Day (aboriginal name, Kekemarke), which should not be confused with the larger stream of this name in eastern Oregon. See our volume v, p. 181, note 104.— ED.

[184] For Cathlamet Point see our volume vii, p. 116, note 20. The old village of the Cathlamet Indians which was located near the present town of Knappa, was visited by Lewis and Clark on their outward journey (1805); see *Original*

A few miles above old Catalamet town, near the top
of the bluff, about four hundred yards from the Columbia,
stands Wilson & Hunt's saw mill, which is driven by a
small stream coming down from the mountain; after
leaving the wheel the stream falls about sixty feet, striking tide water below. A sluice or platform is so constructed as to convey the lumber from the mill to the level
below, where it is loaded into boats and run out to the
river, where it can be loaded into vessels.

Upon our arrival at this place, the bark Toulon was
lying at anchor, about fifty yards from the shore, taking
in a cargo of lumber for the Sandwich Islands, to which
she expected to sail in a few days. This was early in
January, but from some cause she did not leave the
mouth of the river until the last of February.[185]

In the vicinity of the mill there is some better timber
than I have seen in any other part of the country. The
largest trees are about seven feet in diameter, and nearly
three hundred feet high; the usual size, however, is from
eighteen inches to three feet diameter, and about two
hundred feet high.

The country slopes up from the mill gradually, for
several miles, and is susceptible of easy cultivation; the

Journals of the Lewis and Clark Expedition, iii, p. 252. The stream was
that now known as Tillasqua Creek.— ED.

[185] This mill was erected by Henry Hunt, one of the emigrants of 1843, for
the purpose of preparing lumber for the Pacific market, especially that of
the Sandwich Islands. See letter of Tallmadge B. Wood in *Oregon Historical
Quarterly*, iii, pp. 394-398. Later, salmon barrels were made at this place,
the men employed at the task being the only settlers between Astoria and
Linnton on the Willamette; and sometimes they were summoned to serve
as a sheriff's posse. See Oregon Pioneer Association *Transactions*, 1890,
p. 73. Hunt's Mill Point is marked on the federal land office map of 1897
as being opposite the lower end of Puget Island.— ED.

soil is somewhat sandy, and has the appearance of being good.

In leaving this place, we struck directly across the river, which is here over two miles wide. Upon the north side, almost opposite to the mill, is a claim held by Birney, of Astoria, who has made an effort at improvement by cutting timber and raising the logs of a cabin. At this place a rocky bluff commences and continues up the river for ten miles, over which a great many beautiful waterfalls leap into the Columbia. There is one sheet of water ten or twelve feet wide, which plunges over a precipitous cliff two hundred feet into the river, [110] striking the water about thirty feet from the base of the rock, where there is sufficient depth to float vessels of large size.

At the distance of eight or ten miles above the mill, on the south side of the river, there is an indentation in the mountain to the south, and a bend in the river to the north, which forms a body of bottom land several miles in width, and some ten or twelve miles long, the greater part of which, except a strip varying from a quarter to half a mile in width, next to the river, is flooded during high tides. This strip is covered with white oak and cottonwood timber. The remainder of the bottom is prairie, with occasional dry ridges running through it, and the whole of it covered with grass. By throwing up levees, as is done upon the Atlantic coast, most of these fine lands might be cultivated.

At the extreme southern point of the elbow, there comes in a stream, the size of which was not ascertained, but from appearances it is of sufficient size to propel a considerable amount of machinery. There are several islands in the river opposite the lower point of this bottom, and at the northern angle the Columbia is not more than three-fourths of a mile wide. This is called Oak point, and holds out good inducements for a settlement. There is an Indian village half a mile below the point; and opposite, upon the northern side of the river, a good mill-stream, the falls being near the river, and the mountain covered with timber.[100] Immediately above the point, the river spreads out to one and a half or two miles in width, and having several islands, portions of which are covered with cottonwood, oak and ash timber, the remainder being nearly all prairie. From Oak point up to Vancouver, the scenery very much resembles that along the Hudson river through the Catskill Mountains, but much more grand, as the Cascade range of mountains, and many snowcapped peaks, are in view.

Some portions of the way the shore is high rugged cliffs of rocks, at others indentations in the mountain leave bottoms, from a quarter to three miles wide, which are mostly covered with timber. From the lower mouth of the Willamette to Fort Vancouver, the shores are lined with cottonwood timber, and upon the south side, as far up as the mouth of Sandy, or Quicksand river, which comes in at the western base of the Cascade range. But few claims have as yet been taken along the Columbia, but the fishing and lumbering advantages which this part

---

[100] At Oak Point was made the first American settlement in Oregon; see our volume xxi, pp. 261, 287, notes 74, 94. The stream on the south side is the Clatskanie River, in Columbia County, Oregon, flowing southwest and entering the river opposite Wallace Island. For the origin of this word and its relation to the Klaskanine River see H. S. Lyman, "Indian Names," in *Oregon Historical Quarterly*, i, p. 322. The mill stream of the northern bank is Nequally Creek in Cowlitz County, Washington.— Ed.

of the country possesses over many others, holds out great
inducements to settlers.

[111] From Fort Vancouver, for several miles down
upon the north side, the country is sufficiently level to
make good farming land; and the Hudson's Bay Company, or members of the company, have extensive farms,
with large herds of cattle. Fort Vancouver is one of the
most beautiful sites for a town upon the Columbia. It
is about ninety miles from the ocean, and upon the
north side of the river. Large vessels can come up this
far. The banks of the river are here about twenty-five
feet high. Much of the bottom land about the fort is
inclined to be gravelly, but produces well.[187]

A party consisting of nine persons, in two row-boats,
started from Oregon city on the 24th of December, for
Fort Vancouver, and arrived there in the afternoon of
the 25th. In our party was Colonel M'Clure, formerly
of Indiana, and who had been a member of the Oregon
legislature for two years.[188] As soon as we landed, he
made his way to the fort, which is about four hundred
yards from the shore, with the view of obtaining quarters
for the party. He soon returned and conducted us to
our lodgings, which were in an old cooper's shop, or
rather shed, near the river.

Before starting we had prepared ourselves with provisions, and a few cooking utensils. We set to work,

[187] For a brief historical sketch of Fort Vancouver see our volume xxi,
p. 297, note 82.— ED.

[188] Colonel John McClure came to Oregon from New Orleans some time
before 1842. In 1843 he settled at Astoria, where he had a cabin on the site
of the first Astoria mill. He married a native woman, and his portion of the
early town was known as McClure's Astoria. He is described as having
been an old man in 1845, and he had died before 1867.— ED.

and although the wind and rain made it unpleasant, we soon had a comfortable meal in readiness, and we made good use of the time until it was devoured. This was holyday with the servants of the Hudson's Bay Company, and such *ranting* and frolicking has perhaps seldom been seen among the sons of men. Some were engaged in gambling, some singing, some running horses, many promenading on the river shore, and others on the large green prairie above the fort. H. B. Majesty's ship of war Modesté was lying at anchor about fifty yards from the shore.[100] The sailors also seemed to be enjoying the holydays — many of them were on shore promenading, and casting *sheep's eyes* at the fair native damsels as they strolled from wigwam to hut, and from hut to wigwam, intent upon seeking for themselves the greatest amount of enjoyment. At night a party was given on board the ship, and judging from the noise kept up until ten at night, they were a jolly set of fellows. About this time a boat came ashore from the ship, with a few land lubbers most gloriously drunk. One of them fell out of the boat, and his comrades were barely able to pull him ashore. They passed our shop, cursing their stars for this ill luck.

We wrapped ourselves in our blankets, and lay down

---

[100] The British ship of war "Modeste," Captain Baillie commanding, first visited Fort Vancouver in July, 1844. Governor McLoughlin was offered no protection at this time; but the situation having grown more intense, the vessel was ordered to the Columbia in October, 1845, and remained to protect British interests until April, 1847. The officers sought to conciliate the American pioneers, but there was on the whole little intercourse between the two nationalities. Theatrical entertainments were planned and given in the winter of 1845-46, and a ball arranged by these officers was the occasion of an expression of a majority sentiment for the American cause. See Oregon Pioneer Association *Transactions*, 1874, pp. 26, 27.— Ed.

upon [112] a pile of staves. The rain was falling gently, and we were soon asleep. In the after part of the night, several of us were aroused by a strange noise among the staves. In the darkness we discovered some objects near us, which we supposed to be hogs. We hissed and hallooed at them, to scare them away. They commenced grunting, and waddled off, and all was again quiet, and remained so until daylight; but when we arose in the morning, we found ourselves minus one wagon sheet, which we had brought along for a sail, our tin kettle, eighteen or twenty pounds of meat, a butcher knife and scabbard, one fur cap, and several other articles, all of which had been stolen by the Indians, who had so exactly imitated the manœuvres of a gang of hogs, as entirely to deceive us.

After breakfast we visited the fort, where we had an introduction to Dr. McLaughlin, the Governor of the Hudson's Bay Company. He appears to be much of a gentleman, and invited us to remain during the day; but as we were upon an excursion down the river, we only remained to make a few purchases, which being accomplished, we left the place.

As before stated, the fort stands upon the north bank of the Columbia, six miles above the upper mouth of the Willamette, and about four hundred yards from the shore. The principal buildings are included within a stockade of logs, set up endwise close together, and about twelve feet high; the lower ends of the timbers being sunk about four feet in the ground. A notch is cut out of each log near the top and bottom, into which a girth is fitted, and mortised into a large log at each end, the whole being trenailed to this girth. I judge the area contains about four acres. The first thing that strikes a person forcibly upon entering one of the principal gates upon the south, is two large cannons, planted one upon either side of the walk leading to the Governor's house, immediately in front of the entrance. Many of the buildings are large and commodious, and fitted up for an extensive business, others are old fashioned looking concerns, and much dilapidated. East of the fort and along the river bank there is a grassy prairie, extending up for about three miles; it has been cultivated, but an unusually high freshet in the river washed the fence away, and it has since remained without cultivation. The soil is gravelly. North of this, and extending down nearly even with the fort there is a handsome farm, under good cultivation. North of the fort there is a beautiful orchard, and an extensive garden, with several large blocks of buildings. Below the [113] fort, and extending from the river for half a mile north, is the village; the inhabitants of which are a mongrel race, consisting of English, French, Canadians, Indians of different nations, and half breeds, all in the employ of the company. The buildings are as various in form, as are the characteristics of their inmates.

As yet there are but few Americans settled upon the north side of the Columbia. There seems to have been an effort upon the part of the Hudson's Bay Company, to impress the American people with an idea that the entire country north of the river was unfit for cultivation. Not only was this statement made to emigrants, but it was heralded forth to the whole world; and as much of the country along the Columbia corroborated this statement, no effort was made to disprove it. Americans visiting that country being so well pleased with the attentions paid them by the Hudson's Bay Company, took for granted their statements, without examining for themselves, and have asserted it at home, in accordance with British interests, and this I fear has had its influence in the settlement of this question. · For any one acquainted with the character of the claims of the respective governments can but admit, that greater privileges have been granted to Great Britain than that government had any right to expect, or than the justice of our claim would allow. Undoubtedly, the largest part of good agricultural country is south of 49° north latitude, but there is a great deal of excellent land north of that line. But little of it has been explored by Americans, and we have taken only the statements of British subjects, and upon their authority, the question between the two governments was settled. But as we have proven by actual examination the incorrectness of their statements in relation to the country between the Columbia and the 49th degree north latitude, we may reasonably infer that they are also incorrect in relation to the remainder of the country north. That the general features of the country north of the Columbia River are rough and mountainous, is admitted; and the same may be said in relation to the country south of it; but that it is barren and sterile, and unfit for cultivation, is denied.

The country upon the north side of the Columbia abounds with beautiful valleys of rich soil, of prairie and timbered lands, well watered, and adapted to the growth of all the grains raised in the northern, middle, and western States, with superior advantages for grazing; never failing resources for timber [114] and fish;

and its proximity to one of the best harbors in the world, renders it one of the most desirable and important sections upon the Pacific coast. Frazer's river, with its numerous tributaries, will afford a settlement which will compare well with England itself.

Vancouver's Island, an excellent body of land, is equal to England in point of size, fertility of soil, climate, and everything that would constitute great national wealth. And besides these, there are undoubtedly extensive valleys north of Frazer's river, which will compare well with it; but we know nothing positively upon this subject.[100]

The excellent harbors of Puget's sound, with its many advantages, and the delightful country about it, are sufficient to induce capitalists to look that way. This will probably be the principal port upon the coast. Here will doubtless be our navy yard and shipping stores. It is thought by many that an easy communication can be had between the Sound and the middle region, by striking the Columbia above fort Wallawalla. If this can be effected, it will lessen the distance materially from the settlement upon the upper Columbia to a sea-port town; and as the navigation of that river, between the Cascade and Lewis's fork is attended with great danger and difficulty, a route through to the sound in this quarter would be very desirable.[101] That it can be accomplished there is but little doubt. A stream empty-ing into the ocean between the Columbia and the sound, called Shahales, affords a very good harbor, which is

---

[100] For Fraser River and Vancouver Island see Farnham's *Travels*, our volume xxix, pp. 43, 75, notes 52, 91.— ED.

[101] For Puget's Sound see *ibid.*, p. 90, note 108. The first road over the Cascades was built in 1853, from Olympia to Walla Walla.— ED.

called Gray's harbor.[182]   Up this stream there is a country suitable for an extensive settlement. Like most other valleys in the country it is diversified with prairie and timbered land, and well watered. No claims as yet have been taken in this valley.

There are two peaks upon the north side of the river, which remain covered with snow the whole year round. One is called Mount St. Helen, and stands north east of Fort Vancouver, and distant perhaps forty-five or fifty miles.

The other is Mount Regnier, and stands some thirty-five miles from St. Helen, in a northerly direction. This is said to be a volcano.

The distance from Fort Vancouver to Puget's sound, in a direct line, cannot exceed ninety miles; but the high mountains between render the route somewhat difficult, and the distance necessarily traveled would be considerably increased.

About forty miles below fort Vancouver there comes in a [115] stream called Cowlitz; twenty-five miles up this stream there is a French settlement of about twenty families. Like those in the settlement upon the east side of the Willamette river, they have served out their term of years in the H. B. Company, have taken claims, and become an industrious and thriving population.[183]

The people in Oregon have adopted a code of laws for their government, until such time as the United States shall extend jurisdiction over them.

[182] For Gray's Harbor see our volume vi, p. 256, note 64; the Chehalis River is described in Farnham's *Travels*, our volume xxix, p. 81, note 103.— ED.

[183] For the Cowlitz settlement see our volume xxvii, p. 386, note 203.— ED.

The powers of the government are divided into three distinct departments — the legislative, executive, and judicial.

The legislative department is to consist of not less than *thirteen* members, nor more than *sixty-one*; the number not to be increased more than *five* in any one year. The members are elected annually; each district electing a number proportionate to its population.

The executive power is vested in one person, who is elected by the qualified voters of the territory, and holds his office for the term of two years. The judicial power is vested in a supreme court, and such inferior courts of law, equity, and arbitration, as may by law from time to time be established. The supreme court consists of one judge, elected by the legislature, and holds his office four years. They have adopted the Iowa code of laws.[194]

Oregon is now divided into eight counties, viz: Lewis, Vancouver, Clatsop, Yam-hill, Polk, Quality, Clackamis,

[194] Much has been written on the provisional government of Oregon, which was shadowed forth in the action of 1841, and actually established July 5, 1843. Consult J. Quinn Thornton, "History of the Provisional Government," in Oregon Pioneer Association *Transactions*, 1874, pp. 43-96; J. Henry Brown, *Political History of Oregon* (Portland, 1892); James R. Robertson, "Genesis of Political Authority in Oregon," in *Oregon Historical Quarterly*, i, pp. 1-59; and H. W. Scott, "Formation and Administration of the Provisional Government of Oregon," *ibid.*, ii, pp. 95-118. Palmer's brief synopsis is a summary of the revised organic law, drafted by a committee appointed by the legislature in June, 1845, endorsed by popular vote on July 26, and put in operation August 5 (see appendix to the present volume). This government continued until February 16, 1849, when it was superseded by the territorial government provided by Congress under act approved August 14, 1848. The code of Iowa laws appears to have been adopted because of the existence of a copy of Iowa statutes in the country. See F. I. Herriott, "Transplanting Iowa's Laws to Oregon," in *Oregon Historical Quarterly*, v, pp. 139-150.— ED.

and Shampoic.[116] Lewis county includes that portion of country about Puget's sound;—Vancouver, that along the northern side of the Columbia. These two counties comprise all the territory north of the Columbia river.

Clatsop county includes that part of the country west of the centre of the coast range of mountains, and from the river south, to Yam-hill county, and of course includes Astoria, Clatsop Plains, &c.

Quality county includes the territory bounded on the north by the Columbia, on the east by the Willamette, on the south by Yam-hill, and on the west by Clatsop county.

Yam-hill county is bounded on the north by Quality and Clatsop, (the line being about fifteen miles south of Oregon city,) on the east by the Willamette river, on the south by Polk county, and on the west by the Ocean.

[116] Polk county is bounded on the north by Yam-hill county, on the east by the Willamette, on the south by the California line, and on the west by the Pacific ocean.

Clackamis county is bounded on the north by the Columbia, on the east by the Rocky mountains, on the south by Shampoic county, and on the west by the Willamette, including Oregon city.

Shampoic county is bounded on the north by Clackamis county, on the east by the Rocky mountains, on the south by California, and on the west by the Willamette.

[116] The legislature of 1843 erected four districts for the purpose of local government — i.e., Tuaiatin (read for Quality), Yamhill, Champoeg (read for Shampoic), and Clackamas. That of 1845 changed the title to counties and created four more — Clatsop, Polk, Vancouver, and Lewis. Palmer gives their location properly.— ED.

The country will, without doubt, be divided into at least three states.   One state will include all the country north of the Columbia river.   Nature has marked out the boundaries.   Another state will include all that country south of the Columbia river to the California line, and west of the Cascade range of mountains.   This country, however, is large enough to form two states. The country east of the Cascade range, extending to the Rocky mountains, and between the Columbia and California, would make another state.   This would include more territory than all the remainder;   but it would cover all that vast barren region of country which can never be inhabited by the white man.   The western portion of this section is fertile.   The line doubtless would be established between, leaving the eastern portion as Oregon territory, for future generations to dispose of.

The country now contains over six thousand white inhabitants;   and the emigration this year, over land, will be about seventeen hundred souls, and that by water will probably equal it, which will increase the number to near ten thousand.   It may be a safe calculation to set down the number for the first of January, 1847, at twelve thousand souls.

The settlers are labouring under great disadvantages on account of not being able to obtain a sufficient amount of farming implements.   The early settlers were supplied at the Hudson Bay Company's store, and at prices much less than those now charged for the same articles.   At that time the supply was equal to the demand;   but since the tide of emigration has turned so strongly to this region, the demand is much greater than the supply.   This may be said of almost every kind of goods or merchandise.

The supply of goods in the hands of the American merchants has been very limited, being the remnant of cargoes shipped round upon the coast, more for the [117] purpose of treating with the Indians, than with the cultivators of the soil.

Great complaints have been made by the merchants trading in that quarter, that they were not able to compete with the Hudson Bay Company; and this is the cry even at home; but the fact is, the prices were much lower before these American merchants went into the country than they now are. Their mode of dealing is to ask whatever their avarice demands, and the necessities of the purchaser will bear. And not being satisfied with an open field, they have petitioned the Hudson Bay Company to put a higher price upon their goods, as they were selling lower than the American merchants wished to sell. In accordance with this request, the H. B. Company raised the price of goods *when sold to an American*, but sold them at the old prices to British subjects. This arrangement was continued for two years; but an American can now purchase at the fort as cheap as any one. These facts I obtained from various sources, and when apprised of the prices of goods in that country, they are not so hard to be believed.

I paid for a pair of *stoga* shoes, made in one of the eastern states, and a very common article, four dollars and fifty cents; for a common coarse cotton flag handkerchief, which can be had in Cincinnati for five or ten cents, *fifty* cents. The price of calico ranges from thirty-one to eighty-seven and a half cents a yard; common red flannel one dollar and fifty cents per yard; a box of two

hundred and fifty percussion caps, two dollars and fifty
cents; coarse boots, eastern made, six to eight dollars;
calfskin from ten to twelve dollars; coarse half hose,
one dollar; dry goods generally ranging with the above
prices. Iron was selling at twelve and a half cents per
pound. Tools of all kinds are very high; so that whatever may be said against the company, for putting down
the prices to destroy competition by breaking up other
merchants, cannot be "sustained by the facts of the case."
That they prevent them from raising the prices there
is no doubt, and if the American merchants had the
field, clear of competition, the prices would be double
what they now are. They have not capital to enable
them to keep up a supply, nor to purchase the surplus
of the country. The Hudson Bay Company are the
only purchasers to any extent, for there are no others
who have the necessary machinery to manufacture wheat,
which is the staple of the country at present. The
American merchants buy a few fish, [118] hides, and
lumber; but in such limited quantities as to be of very
little advantage to the country.

A few American merchants, with a little capital, would
give an impulse to trade, encourage the settlers, make
it a profitable business to themselves, and add much to
the character of the country. There is scarcely any
branch of business that might not be carried on successfully in Oregon. Flouring mills, saw-mills, carding
machines, fulling and cloth dying, tin shops, potteries,
tanyards, &c., &c., would all be profitable; and in truth
they are all much needed in the country.

The price of a flour barrel is one dollar; that of common split-bottom chairs twenty-four dollars per dozen;

a common dining table without varnish, fourteen dollars; half soling a pair of shoes or boots, two dollars; cutting and splitting rails, one dollar and twenty-five cents per hundred; eighteen inch shingles, four dollars and fifty cents per thousand; cutting cord wood, from seventy-five cents to one dollar per cord; carpenter's wages from two to three dollars per day; laborer's from one to two dollars per day; plough irons fifty cents per pound; stocking a plough, from four to six dollars. Wheat, eighty cents per bushel; potatoes fifty cents; corn sixty-two and a half cents; oats fifty cents; beef four to six cents per pound; pickled salmon by the barrel, nine to twelve dollars for shipment; work cattle are from seventy-five to one hundred dollars per yoke; cows from twenty-five to fifty dollars each; American work horses from one hundred and fifty to two hundred dollars. I have never heard of any sheep being sold, but presume they would bring from five to ten dollars. A tailor will charge from six to twelve dollars for making a dress coat. Hogs are high, though there seems to be plenty of them in the country. The common kinds of poultry are plenty. It is a singular fact that the honey bee is not found in the Oregon territory, neither wild nor domesticated. Beef hides are two dollars each; a chopping axe from four and a half to six dollars; a drawing knife, three to five dollars; hand-saws, six dollars; cross-cut saws, eight to twelve dollars; mill-saws, twenty-five dollars. There is but little hollow ware in the country. No stationery of — any kind could be had when I was there. The people are in great need of school books; some sections being destitute of schools in consequence of not being able to procure books. Good teachers are also much needed.

I had expected to find the winters much more severe than they turned out to be. I had no thermometer, and no means [119] of ascertaining the degrees of heat and cold, but I kept an account of the wet and dry weather, cloudy, clear, &c., &c., commencing on the first day of November and ending on the fifth of March, which was the day I started on my return to the United States.

The 1st and 2d days of November were clear; 3d rainy; then clear until the 11th; cloudy until the 13th. Then cloudy, with slight showers of rain until the 20th; 21st and 22nd clear; 23d rainy; 24th and 25th were cloudy, but no rain; the weather was then clear until the 29th, when it again clouded up.

30th of November and first of December were cloudy; 2d and 3rd clear, with frosty nights. On the 4th a misty rain; 5th and 6th were cloudy; from 7th to 10th clear and cool, with frost every night. On the 11th it rained nearly all day, and on the 12th about half the day. 13th and 14th were cloudy. From the 15th to 22d clear and pleasant, with frosty nights; it thawed through the day in the sun all that froze at night, but in the shade remained frozen. From the 22d to 24th cloudy, with showers of drizzling rain; 25th, 26th and 27th rain nearly all the time, but not very copiously; the mornings were foggy. The 28th and 29th were clear, but very foggy in the forepart of the day; 30th and 31st rain about half the time.

From the 1st to 3d of January it was squally, with frequent showers of rain; 4th cloudy, but no rain; 5th rained nearly all day. From the 6th to the 12th, clear and pleasant, being slightly foggy in the mornings; from

13th to 17th rained about half each day, and nearly all the night; 18th and 19th, cloudy without rain. The 20th and 21st, slight rain nearly all the time; 22d was cloudy; 23d and 24th, rain about half of each day; 25th rained all day, 26th cloudy, without rain, 27th was rainy, some heavy showers; 28th was clear; 29th, 30th and 31st, were showery and blustering, raining about half the time, and foggy.

The 1st of February was clear; 2d cloudy, 3d rainy; 4th and 5th were a little cloudy, but pleasant; 6th and 7th, a few slight showers; 8th and 9th rainy and quite cool; snow was seen on the lower peaks of the Coast range of mountains, but none in the valley. The 10th was cloudy, at night a little frost; 11th was rainy; 12th and 13th rained all the time; 14th and 15th were nearly clear, with light frosts. The weather remained clear until the 23rd, with light frosts, but not cold enough to freeze the ground; 24th cloudy; 25th clear; 26th, 27th, and 28th rained all the time.

[120] First of March, rained half the day; 2d cloudy, 3d rained all day; 4th cloudy, 5th was showery — making in all about twenty days that it rained nearly all the day, and about forty days that were clear, or nearly so; the remainder of the days were cloudy and showery. A number of the days set down as rainy, a person with a blanket coat could have worked out all the day without having been wet. Much of the time it rained during the night, when it was clear through the day. I should think that two-thirds of the rain fell during the night.

No snow fell in the valleys, nor were there frosts more than *fifteen* nights. Ice never formed much over a quarter of an inch in thickness. The little streams and "*swales*" sometimes rise so high as to make it difficult to get about for a few days; but they are short, and soon run down. But little labour has yet been bestowed on the public roads. The Willamette river is the highway upon which nearly all the traveling is done, and upon which nearly all the products of the country are conveyed. The numerous streams can be easily bridged, and when this is done, there will be but little difficulty in traveling at any period of the year.

Upon the 5th of March, 1846, I set out on my return to the States. About one week previous, a party of seven persons had also set out on their return, and we expected to overtake them at Dr. Whitman's station. A few head of lame cattle had been left the preceding fall with a man named Craig, who resided near Spalding's mission;[199] and as the Indians in that vicinity had large bands of horses, which they wished to trade for cattle, I purchased several head of cattle to trade for horses, as also did others of the party. I, however, had purchased two horses and one mule; which, with several horses and mules belonging to the party, had been taken ahead on the 2d of the month, with the view of crossing the Columbia river at fort Vancouver, going up the valley of the Columbia, and recrossing below

---

[199] For the location of Spaulding's mission see our volume xxviii, p. 338, note 215.

William Craig was a mountain man who came to Oregon in 1842. He married among the Nez Percés, and established a farm just east of the Lapwai mission, where he had great influence with this tribe. In 1855 his land was reserved to him by treaty, the Nez Percés "having expressed in council a desire that William Craig should continue to live with them, having uniformly shown himself their friend." In 1856 he was made lieutenant-colonel of Washington volunteers, and in 1857-59, Indian agent at Walla Walla.— ED.

the Dalles.   By this route we would avoid the deep
snow on the Cascade mountains.

We loaded our effects on board a boat which we had
bought for that purpose, and at two o'clock P. M. shoved
off; and although anxious to be on the way back, yet
I left the place with considerable reluctance.   I had
found the people of Oregon kind and hospitable, and my
acquaintance with them had been of the most friendly
character.   Many of the persons who had traveled
through to Oregon with me, resided at Oregon [121]
city.   Attachments had been formed upon the road,
which when about to leave, seemed like parting with
our own families.   We were about to retrace the long
and dreary journey which the year before had been
performed, and again to brave the privations and dangers
incident to such a journey.   Traveling as we expected
to do on horseback, we could not take those conveniences
so necessary for comfort, as when accompanied with
wagons; but we bade adieu to the good people of Oregon,
and rapidly floated down the Willamette to the town of
Portland, twelve miles below the falls.   It commenced
raining quite fast, and we hove to, and procured quarters
with Mr. Bell, one of the emigrants who had recently
settled at this place.   This will probably be a town of
some consequence, as it occupies a handsome site, and
is at the head of ship navigation.   Mr. Petigrew [107] of

---

[107] For the beginnings of Portland see note 136, *ante*, p. 166.

Francis W. Pettygrove was born in Calais, Maine, in 1812. Having
engaged in mercantile business he carried a cargo of goods valued at $15,000
to Oregon by sea, establishing a store at Oregon City (1843).   It was due to
his wish that the newly-founded town near the mouth of the Willamette received
the name of Portland.   In 1848 Pettygrove sold his interest in the Portland
town site, going to California, where he speculated in land at Benicia.   In
1851 he was one of the founders of Port Townsend, in Washington.— ED.

New York is the proprietor. It continued raining nearly all night.

In the morning the rain abated; we again took the oars, and in two hours and a half reached the town of Linton. Here are a few log huts, erected among the heavy timber; but it will not, probably, ever be much of a town.[106] A great portion of the emigrants traveling down the Columbia land at this place, and take the road to Quality plains, which are about twenty-five miles distant; but the road is a bad one.

At 3 o'clock P. M. we arrived at fort Vancouver, where we made a few purchases to complete our outfit, and then rowed up the river two miles and a half, and encamped. Here we found the party with our horses. The Indians had stolen two horses, several trail ropes, &c. The day was showery.

On the 7th we ascended about eighteen miles, to the mouth of a stream coming in upon the north side of the river, about one hundred yards in width, having its source in Mount St. Helen. Here a commencement of a settlement had been made by Simmons, Parker, and others, and about a dozen buildings erected, but were now abandoned on account of its being subject to be overflowed by the annual high freshets of the Columbia river.[107] The soil is good, with several patches of prairie.

---

[106] The town of Linnton was founded in 1843 by M. M. McCarver and Peter H. Burnett, emigrants of that year, who supposed they had chosen a site that would be the head of ship navigation. They spent the first spring cutting the road to Tualatin Plains; but not finding Linnton a profitable speculation, they removed to the Plains and began farming. The town has continued to exist until the present, its population in 1900 being 384.— ED.

[107] The stream is the Washougal River of Clarke County, Washington whose source is not as far north as Mount St. Helens, but near Saddle Peak in Skamania County. A number of the immigrants of 1844 stopped here and

On our way we passed the grist and saw mills of the Hudson's Bay Company. They stand immediately upon the bank of the Columbia. The water power is obtained from small mountain streams. The mills are six and eight miles above the fort. Several islands in the river might be *leveed* and successfully cultivated. The day was cloudy, with occasional showers of rain, and some hail.

[122] On the 8th we advanced sixteen or eighteen miles. For the greater part of the way, the river is hemmed in by high, craggy, rocky cliffs. At a point, called Cape Horn, the rocks project over the stream, presenting a huge mass of black looking rocks of several hundred feet in height.[200] Some of them seem to have broken and slid from their former position, and now stand in detached columns erect in the deep stream, presenting a grand and terrific appearance. At several points, streams of water were tumbling more than a thousand feet from crag to crag, and falling into the river in broken sheets. Upon one of these columns stands a solitary pine tree, and upon the topmost branch sat a large bald-headed eagle. We rowed nearly under it, when one of our men took his rifle and fired, and down came the eagle, striking the water not more than

---

established winter quarters, going on the next year to settle at Puget Sound. Chief among these was Colonel Michael T. Simmons, this title being bestowed because he was second in command of the caravan of 1844. Born in Kentucky in 1814, he had in 1840 removed to Missouri where he built and ran a saw mill, which he sold to obtain his outfit for the Oregon journey. He explored the Puget Sound region in the spring of 1845, settling at Tumwater, where he died in 1867. Simmons is known as the father of Washington; he was sub-Indian agent for several years, and much concerned in building up the settlement.— ED.

[200] For this landmark see our volume xxi, p. 346, note 120.— ED.

ten feet from the boat. A wing had been broken, and
we dispatched him with our oars; he measured over
seven feet from tip to tip of the wings. Round this
point the water is sometimes very rough. Boats have
been compelled to lay to, for two weeks, on account
of the roughness of the water. The day was clear.

Upon the 9th we progressed about ten miles. Seven
miles brought us to the foot of the rapids, called the
Cascade falls, and here for five miles the river is hemmed
in and contracted to not more than three hundred yards
in width, and runs with tremendous velocity.[201] We
were compelled to *cordelle* our boat, and sometimes lift
it over the rocks for several rods. It is not easy to form
an idea of the difficulties to be encountered, in ascending
this rapid. Late in the evening we encamped, after a
day of hard work in wading, pulling and lifting. It
rained nearly all night.

On the 10th we arrived at the head of the portage.
Three times we were compelled to unload our boat,
and carry our effects over the rocks along the shore;
and at the main falls the distance of the portage is nearly
one mile. At night we had completed the portage, and
were all safe above the falls.

At the foot of the rapids we met several families of
emigrants, who had been wintering at the Dalles. One
of them had traveled the most of the way with us, but
being unwilling to travel as fast as we wished, had not
arrived in time to get through before winter set in. In
this family was a young woman, who so captivated one
of our party, that he turned back with them.

On the 11th we made but about eight miles; the wind

[201] For the Cascades see our volume xxviii, p. 371, note 233.— ED.

causing [123] a swell that rendered boating dangerous. The day was clear, and at night there was a hard frost.

We progressed twelve or fourteen miles on the 12th; the day was cloudy. Here we had designed crossing the river with our horses.

The morning of the 13th was too windy to swim our horses over. We attempted to take them up the north side of the river; but after clambering about three miles, we were compelled to halt, the cliffs being so abrupt that we were unable to pass them with horses. We remained at this place through the day.

On the morning of the 14th the wind had so abated that we could swim our animals. We commenced by taking four at a time; two upon each side of the boat, with four men rowing. In this manner by ten o'clock A. M., all had crossed. The water was very cold. The width of the river at this place, is more than a mile. The party with the horses then took the trail, and we saw no more of them, until we arrived at the Dalles, which we reached on the 15th. Here we found five of the party who had started a week in advance of us. Two of their company had gone on to Whitman's station. We sold our boat to the Missionaries, and remained here until the morning of the 19th, endeavoring to hire and buy horses to pack our effects to Dr. Whitman's. There were hundreds of horses belonging to the Indians, but their owners knew our situation, and wished to extort a high price from us. We so arranged our effects as to pack them on the mules and horses we had, and we ourselves traveled on foot.

On the evening of the 18th, we packed up and proceeded two miles, when we encamped. Two Indians came and encamped with us. In the night our mules began to show signs that a thief was approaching. The guard apprised us of it, and we prepared our arms. Our two Indian friends seeing that we were prepared to chastise thieves, roused up and commenced running around the camp, and hallooing most lustily; probably to give warning that it was dangerous to approach, as they soon disappeared.

During the day we had seen some sport. As we were nearly all *green* in the business of packing, and many of our animals were quite wild, we frequently had running and kicking "sprees," scattering the contents of our packs over the prairie, and in some cases damaging and losing them. In one instance, while traveling along a narrow, winding path upon the side of [124] a bluff, a pack upon a mule's back became loose; the mule commenced kicking, and the pack, saddle and all, rolled off, and as the trail rope was tied fast to the mule's neck, and then around the pack, it dragged the mule after it. The bank for six or eight hundred feet was so steep that a man could scarcely stand upright. The mule was sometimes ahead of the pack, at others the pack was ahead of the mule. At length, after tumbling about one thousand feet, to near a perpendicular ledge of rocks, they stopped. Six feet farther would have plunged them over a cliff of two hundred feet, into the river. We arrived at and crossed Falls river, receiving no other damage than wetting a few of our packs.[102] We encamped two miles above Falls river, having traveled about sixteen miles. The weather was

---

[102] This is an alternate name for Deschutes River, for which see *ante*, p. 119, note 102.— ED.

clear and warm. We traveled leisurely along, nothing remarkable occurring; but as some of the party were unaccustomed to walking, they soon showed signs of fatigue and sore feet. We were often visited by a set of half-starved and naked Indians.

On the 26th we reached Fort Wallawalla, or Fort Nez Percés, as it is sometimes called. This fort stands upon the east side of the Columbia, and upon the north bank of the Wallawalla river. We went about three fourths of a mile up the Wallawalla river, and encamped. Near us was a village of the Wallawalla Indians, with their principal chief.[300] This old chief was not very

---

[300] For this fort see our volume xxi, p. 278, note 73. The chief of the Wallawalla was Peupeumoxmox, or Yellow Serpent. He early came under missionary influence, and sent one of his sons to the Willamette to be educated under Methodist influences. This young man was christened Elijah Hedding, for a bishop of the church. He remained with the missionaries for over six years and acquired a command of English. In the autumn of 1844 a number of Cayuse, Nez Percé, and Wallawalla chiefs decided to visit the California settlements in order to trade for cattle. From Sutter's fort they made a raid into the interior, capturing some horses from a band of thieves. These animals were claimed by the Spanish and American settlers while the Indians maintained that they were their own property. In the course of the dispute Elijah was shot and killed. The Oregon Indians were greatly exasperated by this incident, threatening to raise a war-party against California, or to make reprisal upon any or all whites. The affair was quieted by the Hudson's Bay agent and the missionaries, but was undoubtedly one of the causes of the Whitman massacre. Yellow Serpent took no part in this latter event, but was active in the war of 1855, in which he perished while a hostage in the hands of the whites.

John Augustus Sutter was a German-Swiss born in 1803. After serving in the Franco-Swiss guards (1823-24) he came to America (1834) and embarked in the Santa Fé trade (1835-37). In 1838 he started for California, going via Oregon, the Sandwich Islands, and Alaska. Arriving in San Francisco Bay (1839) he secured from the Mexican government a concession on the Sacramento River, where he built a fort (1842-44) and named his possessions New Helvetia. In 1841 Sutter bought the Russian establishment known as Ross (see our volume xviii, p. 283, note 121), whose materials he used in fitting up his own fort. Sutter was friendly to the American cause, and received

friendly to Americans. The season before, a party of
the Wallawallas had visited California, by invitation of
Capt. Suter; and whilst there, a difficulty arose about
some horses, and the son of the old chief was killed in
the fort. The Indians left immediately, and as Suter
claimed to be an American, the chief's feelings were
excited against all Americans. He had showed hostile
demonstrations against a party of Americans the summer
previous; and when we arrived, we were told that he
was surly, and not disposed to be friendly. The grazing
about the camp was poor, and we sent a few men with
the animals to the hills, three miles distant, to graze.
Near night we observed quite a stir among the Indians.
We gave a signal to drive in the horses; they soon came
in, and we picketed them near the camp. As soon as
it was dark the Indians commenced singing and dancing,
accompanied with an instrument similar to a drum, and
giving most hideous yells, running to and fro. We
began to suspect that they meditated an attack upon
our camp; and we accordingly prepared to meet them
by building a fortification of [125] our baggage, and post-
ing a strong guard. We remained in this position until
day-light, when we packed up, and traveled up the Wallawalla eight or ten miles, when we stopped, cooked breakfast, and allowed our animals to graze.

Before starting, the old chief and a few of his principal

emigrants with hospitality. He aided Frémont in the revolt against Mexican
authority. In 1848 gold was discovered upon his property. He profited
but little by this event, however, and became so poor that he was pensioned
by the California legislature. About 1865 he went East to live, dying in Washington, D. C., in 1880. H. H. Bancroft secured from Sutter, by means of
interviews, a detailed narrative of his career, and the manuscript is now in the
Bancroft Library, purchased for the University of California in November
1905.— ED.

men made us a visit. They appeared friendly, and wished to trade. We gave them some provisions, and made them a few presents of tobacco, pipes, &c. After shooting at a mark with the chief, to convince him of our skill, we conversed on various subjects, among which the death of his son was mentioned, and he expressed his determination to go to California this season. We parted, he and his people to their village, and we upon our route to Dr. Whitman's.

We were here joined by a party of Nez Percé Indians; among whom were four of their principal chiefs. Ellis the great chief was with them. He speaks very good English, and is quite intelligent. He was educated at the Hudson's Bay Company's school, on Red river.[194] They traveled and encamped with us, making heavy drafts upon our provisions; but as we expected to replenish at Whitman's, we gave them freely. We encamped on a branch of the Wallawalla. This is a most beautiful valley of good land, but timber is limited to a few cottonwood and willows along the streams.

In the afternoon of the 28th we reached Dr. Whitman's station.[195] Here we remained until the 31st, when in company with four others, and the Nez Percé

[194] Ellis (or Ellice) was the son of Bloody Chief. Having been educated by the Hudson's Bay Company, he had acquired much influence with his tribe. In 1842, being then about thirty-two years old, he was, at the instigation of Dr. Elijah White, Indian sub-agent, chosen head chief of the Nez Percés, and ruled with considerable tact and wisdom, being favorable to the whites. During the Cayuse War of 1848, Ellis was reported as hunting in the buffalo country; later, it was stated that having gone with sixty braves to the mountains for elk, they all perished from an epidemic of measles. Lawyer was chosen as head-chief in Ellis's place.— ED.

[195] For the location of Whitman's mission, see our volume xxviii, p. 333, note 210.— ED.

Indians, we started for Spalding's mission — Mr. Spalding being of our party. The rest of our party remained at Whitman's. Our object was to purchase horses and explore the country. The distance from Dr. Whitman's to Spalding's was about one hundred and fifty miles, in a north-east direction. The first day we traveled but about twenty-five miles, over a most delightful prairie country, and encamped on a beautiful clear stream coming down from the Blue mountains, which are about twelve miles distant.[300]

The first of April we traveled about fifty-five miles, also over a delightful, rolling, prairie country; crossing several beautiful streams, lined with timber, and affording desirable locations for settlement. The soil is rich, and covered with an excellent coat of grass. This region possesses grazing advantages over any other portion of Oregon that I have yet seen. The day was blustering, with a little snow, which melted as it reached the ground.

On the 2d of April we arrived at Mr. Spalding's mission, [126] which is upon the Kooskooskee or Clear Water,[307] and about twenty miles above its mouth or junction with Lewis's fork of the Columbia. Ten miles from our camp we struck Lewis's fork, and proceeded up it for five miles, and crossed. On our way up we passed a ledge of rocks of fluted columns, two or three hundred feet high. The bluffs of Lewis's fork and the Kooskoos-

---

[300] For the Blue Mountains see our volume xxi, p. 273, note 71. The stream was probably Touchet River, the largest affluent of the Walla Walla. Rising in the Blue Mountains in Columbia County, Washington, it flows northwest to Dayton, then turns southwest and south, debouching into the Walla Walla at the present town of Touchet.— Ed.

[307] For this stream see Farnham's *Travels* in our volume xxix, p. 79, note 98.— Ed.

kee are very high, sometimes more than three thousand feet. The hills are nearly all covered with grass.

As the time I could remain in this region would not allow me to explore it satisfactorily, I requested Mr. Spalding to furnish me with the result of his experience for ten years in the country. He very kindly complied, and the following is the information obtained from him.[300] As he goes very much into detail, it is unnecessary for me to add any further remarks here, in relation to this region of the country.

We remained at this missionary establishment until the 10th of April. During our stay, we heard related many incidents common to a mountain life. At one time, when Mr. Spalding was on an excursion to one of the neighboring villages, accompanied by several Indians and their wives, they espied a bear at a short distance clambering up a tree. He ascended thirty or forty feet, and halted to view the travelers. A tree standing near the one upon which sat the bear, with limbs conveniently situated to climb, induced Mr. Spalding to attempt to *lasso* master bruin. He accordingly prepared himself with a *lasso* rope, and ascended the tree until he attained an elevation equal to that of the bear. He then cut a limb, rested the noose of the rope upon one end, and endeavored to place it over the head of the bear; but as the rope approached his nose, bruin struck it with his paw, and as Mr. S. had but one hand at liberty, he could not succeed, the weight of the rope being too great. He called to some of his Indian friends, to come up and assist him; but none seemed willing to risk themselves so near the formidable animal. At length

[300] See Appendix.— PALMER.

one of the squaws climbed up, and held the slack of the rope, and Mr. S. succeeded in slipping the noose over bruin's head. He then descended from the tree, and as the rope extended to the ground, they gave it a jerk, and down came the bear, which fell in such a way as to pass the rope over a large limb, thus suspending him by the neck.

The cattle which we had purchased were scattered over the [127] plain. On the 3d they were brought in, and the chief Ellis bought the whole band, agreeing to give one horse for each head of cattle. His place of residence was about sixty miles further up the Kooskooskee, but his father-in-law resided near the mission. Ellis made arrangements with the latter for six horses, and delivered them to us, and his father-in-law took possession of the cattle. We left the horses in his possession, until Ellis could return with the remainder of the horses. In his absence many of the natives came in with their horses to trade for the cattle, and when informed that Ellis had bought them all, they were very much displeased, and charged Ellis with conniving with the whites against his people. In a few days Ellis returned, when the feelings of his people were so much against him, that he was forced to abandon the trade. His father-in-law drove down his band of horses according to agreement, but instead of bringing the horses which had been selected, he brought some old, broken-down horses that could not stand the trip. We objected to receive these horses, and thus broke up the whole arrangement. They had the horses and cattle; of course we demanded the cattle; the Indians showed us that they were on the plains, and that we must hunt them up. We dispatched a party, and they soon brought us all but one heifer.

Our intention then was to drive the cattle down to Dr.
Whitman's, and trade with the Cayuses; but as we
would be compelled to travel on foot for nearly one
hundred and fifty miles, we abandoned the project.
The neighboring Indians soon drove in some horses to
trade, and before night we had disposed of all but four
head of our cattle, one yoke of oxen, one yearling heifer,
and a yearling calf. The oxen belonged to me. I left
them in charge of Mr. Spalding, until my return. In
the exchange one horse was given for a cow or heifer.
A few horses were purchased for other articles of trade,
such as blankets, shirts, knives, &c. The value of
fourteen dollars in trade would buy an ordinary horse;
if it was an extra horse something more would be asked.
Four blankets was the price of a horse. None of the
Indians would take money except Ellis. In fact they
did not seem to know the value of money.

During our stay at this place, the Indians flocked in
from all quarters. It is but seldom that the whites visit
this portion of the country, and the Indians all seemed
anxious to see us. The house was literally filled from
morning until night with men, women, and children.
They are usually much better [128] clad than any other
tribe east or west of the mountains, are quite cleanly,
and are an industrious people. They have made considerable advances in cultivating the soil, and have large
droves of horses, and many of them are raising large
herds of cattle. Mr. and Mrs. Spalding have kept up a
school, and many of the Indians have made great profi-
ciency in spelling, reading, and writing. They use the
English alphabet to the Nez Percé language. Mr.
Spalding has made some translations from the Scrip-
tures, and among others from the book of Matthew.

From this printed copy [300] many of the Indians have printed with a pen fac similes of the translation, which are neatly executed. I have several copies in my possession of these and other writings, which can be seen at any time in Laurel, Indiana. They are a quiet, civil people, but proud and haughty; they endeavor to imitate the fashions of the whites, and owe much of their superior qualifications to the Missionaries who are among them.

Mr. Spalding and family have labored among them for ten years assiduously, and the increasing wants and demands of the natives require an additional amount of labor. A family of their own is rising around them, which necessarily requires a portion of their time; and the increasing cares of the family render it impossible to do that amount of good, and carry out fully that policy which they have so advantageously commenced for the natives. It is impossible for one family to counteract all the influences of bad and designing men, of whom there are not a few in the country. They need more assistance. There are a sufficient number of establishments, but not a sufficient number of persons at those establishments. For instance: Mr. Spalding must now attend not only to raising produce for his own family, but also to supply in a great measure food to numerous families of Indians; to act as teacher and spiritual guide, as physician, and perform many other duties incident to his situation. With such a multitude of claims on

---

[300] For the history of the printing press in use at this mission, see our volume xxviii, p. 333, note 211. The first book in the Nez Percé language was a little compilation of texts, consisting of eight pages. The translation of Matthew was printed at Lapwai; that of John was later published by the American Bible Society.— ED.

his attention, his energies are too much divided, and on the whole his influence is lessened. Could not the Missionary board send out an assistant?

There is one thing which could be accomplished with a small outlay, that would be of lasting advantage to these people. They are raising small flocks of sheep, and have been taught to card and spin and weave by hand, and prepare clothing — but the process is too tedious. A carding machine and machinery for fulling cloth would be a saving to the board of [129] missions, and of lasting benefit to the natives. There are no such machines in that country. The wood work of those machines could nearly all be done in the country; the cards and castings are all that would be necessary to ship. A mechanic to set up the machines would be necessary.

Perhaps no part of the world is better adapted to the growth of wool than this middle region, and it abounds with water-power to manufacture it. Farmers, mechanics and teachers, should be sent among these people by the missionary board, or by the government. A division is about being made in this nation, which if not counteracted, will doubtless lead to bad consequences. Three Delaware Indians have crossed the mountains, and settled on the Kooskooskee among the Nez Percé Indians. One of them, named Tom Hill, has so ingratiated himself into the feelings of the Nez Percé Indians, that he has succeeded in persuading about one hundred lodges to acknowledge him as their chief. It was formerly, as among other tribes, customary for an Indian to have as many wives as he could maintain; but the missionaries taught them otherwise, and succeeded in abolishing this heathen custom. But Tom Hill tells them that they can have as many wives as they please. He says to them, You make me chief, and I will make you a great people. The white men tell you not to steal — I tell you there is no harm in it; the bad consists in being caught at it. These men will mislead you, &c., &c.

Ellis and the other chiefs have exerted themselves to recall their people, but they cannot succeed. In conversing with Ellis, I enquired whether cases of insanity were common among his people. He answered that he never knew a case of insanity, but this one of Tom Hill's. He looks upon him as a crazy man. The two other Delaware Indians are young men, and are industrious and peaceable. They have commenced cultivating the soil, and are raising a fine herd of cattle. Ellis is considered wealthy. He has about fifteen hundred horses, a herd of cattle, some hogs, and a few sheep. Many persons in this nation have from five to fifteen hundred head of horses. In traveling from Dr. Whitman's to this place, I saw more than ten thousand horses grazing upon the plains. They are good looking, and some of them large.

In the fall I had made enquiries as to whether it was practicable to obtain the necessary supplies at these missions for our home journey; and in the winter Mr. Spalding wrote to us that he could furnish us with flour and meat. We had accordingly [130] contemplated procuring a part of our outfit at this place. A few bad designing Indians had frequently given Mr. Spalding trouble about his place, and had made severe threats. At one time they had threatened to tie him, and drive his family away. They complained that the whites never came through their country, giving them the advantages of trade; but that the white men passed through the Cayuse country, selling their cattle, clothing, &c.; and that if they could not have all the benefits of trade, the whites should leave the country.

Early in the spring some of them had got into a fit of ill humour, and had ordered Mr. Spalding from the place, cut open his mill-dam, threw down his fences, broke the windows of the church, crippled some of his hogs, and took possession of the whole premises. This time they seemed to be determined to carry their threats into execution. Mr. S. allowed them to take their own course, putting no obstacle in their way. The principal men seemed to look on with indifference; but they evidently saw that it was likely to injure them, more than it would Mr. Spalding; for they relied upon the mill and farm for their support to a great extent.

In the meantime Mr. Spalding had written a letter to us, informing us of his situation, and that we could not rely on him for furnishing us with supplies. He gave the letter to an Indian to carry to Dr. Whitman's, that it might be forwarded to us. The Indians being apprised of the contents of the letter, stopped the carrier, and took from him the letter, and after a consultation determined to abandon their rash course; as it would be likely to deprive them of the benefit of our trade, and be a barrier against the white men ever coming to trade with them. They accordingly brought the letter to Mr. Spalding, acknowledging they had done wrong, and placed him in full possession of his premises, promising to behave better for the future; and when we arrived he was enjoying their full confidence.

The Indians informed us that there was a good pass-

way upon the north side of Lewis's fork, by proceeding
up the Kooskooskee some sixty miles, and then striking
across to Salmon river, and then up to Fort Bois. By
taking this route in the winter season, we would avoid
the deep snow upon the Blue Mountains, as the route
is mostly up the valley of Lewis' river, and it is undoubtedly nearer to Puget Sound than by the old route. Those
wishing to settle about the Sound would do well to take
this route, or at least the saving in the distance [131]
would justify an examination of the route, to ascertain
its practicability.

We were very hospitably entertained by Mr. Spalding,
and his interesting family. With the exception of Mr.
Gilbert, who is now engaged on the mission farm, and
Mr. Craig, who has a native for a wife, and lives six
hundred yards from Mr. Spalding's dwelling, the nearest
white families are Messrs. Walker and Ellis, who have a
mission one hundred and thirty miles to the north, among
the Flathead nation; and Dr. Whitman, nearly one hundred and fifty miles distant, among the Cayuses.[210]
In this lonely situation they have spent the best part
of their days, among the wild savages, and for no compensation but a scanty subsistence. In the early part
of their sojourn they were compelled to use horse meat
for food, but they are now getting herds of domestic
animals about them, and raise a surplus of grain beyond
their own wants. At Mr. Spalding's there is an excuse

---

[210] For this mission and its missionaries see our volume xxvii, p. 367, note
187. The farmer at Lapwai mission was Isaac N. Gilbert, who was born in
New York (1818). He early emigrated to Illinois, and came to Oregon with
the party of 1844. Late in 1846 he proceeded to the Willamette valley, and
settled near Salem, where he was county clerk and surveyor, dying in 1879.
See Oregon Pioneer Association *Transactions*, 1878, pp. 82, 83.— Ed.

for a grist mill, which answers to chip up the grain, but they have no bolting cloth; in place of which they use a sieve. The meal makes very good bread. There was formerly a saw mill, but the irons have been taken and used in a mill which Dr. Whitman has recently built about twenty miles from his dwelling, at the foot of the Blue mountains. The Catholics have several missionary establishments upon the upper waters of the Columbia.[211]

On the 10th of April we had made the necessary arrangements, and started on our return to Dr. Whitman's, where we arrived on the 14th. On my way down in the fall, I had left a horse and a heifer with the Doctor. They were now running on the plains. Several persons were engaged in hunting them up; the horse was found and brought in, and was in good condition. The Indians had concealed the horse, in order to force a trade, and offered to buy him, they to run the risk of finding him; but as he was a favorite horse, that I had brought from home, I felt gratified when he was found. The heifer I traded for a horse, the purchaser to find her. My two oxen, which I had left at Mr. Spalding's, I traded for a horse. An Indian who had stolen a horse from a company in the fall, had been detected, and the horse taken to fort Wallawalla. He had again stolen the horse, and traded him off. He was at Dr. Whitman's, and as the owner was of our party, he made a demand for the horse, and the Indian gave up a [132] poor old horse in its stead. This was the same fellow that had bought my heifer.

---

[211] For these missions see De Smet's reports in our volumes xxvii, p. 365, note 184; xxix, p. 178, note 73.— ED.

We remained at Dr. Whitman's until the 17th, when all was prepared, and we made a formal start. Our party consisted of eighteen persons, and fifty-one horses and mules. We traveled about eight miles, and encamped. On the 18th, we traveled to the Umatillo. On the way the fellow who had bought the heifer overtook us and demanded the horse, as he said he had not time to hunt up the heifer. I refused to give it up, and he insisted. At this juncture Dr. Whitman overtook us, and the Indian made complaint to him. It was arranged that we should all go on to Umatillo, where several of the chiefs resided, and have the matter amicably settled. We reached the river in the afternoon, and repaired to the chief's. The Indian told his story, and I told mine. The chief decided that I should give up the horse, and he would give me a horse for the heifer. I agreed that in case the heifer could not be found, to give him another on my return to Oregon. The Indian set out with his horse, and the chief soon brought me one in its place, worth at least two such as the first. Of course I was much pleased with the exchange.

At night it commenced raining, and then snowing, and in the morning the snow was four or five inches deep on the ground. We were then immediately at the foot of the mountain, and as we expected the snow had fallen deep upon the mountain, we remained in camp all day. The 20th was unfavorable for traveling, and we remained in camp.

On the 21st we took up the line of march, ascended the mountain, and advanced about twenty-five miles, which brought us over the dividing ridge. We found the snow in patches, and sometimes three feet deep — that is, the old snow, for the new fallen snow had all melted away. The grazing was poor, but at night we found a prairie upon the south side of the mountain, which afforded a scanty supply of grass; here we encamped for the night.

The 22d was very blustery, sometimes snowing; very disagreeable traveling. We reached the Grand Round at 2 o'clock P. M. and encamped. Here we found an abundance of good grass, and halted for the night. During the night the horse which I had obtained of the old chief broke from his picket, and in company with one that was running loose, took the back track. In the morning we dispatched two men, who followed them about four miles, when it was found that the [133] horses had left the road. The two men went back ten or twelve miles, but could see nothing of the horses. They then returned to camp. We in the mean time had packed up, and traveled across Grand Round about eight miles, when we encamped. In the morning we started back four men to hunt for the horses. On the evening of the 24th our men returned, but without the horses.

On the morning of the 25th we packed up, traveled about twenty-six miles, and encamped on Powder river, near the lone pine stump.[212]

On the 27th we traveled about twenty-five miles. On the 28th we traveled about twenty-three miles, and encamped near Malheur.

On the 29th we reached fort Bois. The people at the fort, and the Indians in the vicinity, were evidently much alarmed. Before reaching the fort, I saw at a

---

[212] For this landmark see our volume xxviii, p. 324, note 204.— ED.

distance numerous columns of smoke, alternately rising and disappearing; and then another column would rise at a great distance. These columns of smoke seemed to be signals that enemies were in the country. The people at the fort were seemingly friendly, and supplied us with milk and butter. We selected our camping ground with caution, and with an eye to the defence both of horses and men. Our guard was doubled. We were visited by many Indians, but no hostile demonstration was exhibited. Here the wagon road crosses the river, but as there were no canoes at the upper crossing, and the river was too high to ford, we decided upon traveling up the south side of the river.

On the 30th of April we packed up, and left fort Bois. The trail led us up to the mouth of a stream coming in on the south side of Lewis river, about one hundred yards in width. This we reached in about three miles. Immediately at the crossing is an Indian village of the Shoshonee tribe. When within one fourth of a mile from the crossing, an Indian who had been at our camp the evening before, was seen riding furiously towards us. He came up directly to me, extending his hand, which I took of course; two or three were riding in front with me, who all shook hands with him. He then turned and led the way through the bushes to the crossing. At the point where we came out, the bank was some fifteen feet high. A narrow place had been cut down, so as to admit but one horse at a time to go up the bank; the village was immediately upon the bank, and I discovered some thirty or forty Indians standing near the point where the trail ascended the bank. I rode [134] to the top of the bank, where about fifteen ugly looking Indians were standing, all striving to shake hands, but my horse would not allow them to approach.

I passed on, the company following, and as we formed a long train, being in single file, by the time those behind were out of the creek, those in the lead were five or six hundred yards from the bank, and over a ridge. I halted the front, for all to come up, when I discovered that Buckley, who was in the rear riding one horse and leading another, had not appeared over the ridge. Two of the men who were in the rear went back for him. The horse which he was leading soon came running over the ridge, and as Buckley did not make his appearance, we supposed that something was wrong. Others started back, but they all soon returned, and we went on. In a few minutes, however, one of the party came riding up, and stated that the Indians were going to charge upon us.

At this instant a gun was fired by them, and a hideous yelling was heard at our heels. The Indians were drawn up in line upon the ridge, all armed, some with muskets, and others with bows and arrows. The fellow who had met us, was still mounted, and running his horse from one end of the line to the other, and all were yelling like fiends. I thought it could not be possible that they would charge upon us, and ordered all hands to move along slowly but cautiously, to have their arms in readiness, and to keep the pack animals together, so that they could be stopped at any moment. We marched along slowly in close order, and paid no further regard to the Indians, than to carefully watch their movements. They followed along a few hundred yards, and halted, their yells then ceased, and we saw nothing more of them.

When the two men returned to Buckley, the mounted Indian spoken of had Buckley's horse by the head; he had proposed an exchange, but Buckley did not wish to swap, and asked him to let go the bridle: the Indian held on, Buckley pulled and he pulled; Buckley rapped his knuckles with a whip, and in the scuffle the horse that B. was leading broke loose, and ran over the ridge, they not being able to catch him. At this juncture the two men arrived; one of them raised his rifle in the attitude of striking the Indian on the head, but he paid no regard to it; the other, seeing his determined manner, rushed at him with his bowie knife; he then let go the bridle, and our men came up to the company. What his object was, or what their object in rallying their forces, I could not conjecture: but it [135] put us on our guard. At our night encampment there were Indians prowling about, but they were afraid of our riding too near them, and made no attempt to steal, or otherwise molest us. The country was extremely dry and barren; grazing was very poor.

On the 5th of May we arrived at the upper crossing of Snake river. On our way we had seen several villages of Shoshonee Indians, but were not disturbed by them. The grazing was poor, and the country very barren. We crossed several warm streams running down from the mountains, which appeared at a distance of from five to ten miles on our right. A wagon road can be had along the south side of the river, by hugging the base of the mountains for twenty or thirty miles, when it would take down the low bottom of Snake or Lewis river; but the distance is greater than by crossing the river.

On the 6th of May we reached Salmon falls, and went up six miles to Salmon Fall creek, and encamped. On the 8th and 9th it rained and snowed, so that we were compelled to lay by most of the time. On the 10th it cleared up, and in the afternoon we had fair weather and pleasant traveling. On the 12th we reached Cassia creek. At this place the California trail turns off.

On the 14th we arrived at Fort Hall. On the 16th we reached the Soda Springs. On the 18th we met about six hundred lodges of Snake Indians; they were moving from Big Bear river to Lewis' fork. On the 23d we reached Green river, taking the northern route. Much of the time the weather has been cool with frosty nights, and several days of rain and snow.

On the 24th we crossed Green river, and traveled about forty miles to the Big Sandy. The day was blustering, with rain and snow. Along the bottoms of the Sandy we found very good grazing for our animals.

On the 25th we traveled to the Little Sandy. On the 26th we arrived at the *South Pass*, and encamped on Sweet Water. Here we saw a few buffalo. The ride from Little Sandy to Sweet Water was extremely unpleasant on account of the wind and snow. We were sometimes compelled to walk, in order to keep warm. We here found a horse, which we supposed had been lost by some emigrants the year before. He came running to our band, and exhibited signs of the greatest joy, by capering and prancing about. He was quite fat, and seemed determined to follow us.

[136] On the 27th we traveled down the valley of Sweet Water about twenty-five miles. On our way we saw some hundreds of buffalo and antelope, and two grizzly bears. We gave the latter chase, but did not succeed in taking them. We had some difficulty in preventing our pack animals from following the numerous bands of buffalo which came rolling past us.

We traveled down this valley until the 30th, and encamped about four miles east of *Independence Rock*, at a spring near a huge mountain of gray granite rock. Soon after encamping it commenced raining, which turned to snow, and in the morning we had about five inches of snow upon us. We were uncomfortably situated, as we could procure but little fuel, and had no means of sheltering ourselves from the "peltings of the pitiless storm." Our horses too fared poorly.

On the 31st of May we remained in camp. By noon the snow had disappeared, and we succeeded in finding a few dry cedar trees, built a fire, and dried our effects. We had an abundance of buffalo marrow-bones, tongues, and other choice pieces, on which we feasted. We saw large droves of mountain sheep, or big-horn, and thousands of antelope.

On the 2d of June we arrived at the north fork of Platte. The plains during this day's travel were literally covered with buffalo, tens of thousands were to be seen at one view; antelope and black-tailed deer were seen in great abundance, and a few elk and common deer. One panther, and hundreds of wolves were also seen. We found the river too high to ford. Soon after encamping, snow commenced falling, which continued all night, but melted as it reached the ground. The grazing on the bottom was excellent, the grass being about six inches high. This was the best grass we had seen since leaving Burnt river.

On the 3d we succeeded in finding a ford, and in the evening we crossed. On the 4th we reached Deer creek, having traveled about thirty miles. On the way we saw a band of Indians whom we supposed to be of the Crow nation, and as they are generally for fight, we prepared to give them a warm reception; but it seemed that they were as fearful of us, as we were of them.[213] They were soon out of sight. After traveling about five miles, we saw them drawn up into line two miles from the road. As they were at a respectful distance, we did not molest them. We however kept a sharp look out, and at night were cautious in selecting camp ground. The grass was good, and our animals fared well.

[137] On the 5th we traveled about fifteen miles, and encamped on Mike's-head creek.[214] Here we found two trappers, who had been out about three weeks. They accompanied us to Fort Laramie, which we reached on the 8th of June. In the morning H. Smith, one of our party, in catching a mule was thrown, and his shoulder dislocated.[215] We attempted to set

---

[213] For the Crow Indians see our volume v, p. 226, note 121.— ED.

[214] Mike's Head is probably a popular name for the rush of the Equisetum species, known as "horsetail." The creek is known by the French form of this plant — à la Prêle; it is a tributary of the Platte, in Converse County, Wyoming.— ED.

[215] Hiram Smith was born in New York, early emigrated to Ohio, and crossed the Plains with the party of 1845. Having returned with Palmer he remained in the states until 1851, coming again to Oregon with a large drove of cattle and horses. He settled at Portland, and became wealthy and influential.

it, but could not succeed. He traveled on to the fort, but in great misery. We remained here until the afternoon of the 10th. Mr. Smith's shoulder was so much injured that he could not travel. He concluded to remain at the fort a few days; three men were to stay with him, and the rest of us had made arrangements for starting, when a company of Oregon emigrants came in sight. We awaited their arrival, and had the gratification of hearing from the States, it being the first news we had received since leaving our homes. A part of us remained a few hours to give them an opportunity of writing to their friends; while five of the party took the road. In the evening we traveled about eight miles, and encamped.

We continued for a distance of two hundred miles meeting companies of from six to forty wagons, until the number reached five hundred and forty-one wagons, and averaging about five souls to each wagon. They were generally in good health and fine spirits. Two hundred and twelve wagons were bound for California; but I have since learned that many of those who had designed to go to California had changed their destination and were going to Oregon.[216]

At Ash hollow we met a company who had lost many of their cattle and horses; but they were still going on.

He crossed again to the states, returning in 1862 — in all, making six journeys of this character. He died in San Francisco in 1870.— ED.

[216] The Oregon immigration of 1846 was not as large as that of the previous year. Apparently reliable estimates make the number about two thousand that finally reached that territory. For a description of these emigrants see Francis Parkman, *The Oregon Trail* (Boston, 1849, and later editions), chapters i, vi, vii. See also an itinerary of the journey by J. Quinn Thornton, *Oregon and California* (New York, 1849). Among the California emigrants of this year were the ill-fated Donner party, many of whom perished in the Sierras.— ED.

A short distance below the forks of Platte, we met a company of forty-one wagons, under the command of a Mr. Smith, which company had lost about one hundred and fifty head of cattle; they were encamped, and parties were out hunting cattle.[217] We remained with them a short time, and then passed on. This was on the 18th of June. Two of Smith's company had taken the back track in search of a band of their cattle, which had traveled nearly forty miles on the return to the States. Near night, and after we had encamped, two others of the company came up in search of the two men who had started in the morning. We had also met a boy belonging to their company, who had been in search of cattle, but had found none; and as it was nearly night, and he was about thirty miles from their camp, we induced him to remain with us through the night.

[138] The two men who had arrived after we had encamped, concluded to continue their search until they found the two other men who had preceded them. Accordingly after taking some refreshments, they mounted and followed on. Soon after dark, they came running their horses up to our camp, one of them having behind him one of the men who had started out in the morning. They had proceeded from our camp about seven or eight miles, when rising over a small swell in the prairie, they discovered a few head of cattle, and saw ten or twelve Indians, a part of them engaged in catching a horse which Mr. Trimble (one of the men who had started out in the morning) had been riding, and some

---

[217] Probably this was Fabritus R. Smith, a native of Rochester, New York (1819). Settling at Salem, Oregon, he was in the state legislature of 1876, and still living at Salem in 1896.— Ed.

were engaged in stripping the clothes from Mr. Harrison, the other of the men. The men who had left our camp put whip to their horses, and ran towards the Indians, hallooing and yelling. The Indians seeing them approach, and probably supposing that there was a large company, left Harrison, and ran under a bluff, but they took the horses with them.

Harrison put on his clothes and mounted behind Bratten, (one of the men who had come to their rescue,) stating that the Indians had killed Trimble,[20] and as none of the emigrants had fire-arms, the Indians would soon return upon them. They then came to our camp. Harrison stated that he and Trimble had traveled nearly all day with that portion of our party who had started from the fort in advance of us, and near night had found five head of their cattle, with which they were return- ing to the company; and as they were traveling leisurely along, about dusk, whilst in a small hollow, ten or twelve Indians came suddenly upon them, seized his horse, and endeavored to get hold of Trimble's horse, but he jumped away, and ran his horse off. Harrison in the mean time had dismounted, and three of the Indians rifled him of his clothes. On looking to see what had become of Trimble, he saw him riding in a circuitous manner towards the place where Harrison was; at this instant some half dozen arrows were let fly at Trimble by the Indians, some of which took effect. He leaned a little forward, his horse at the time jumping; at that instant the crack of a gun was heard, and Trimble fell

---

[20] This unfortunate victim of the Pawnee Indians was Edward Trimble of Henry County, Iowa. See another account of his death in *Niles' Register*, lxx, p. 341.— ED.

from his horse upon his face, and did not move afterwards. His horse ran round for some minutes, the Indians trying to catch him; and at that instant Bratten and his friend came up.

Several of our party, supposing that we had passed all danger, had sold their arms to the emigrants, and we had but five [139] rifles in the company. It was quite dark, and there would be but little prospect of finding Trimble, if we attempted a search. We therefore remained in camp until morning. About eleven o'clock at night we dispatched two persons back to inform the company of what had occurred, with a request that a force might be sent, which would be able to chastise the Indians, if found.

Early in the morning we packed up and traveled to the spot where the murder had been committed. We found there Trimble's hat, whip, and pocket knife; and several large pools of blood where he had fallen from his horse, and where the Indians had evidently stripped him. We also found several arrows, two of which appeared to have struck him; but nothing could be found of his body. The river Platte was about a quarter of a mile distant; we searched the shore diligently, but could see no sign. As we approached the spot a gun was fired on a large island opposite, but we saw no Indians. Eight beds in the grass near where the attack was made, showed the manner in which the Indians had been concealed.

It is highly probable that the Indians had driven the cattle off, and that some of the Indians concealed themselves, and as Trimble and Harrison had no fire-arms, and carried long ox-whips, they could be easily dis-

tinguished as cattle hunters, and the Indians knowing
that the white men must come back, selected a favorable
spot, and attacked them as above related. The proba-
bility is, that had Trimble and Harrison been armed,
they would not have been molested.

We remained upon the ground until late in the afternoon, waiting the arrival of the force from the company. We finally began to despair of their coming,
and feared that the two men whom we had sent back
had been cut off; and as we had two of the company
with us, and one of our party was back, we packed up
and took the back track, and after traveling about five
miles, we discovered a band of their cattle crossing the
river a mile above us. We made to the shore, when
the cattle turned down the river, in the direction of the
head of the big island. We judged that the Indians
had been driving the cattle, but upon our approach
had left them. The river was quite shoal, and Buckley
waded out and turned them to the shore. There were
in this band twenty-one head of work cattle; two of
them carried marks of the arrow. After traveling three
miles farther, we espied the party coming to our assistance, but it consisted of only seven persons.

[140] Mr. Trimble had left a wife and four children.
She had sent by the party a request that we might come
back, and allow her and family to travel with us to the
U. States. We accordingly all took the road to the
company's camp, (driving the cattle) which we reached
at day-break on the morning of the 20th June. Here
we remained until the afternoon. By the persuasion
of her friends, Mrs. Trimble concluded to continue
her journey to Oregon. But there were four families
who had lost so many of their cattle, that they were

unable to proceed on their journey. They had four wagons, and only five yoke of cattle, and some of them were very small. They wished us to travel with them through the Pawnee country, as the Pawnees were the perpetrators of the act which had caused them so much difficulty. We accordingly traveled with them until the 30th, when we left them, and resumed our journey towards home.

On the morning of the 21st we were joined by Mr. Smith, and the three men who had been left at the fort. We traveled on rapidly day and night, barely giving our animals time to rest. The weather was becoming warm; the flies and musquitoes were very annoying. We arrived at the Mission or Agency on the morning of the 6th of July.[219] Here are extensive farms, and a most delightful country. The first view of cultivated fields, and marks of civilization, brought simultaneous shouts from the whole party. Our troubles and toils were all forgotten.

On the 7th of July, at 10 o'clock A. M., we arrived at the St. Joseph's mission, where we all hoped to meet with friends.[220] We had been so long among savages,

[219] On this return journey, Palmer took the St. Joseph Trail, which branched off from the usual Oregon Trail near the Little Blue, and followed the valley of the Great Nemaha through the Iowa, Sauk, and Fox reservation to the Missouri opposite St. Joseph. An excellent map of Nebraska and Kansas, presumably issued in 1854, but lacking name of place or publisher, plainly indicates this road. For the removal of these Indians to the reservation in northeast Kansas and southeast Nebraska see our volume xxviii, pp. 141, 145, notes 87, 89. The agency was known as the Great Nemaha; it was situated near the mission begun (1837) by the Presbyterians under the direction of Rev. S. M. Irvin. He crossed from Missouri with the Indians, and established his mission twenty-six miles west of St. Joseph, not far from the site of the present Highland, Doniphan County, Kansas. At the time of Palmer's visit, Irvin was being assisted by William Hamilton, and a mission school was in course of establishment.— ED.

[220] For St. Joseph see our volume xxii, p. 257, note 210. This was not a

that we resembled them much in appearance; but when attired in new apparel, and shaved as became white men, we hardly knew each other. We had been long in each other's company; had undergone hardships and privations together; had passed through many dangers, relying upon each other for aid and protection. Attachments had grown up, which when we were about to separate were sensibly felt; but as we were yet separated from our families, where still stronger ties were felt, each one took his course, and in a few hours our party was scattered, and each traveling in a different direction.

Those of us who had mules found ready sales; but as the horses were much reduced in flesh, they could not be disposed of. Our horses had stood the trip remarkably well, until within two hundred and fifty miles of Missouri. But the flies [141] had so annoyed them, the weather being warm, and the grass of an inferior quality, that they had failed much. I had five horses; the one which I had taken from home was quite lame, and I left him at St. Joseph's; the other four were Indian horses, and Mr. Buckley agreed to take them by land, across Missouri and Illinois, and home; but he was unsuccessful, and arrived with only one of them.

I took steamboat passage to St. Louis [221] and Cincinnati, and thence by stage to Laurel, Indiana, where I arrived on the 23d of July; having been gone from home one year three months and one week. I had the pleasure of finding my family enjoying good health.

mission site, but a trading post. The first church built (1845) was the Presbyterian, under the care of Rev. T. S. Reeve.— ED.

[221] For a contemporary notice of Palmer's arrival in St. Louis, see *Niles' Register*, lxx, pp. 341, 416.— ED.

NECESSARY OUTFITS FOR EMIGRANTS
TRAVELING TO OREGON

For burthen wagons, light four horse or heavy two horse wagons are the size commonly used. They should be made of the best material, well seasoned, and should in all cases have falling tongues. The tire should not be less than one and three fourth inches wide, but may be advantageously used three inches; two inches, however, is the most common width. In fastening on the tire, bolts should be used instead of nails; it should be at least ⅝ or ¾ inches thick. Hub boxes for the hubs should be about four inches. The skeins should be well steeled. The Mormon fashioned wagon bed is the best. They are usually made straight, with side boards about 16 inches wide, and a projection outward of four inches on each side, and then another side board of ten or twelve inches; in this last, set the bows for covers, which should always be double. Boxes for carrying effects should be so constructed as to correspond in height with the offset in the wagon bed, as this gives a smooth surface to sleep upon.

Ox teams are more extensively used than any others. Oxen stand the trip much better, and are not so liable to be stolen by the Indians, and are much less trouble. Cattle are generally allowed to go at large, when not hitched to the wagons; whilst horses and mules must always be staked up at night. Oxen can procure food in many places where horses cannot, and in much less time. Cattle that have been raised in Illinois or Missouri, stand the trip better than those raised in Indiana or Ohio; as they have been accustomed to eating the prairie grass, upon which they must wholly rely while on the road. [142] Great care should be taken in selecting cattle; they should be from four to six years old, tight and heavy made.

For those who fit out but one wagon, it is not safe to start with less than four yoke of oxen, as they are liable to get lame, have sore necks, or to stray away. One team thus fitted up may start from Missouri with twenty-five hundred pounds and as each day's rations make the load that much lighter, before they reach any rough road, their loading is much reduced. Persons should recollect that every thing in the outfit should be as light as the required strength will permit; no useless trumpery should be taken. The loading should consist of provisions and apparel, a necessary supply of cooking fixtures, a few tools, &c. No great speculation can be made in buying cattle and driving them through to sell; but as the prices of oxen and cows are much higher in Oregon than in the States, nothing is lost in having a good supply of them, which will enable the emigrant to wagon through many articles that are difficult to be obtained in Oregon. Each family should have a few cows, as the milk can be used the entire route, and they are often convenient to put to the wagon to relieve oxen. They should be so selected that portions of them would come in fresh upon the road. Sheep can also be advantageously driven. American horses and mares always command high prices, and with careful usage can be taken through; but if used to wagons or carriages, their loading should be light. Each family should be provided with a sheet-iron stove, with boiler; a platform can easily be constructed for carrying it at the hind end of the wagon; and as it is frequently quite windy, and there is often a scarcity of wood, the stove is very convenient. Each family should also be provided with a tent, and to it should be attached good strong cords to fasten it down.

The cooking fixtures generally used are of sheet iron; a dutch oven and skillet of cast metal are very essential. Plates, cups, &c., should be of tin ware, as queens-ware is much heavier and liable to break, and consumes much time in packing up. A reflector is sometimes very useful. Families should each have two churns, one for carrying sweet and one for sour milk. They should also have one eight or ten gallon keg for carrying water, one axe, one shovel, two or three augers, one hand saw, and if a farmer he should be provided with one cross-cut saw and a few plough moulds, as it is difficult getting such articles. When I left the country, ploughs cost from twenty-five to forty dollars each. A good supply of ropes for [143] tying up horses and catching cattle, should also be taken. Every person should be well supplied with boots and shoes, and in fact with every kind of clothing. It is also well to be supplied with at least one feather bed, and a good assortment of bedding. There are no tame geese in the country, but an abundance of wild ones; yet it is difficult procuring a sufficient quantity of feathers for a bed. The Muscovy is the only tame duck in the country.

Each male person should have at least one rifle gun, and a shot gun is also very useful for wild fowl and small

game, of which there is an abundance. The best sized
calibre for the mountains is from thirty-two to fifty-six
to the pound; but one of from sixty to eighty, or even
less, is best when in the lower settlements. The buffalo
seldom range beyond the South Pass, and never west
of Green river. The larger game are elk, deer, antelope, mountain sheep or bighorn, and bear. The small
game are hare, rabbit, grouse, sage hen, pheasant, quail,
&c. A good supply of ammunition is essential.

In laying in a supply of provisions for the journey,
persons will doubtless be governed, in some degree, by
their means; but there are a few essentials that all will
require.

For each adult, there should be two hundred pounds
of flour, thirty pounds of pilot bread, seventy-five pounds
of bacon, ten pounds of rice, five pounds of coffee,
two pounds of tea, twenty-five pounds of sugar, half
a bushel of dried beans, one bushel of dried fruit, two
pounds of saleratus, ten pounds of salt, half a bushel of
corn meal; and it is well to have a half bushel of corn,
parched and ground; a small keg of vinegar should also
be taken. To the above may be added as many good
things as the means of the person will enable him to
carry; for whatever is good at home, is none the less
so on the road. The above will be ample for the journey;
but should an additional quantity be taken, it can readily
be disposed of in the mountains and at good prices, not
for cash, but for robes, dressed skins, buckskin pants,
moccasins, &c. It is also well for families to be provided
with medicines. It is seldom however, that emigrants
are sick; but sometimes eating too freely of fresh buffalo
meat causes diarrhœa, and unless it be checked soon

prostrates the individual, and leaves him a fit subject for disease.

The time usually occupied in making the trip from Missouri to Oregon city is about five months; but with the aid of a person who has traveled the route with an emigrating company the trip can be performed in about four months.

[144] Much injury is done to teams in racing them, endeavoring to pass each other. Emigrants should make an every day business of traveling — resting upon the same ground two nights is not good policy, as the teams are likely to ramble too far. Getting into large companies should be avoided, as they are necessarily compelled to move more tardily. From ten to twenty-five wagons is a sufficient number to travel with safety. The advance and rear companies should not be less than twenty; but between, it may be safe to go with six. The Indians are very annoying on account of their thieving propensities, but if well watched, they would seldom put them into practice. Persons should always avoid rambling far from camp unarmed, or in too small parties; Indians will sometimes seek such opportunities to rob a man of what little effects he has about him; and if he attempts to get away from them with his property, they will sometimes shoot him.

There are several points along the Missouri where emigrants have been in the practice of fitting out. Of these Independence, St. Joseph, and Council Bluffs, are the most noted. For those emigrating from Ohio, Indiana, Illinois and northern Missouri, Iowa and Michigan, I think St. Joseph the best point; as by taking that route the crossing of several streams (which at the early season we travel are sometimes very high) is avoided. Outfits may be had at this point, as readily as at any other along the river. Work cattle can be bought in its vicinity for from twenty-five to thirty dollars per yoke, cows, horses, &c., equally cheap.

Emigrants should endeavor to arrive at St. Joseph early in April, so as to be in readiness to take up the line of march by the middle of April. Companies, however, have often started as late as the tenth of May; but in such cases they seldom arrive in Oregon until after the rainy season commences in the Cascade range of mountains.

Those residing in northern Ohio, Indiana, Illinois, Michigan, &c., who contemplate traveling by land to the place of rendezvous, should start in time to give their teams at least ten days rest. Ox teams, after traveling four or five hundred miles in the states, at that season of the year, would be unfit to perform a journey across the mountains; but doubtless they might be exchanged for others, at or near the rendezvous.

Farmers would do well to take along a good supply of horse gears. Mechanics should take such tools as are easily carried; as there are but few in the country, and those are held at exorbitant [145] prices. Every family should lay in a good supply of school books for their children.

In case of an emergency, flour can be bought at Fort Hall, and Fort Bois, two trading posts of the Hudson's Bay Company, at twenty dollars per hundred; and by forwarding word to Spalding's mission, on the *Koos-kooskee*, they will pack out flour to Fort Bois, at ten dollars per hundred, and to the Grand Round at eight dollars, and will take in exchange dry goods, groceries, &c.; but at Forts Hall and Bois, the company will take nothing in payment but cash or cattle. At Dr. Whitman's station, flour can be bought at five dollars per hundred, corn meal at four dollars, beef at six and seven cents per pound, potatoes, fifty cents per bushel. It is proper to observe that the flour at Spalding's and Whitman's stations will be unbolted. Emigrants however, should be cautious, and lay in a sufficient supply to last them through.

WORDS USED IN THE CHINOOK JARGON

This is a tongue spoken by a few in each of the tribes residing in the middle and lower divisions of Oregon. It is also used by the French, and nearly all the old settlers in the country.

Aach
Sister

Aha
Yes

Alka
Future, by and by

Alta
Present, now

Ala
I wonder

Ankote
Past time

Chawko
Come

Chee
New

Chinkamin
Iron, chain

Chuck
Water

Deob
Satan

Ekik
Fish-hook

Elitah
Slave

Esick
Paddle

Esil
Corn

Geleech
Grease

Halo
None

Hankachim
Handkerchief

Hous
House

How
Let us

Hoel-hoel
Mouse

High-you
Quantity, many

Hu-e-hu
Swop, exchange

Hol
Drag, or pull

Ilips
First

Ith-lu-el, or *Ituel*
Meat, flesh

I-yak
Quick, or hurry

Il-a-he
Soil, dirt

Ichwet
Bear

Is-kum
Take

In-a-ti
Overdress

Ith-lu-k-ma
Gamble

I-wa
Beaver

Delie	*High-you-k-wah*	*Ips-wet*
Dry	Ring	Hide
Ekih	*Hul-u-e-ma*	*Ik-ta*
Brother-in-law	Strange, different	What
Kah	*K-wathen*	*Kilaps*
Where	Bell	Turn over
K-u-ten	*K-macks*	*Klips*
Horse	Dog	Upset
Kaw-lo-ke-lo	*Klugh*	*Ko-el*
Goose	Split, or Plough	Cold
Ka-luck	*Ko-pet*	*Kap-wah*
Swan	Done, finished	Alike
K-puet	*Kop-po*	*Kon-a-maxt*
Needle	Older brother	Both
Kot-suck	*Kow*	*Kla-hum*
Middle	Is to tie	Good-bye
Kap-o	*K-wat*	*Kla-hi-you*
Coat	Hit	How do you do
Ka-nim	*Kop-shut*	*Kaw-a-nassim*
Canoe	Broken	Always
Ka-ta	*Ko*	*Kla-ha-na*
Why	Arrived	Out
Kap-su-alla	*Kim-to*	*Klim-in-wit*
Theft, steal	Behind	A falsehood
K-liten	*Kollo*	*Krap-po*
Lead	Fence	Toad
Kaw-kaw	*Kutt*	*Klose*
Crow	Hard	Good
Klat-a-wah	*Klimin*	*Klas-ko*
Go, Walk	Fine	Them, those

Kul-a-kulla
Fowl

Kum-tux
Know, or understand

Ke-a-wale
Love

Ka-wah-we
All

Klow-e-wah
Slow

K-wallen
The ear

Kee-kool
Down

Lepo-lo
Pan

Le-por-shet
Fork

Lehash
Axe

Leg-win
Saw

Lima
The hand

Lita
Head

Le-pe-a
Feet

Lo-ma-las
Molasses

Kle-il
Black

Ka-was
Afraid

Kom-suck
Beads

Ko-ko-well
Eel

Klaps
Find

Kow-ne-aw
How many

La-sel
Saddle

Le-lo-im
Sharp

Le-poim
Apple

La-bush
Mouth

Le-da
Teeth

Le-ku
Neck

Le-mora
Wild

Lashimney
Chimney

Lemitten
Mitten

Ka-so
Rum

Ko-pa
There

Kit-lo
Kettle

Klone-ass
I do not understand

Klop-sta
Who

Klouch-man
Female

Le-lu
Panther

Le-pul
Chickens

Lecorset
Trunk

Laport
Door

Le-pip
Pipe

Lo-lo
Carry, or tote

Leb-ya
Old woman

La-lure
Hoe

La-cope
White

Lemon-to
Sheep

Lavest
Jacket, or vest

La-ep
Rope

Lep-lash
Boards

Lep-wa
Peas

Lep-well
Skillet

La-win
Oats

La-ram
Oar, for boats

Le-wash
Snow

Lemonti
Mountain

Muck-a-muck
Provisions, eat

Musket
Rifle, or gun

Moon
Month

Mo-kah
Buy

Mim-a-loosheb
Die, or dead

La-ha-la
Feel

Le-le
A long time

Las-well
Silk

La-tem
Table

Lep-o-lip
Boil

Le-sit-well
Stars

Le-mit-rem
Medicine

Le-shaw
Shoe

Le-sack
Sack, or bag

Le-quim
White bear

O-ep-can
Basket

O-ep-in-pin
Skunk

O-e-lile
Berries

O-e-pick
Both

O-elk
Snake

La-cre-me
Yellow

Mas-a-tro
Bad

Met-lite
Residence, Sitting
  down, &c.

Mal-ha-na
As, in the river; or,
  push off the boat

Man
Male

Mow-etch
Deer

Mu-lack
Elk

Muse-a-muse
Cattle

Me-si-ka
Plural of you

Papo
Father

Pil
Red

Pe-chi
Green

Pat-le
Full

Poo
Shoot

Mal-hu-ale	*O-lo*	*Pe-teck*
Back	Hungry	The world
Mi-ka	*Oel-hin*	*Pilton*
You	Seal	Foolish
Ni-ka	*O-koke*	*Pal-a-k-lo*
I, or me	This, or that	Night
Nan-ach	*Pi-yah*	*Pes-hocks*
Look, or see	Fire	Thickety
Na-ha	*Pos-ton*	*Pis-say-ukes*
Mother	Americans	French
New-ha	*Pee*	*Quack-quack*
Let	And	Duck
Now-it-k	*Pus*	*Si-wash*
Yes, certainly	If	Indians
Ne-si-ka	*Puss*	*Swas*
We, us	Cat	Rain
Nein	*Pish-hash*	*Sah-lee*
Name	Polecat	High
O-es-km	*Pos-seas*	*Stick*
Caps	Blanket	Wood
Oel-man	*Pot-latch*	*Seck-um*
Old	Give	Swim
O-pet-sa	*Pole-ally*	*Si-yaw*
Knife	Powder	Far
O-pes-wa	*Po-et*	*Sap-a-lil*
Wonder, astonishment	Boat	Flour
Ow	*Pa-pa*	*Su-ga*
Brother	Paper	Sugar
Sec-a-lukes	*Shot*	*To-lo*
Pantaloons	Shot	Win, or gain

Sap-a-pul
Hat

Sto-en
Rock

Sil
Shirting

Sko-kum
Strong, stout

Sec-pee
To miss

See-ah-os-ti
Face, or eyes

Sam-mon
Fish

Sto-gon
Sturgeon

Son-dra
Roan

Salt
Salt

Shu-es
Shoes

Sun
Sun, or day

Silk-um
Half, or a part

Smo-ek
Smoke

Sul-luks
Mad, angry

Sup-ner
Jump

Til-a-kum
People

Til-the-ko-ep
Cut

Tum-tum
The heart

Te-o-wit
Leg

Tum-pe-lo
Back

Tam-o-lack
Barrel

Ti-ye
Master, or chief

Tes-um
Pretty

To-lo-bus
Wolf

Te-ko-ep
White

Te-mo-lo
To-morrow

Tu-lusk
Milk

Tip-so
Grass

Tum-tuk
Water-falls

Te-ma-has
Poison

Ti-pee
An ornament

Te-kah
Want

Till
Heavy, or tired

Toc-ta
Doctor

Wah-wah
Talk, conversation

Wake
No, not

Wap-a-to
Potato

Win
Wind

Wam
Warm

Wetch
More

Ya-ka
Him, she, it

Yaw-wah
Yonder

Yok-sa
Hair

Ya-ha-la
Name

Six	*Ton-tle-ke*	*Yult-cut*
Friends	Yesterday	Long
Sick	*T-sit-still*	*You-till*
Sick, or sore	Buttons, or tacks	Glad, proud
Shut	*Tee-see*	
Shirt	Sweet	

CHINOOK MODE OF COMPUTING NUMBERS

Iht	1	*Dilo-p-sin-a-maxt*	17
Makst	2	*Dilo-p-sow-skins*	18
Klone	3	*Dilo-p-k-wi-etst*	19
Lakst	4	*Tath-la-hun makst*	20
K-win-nim	5	*Tath-la-hun klone*	30
Ta-hum	6	*Tath-la-hun lakst*	40
Sina-maxt	7	*Tath-la-hun k-win-ma*	50
Sow-skins	8	*Tath-la-hun ta-hum*	60
K-wi-etst	9	*Tath-la-hun sin-a-maxt*	70
Tath-la-ham	10	*Tath-la-hun sow-skins*	80
Dilo-pe-iht	11	*Tath-la-hun k-wi-etst*	90
Dilo-p-maxt	12	*Tak-o-mo-nuxt*	100
Dilo-p-klone	13	*Tak-o-mo-maxt*	200
Dilo-p-lakst	14	*Tak-o-mo-nuxt klone*	300
Dilo-p-k-winnim	15	*Tak-o-mo-nuxt lakst*	400
Dilo-p-ta-hum	16	*Tak-o-mo-nuxt k-win-nim*	500

WORDS USED IN THE NEZ PERCÉ LANGUAGE

Hama	*Talonot*	*Ipalikt*
Man	Ox	Clouds
Aiat	*Talohin*	*Wakit*
Women	Bull	Rain
Haswal	*Kulkulal*	*Hiwakasha*
Boy	Calf	Rains
Pitin	*Shikam*	*Maka*
Girl	Horse	Snow
Silu	*Tilipa*	*Hatia*
Eye	Fox	Wind
Huku	*Tahspul*	*Yakas*
Hair	Beaver	Hot
Ipsus	*Kelash*	*Yamits*
Hand	Otter	Cold
Ahwa	*Hisamtucks*	*Tiputput*
Feet	Sun	Warm
Simusimu	*Hayaksa*	*Silakt*
Black	Is hungry	Body
Ilpilp	*Husus*	*Katnanas*
Red	Head	Salt
Yosyos	*Kohalh*	*Haya*
Gray	Cow	Salmon-trout
Shukuishukui	*Kaih*	*Wahwahlam*
Brown	Colt	Trout
Kohatu	*Highwayahwasa*	*Ilat*
Short	Snows	Weak

Kohat — Long	*Haihai* — White	*Wals* — Knife
Kalinin — Crooked	*Ashtai* — Fork	*Ilatama* — Is blind
Tukuk — Straight	*Ashtai* — Awl	*Lakailakai* — Gentle
Silpsilp — Money	*Wawianas* — Axe	*Shiau* — Skittish
Tasitasi — Flat	*Kimstam* — Near	*Waiat* — Far
Hamoihamoi — Soft	*Maksmaks* — Yellow	*Shakinkash* — Saw
Sisyukas — Sugar	*Shapikash* — File	*Wishan* — Poor
Pishakas — Bitter	*Takai* — Blanket	*Ilakai* — Many
Komain — Sickness	*Sham* — Coat	*Milas* — Few
Hickomaisa — Is sick	*Ahwa* — Foot	*Animikinikai* — Below
Aluin — Is lame	*Silpsilp* — Round	*Tokmal* — Hat
Wakaas — Is well	*Tohon* — Pantaloons	*Huwialatus* — Weary
Tinukin — Is dead	*Ilapkit* — Shoe	*Ahat* — Down
Hiswesa — Is cold	*Hikai* — Kettle	*Akamkinikai* — Above
Yahet — Neck	*Sham* — Shirt	*Koko* — Raven

Nahso	*Laka*	*Houtat*
Salmon	Pine	Goose
Tushti	*Isa*	*Houtat*
Up	Mother	Geese
Atim	*Nisu*	*Yaya*
Arm	Child	Swan
Matsayee	*Mamaias*	*Yatin*
Ear	Children	Crane
Piama	*Hikai*	*Paps*
Brothers	Pail	Fir, (tree)
Kelah	*Sishnim*	*Kopkop*
Sturgeon	Thorns	Cottonwood
Wayu	*Sikstua*	*With*
Leg	Friend	Alder
Kupkup	*Lantuama*	*Tahs*
Back	Friends	Willows
Timina	*Walatakai*	*Tims*
Heart	Pan	Cherry
Sho	*Kuish*	*Satahswakkus*
Spoon	Risk	Corn
Kahno	*Shushai*	*Paks*
Prairie-hen	Grass	Wheat
Huhui	*Suyam*	*Lapatat*
Shoulder	Sucker	Potatoes
Pisht	*Hashu*	*Papa*
Father	Eel	A spring
Walpilkash	*Shakantai*	*Wawahp*
Auger	Eagle	Spring (season)
Katkat	*Sholoshah*	*Tiam*
Duck	Fish-hawk	Summer

Askap	*Washwashno*	*Shahnim*
Brother	Hen	Fall
Asmatan	*Koun*	*Anim*
Sisters	Dove	Winter
Kinis	*Aa*	*Pelush*
Sister	Crow	Gooseberry
Kikaya	*Timanawat*	*Yaka*
Serviceberry	A writer	Black bear
Kahas	*Sapaliknawat*	*Kemo*
Milk	A labourer	Old man
Katamnawakno	*Hania*	*Tahat*
Peas	Made	Young man
Hahushwakus	*Hanishaka*	*Otwai*
Green	Have made	Old woman
Inina	*Hanitatasha*	*Timai*
House	Will make	Young woman
Sanitwakus	*Hanikika*	*Pishas*
Parsnips	Made going	Father-in-law
Initain	*Hanisna*	*Pishas*
For a house	Made coming	Son-in-law
Initpa	*Ipna hani aisha*	*Siwako*
To the house	Make for him	Mother-in-law
Initkinai	*Hanitasa*	*Siwaka*
From the house	Go and make	Daughter-in-law
Initrim	*Tash hama*	*Inaya*
House only	Good man	Brother-in-law
Ininm	*Tash timina*	*Siks*
Of a house	Good heart	Sister-in-law
Initki	*Tash shikam*	*Pimh*
By a house	Good horse	Step-father

Initph	*Tiskan shikam*	*Kaka*
To a house	Fat horse	Step-mother
Haniai	*Hamtis shikam*	*Lemakas*
Not made	Fast horse	Deep
Haniawat	*Kapskaps shikam*	*Pakas*
A mechanic	Strong horse	Shallow
Hanishimai	*Sininish shikam*	*Mul*
Not a mechanic	Lazy horse	Rapids
Tamtainat	*Kapsis shikam*	*Amshah*
Preacher	Bad horse	Breaker
Himtakewat	*Haihai shikam*	*Watas*
Teacher	White horse	Land
Tamiawat	*Hahas*	*Pishwai*
Trader	Gray bear	Stones
Mahsham	*Hitkakokaiko*	*Watoikash*
Mountain	He gallops	It is fordable
Kuhsin	*Hitksilsilsa*	*Hatsu hiyaniksa*
Hill	He trots	Wood is floating
Tahpam	*Himilmilisha*	*Hiwalasa*
Plain	He paces	The water runs
Hantikam	*Hiwalakaiks*	*Hahanwasam*
Bough	He walks	The day is dawning
Tepitepit	*Hishaulakiks*	*Wako hikaaun*
Smooth	He runs	It is daylight now
Wilpwilp	*Titishka shikam*	*Hitinatra hisamtuks*
Round	Fat horses	The sun is rising
Pohol	*Maksmaks shikam*	*Naks halaps*
Valley	Sorrel horse	One day
Tasham	*Hihaihai shikam*	*Hikulawitsa*
Ridge	White horse	It is evening

Iwatam	*Tamsilps shikam*	*Kaaun*
Lake	Spotted horse	Daylight
Tikim	*Tilamselp shikam*	*Hatsu hialika*
Falls	Spotted horses	The wood is lodged
Hitkawisha	*Minsahsminko*	*Kia waaiikshi*
He falls	Read	We are crossing
Kohat tawish	*Kokalh*	*Ka apapinmiks*
Long horn	Cattle	Let us sleep
Wishan kokalk	*Hiwaliksa*	*Ka apahips*
Poor ox	The river is rising	Let us eat
Lilkailakikokal	*Hitaausa*	*Ka apakus*
Gentle cows	The river is falling	Let us go
Hiwasasha	*Hiwalasa*	*Ka apasklin*
He rides	The water runs	Let us go back

NEZ PERCÉ MODE OF COMPUTING NUMBERS

Naks	1	*Putimpt wah wimatat*	18
Lapit	2	*Putimpt wah kuis*	19
Mitat	3	*Laptit*	20
Pilapt	4	*Laptit wah naks*	21
Pahat	5	*Mitaptit*	30
Wilaks	6	*Piloptit*	40
Winapt	7	*Pakaptit*	50
Wimatat	8	*Wilaksaptit*	60
Kuis	9	*Winaptit*	70
Putimpt	10	*Wimitaptit*	80
Putimpt wah naks	11	*Kuisaptit*	90
Putimpt wah lapit	12	*Putaptit*	100
Putimpt wah mitat	13	*Laposhus*	200
Putimpt wah pilapt	14	*Mitoshus*	300
Putimpt wah pahat	15	*Pelaposhus*	400
Putimpt wah wilaks	16	*Pakoshus*	500
Putimpt winapt	17		

TABLE OF DISTANCES FROM INDEPENDENCE, MISSOURI; AND ST. JOSEPH, TO OREGON CITY, IN OREGON TERRITORY

		MILES
FROM Independence to Rendezvous	. . .	20
" Rendezvous to Elm Grove	. . .	13
" Elm Grove to Walkarusha	. . .	20
" Walkarusha to crossing of Kansas river	.	28
" Kansas to crossing of Turkey creek	. .	14
" Turkey creek to Little Vermilion	. .	24
" Little Vermilion to branch of same	. .	12
" To Big Vermilion, with intermediate camps.		29
" Vermilion to Lee's branch .	. . .	8
" Lee's branch to Big Blue .	. . .	6
" Big Blue to the junction with St. Joseph's trail	. . . .	10

The distance from St. Joseph, Missouri, to the Independence trail, striking it ten miles west of Blue river, is about one hundred miles. Good camps can be had from eight to fifteen miles apart.

From forks of road as above, to Big Sandy, striking it near its junction with the Republican Fork of Blue river, with intermediate camps	42
" Sandy to Republican fork of Blue river .	18
" up Republican fork, with good camps. .	53
" Republican fork to Big Platte . . .	20
" up Big Platte to the crossing of South fork .	120

Camps can be had at suitable distances, with wood for fuel upon the islands.

From lower to upper crossings of South fork .	45

There is a road on each side of the river, and but little choice in them.

From South to North fork, at Ash Hollow . .	20
" Ash Hollow to opposite Solitary Tower, on Little creek	42
" Little creek to opposite Chimney rock .	16
" Chimney Rock to where the road leaves the River	15
" thence to Scott's Bluffs (Good Spring) .	10
" Scott's Bluffs to Horse creek . . .	12
" Horse creek to Fort Laramie . . .	24
" Laramie to Dry Branch and Big Spring .	12
" to Bitter Cottonwood	10
To Willow Branch	7
" Horse Shoe Creek	7
" River	8
Thence to where the Road leaves the River . .	8
To Big Timber creek	16
" Marble creek	5
" Mike's-head creek	12
" the River, crossing several streams . . .	10
" Deer creek	6
Thence to crossing of North fork of Platte . .	25
From crossing of Platte to Spring . . .	10
Thence to Mineral Springs (bad camp) . .	8
" Willow Spring (good camp) . . .	5
" Independence Rock on Sweet Water . .	22
" Devil's Gate	5

Up Sweet Water to South Pass (good camps)   .   104
Over the dividing ridge to Pacific Spring, the waters
     of which run into Green river .   .   .   5

HERE, HAIL OREGON !

From Spring to Little Sandy   20
  Here the road forks, the southern trail going by
way of Bridger's Old Fort, and thence to Bear
river.   The northern (which is two and a half days
less driving) strikes Green river about forty miles
above the southern trail; I will give the distance
on both routes.
The northern route, from Little Sandy to Big Sandy   6
From Big Sandy to Green river   40
     (No water and but little grass between.)
 "   thence to Bear river, (with good camps,)   .   64
On the southern route: —
From Little Sandy to Big Sandy   12
Down Big Sandy to Green river   24
Cross Green river and down   8
From Green river to Black's fork   .   .   .   15
Up Black's fork to Bridger's Old Fort .   .   .   30
From Old Fort to Little Muddy (poor camp)   .   8
 "   thence to Big Muddy (poor camp)   .   .   10
Up Big Muddy to the dividing ridge (good camp
     near head of creek)   32
Over dividing ridge to spring   10
From spring to camp on Bear river   .   .   .   6
 "   thence to where the northern trail comes in .   10
To Smith's fork three miles, to Narrows four miles,
     and thence to crossing of Bear river three
     miles   10

Here the road forks; the nearest is to follow up
the creek two miles, cross and then go over the ridge
five miles to foot of Big Hill, where the roads again
unite   7

The other road crosses the river, follows up the
bottom about ten miles, re-crosses and is then about
seven miles to junction.

From foot of Big Hill, to top of ridge is about .	3
" thence to Big Timber on Bear river . .	4
Here is a company of American traders and trappers	—
From Big Timber to Soda Springs . . .	36
" Spring to Soda Pool seven miles, to Spring Branch three.	10
" Spring to Running Branch . . .	9
" thence to foot of hill	8
" foot of hill over dividing ridge and down to camp	12
" thence to Lewis's river bottom at Springs .	18
and to Fort Hall	5
" Fort Hall to the crossing of Portneth . .	6
" Portneth to American falls . . .	12
" American falls to Levey creek . . .	15
" thence to Cassia creek, (here the California trail turns off)	8
" Cassia to Big Marsh	15
" Marsh to River	11
" River to Goose creek four miles, seven miles to river, and twelve miles to Dry Branch, (water in pools)	23
To Rocky Creek	8

MILES

To crossing of Rocky creek, eight miles, down
   to where the road leaves the bluff of creek,
   seven   15
" Salmon Falls creek   20
From thence to Salmon falls   6
"   Falls to first crossing of Lewis river .   .   23
"   crossing to Bois river is about .   .   .   70
Camps can be had from six to fifteen miles
Down Bois river to Fort Bois (good camps) .   .   46
Cross Lewis river and thence to Malheur .   .   15
"   Malheur to Birch creek, about .   .   .   20
"   Birch creek to river three miles, and thence
   five miles to Burnt river .   .   .   8
Up Burnt river about (good camps) .   .   .   26
From where the road leaves Burnt river, to the lone
   pine stump in the bottom of Powder river,
   (the last thirteen miles no water) .   .   28
To the crossing of Powder river   10
To Grand Round   15
Across the southern end of Grand Round .   .   7
Up Big Hill and on to Grand Round river .   .   8
Over the Blue Mountains to Lee's encampment .   19
To Umatillo river   16
Down Umatillo river   44
"   Columbia river to John Day's river .   .   33
From thence to Falls river   22
And thence to the Dalles of the Columbia .   .   16
From the Dalles to Oregon city, by way of wagon
   road south of Mount Hood about .   .   160
   Upon reaching the Columbia, emigrants should

have persons in advance to select suitable places for camp ground: as the country along the river is extremely barren, and the grazing limited to small patches.

APPENDIX

LETTER OF THE REV. H. H. SPALDING TO JOEL PALMER

(Referred to on page 126 *[our page* 233*])*

NEZ PERCÉ MISSION, CLEAR WATER RIVER,
Oregon Territory, April 7, 1846.

To JOEL PALMER ESQ. OF INDIANA.

MY DEAR SIR : — Agreeably to your request I most cheerfully give you my views concerning the Oregon territory, its extent, its most desirable climate, fertility of soil, rivers and mountains, seas and bays, and its proximity to one of the most extensive markets opening upon the world.

The Oregon territory is usually divided into three great divisions, the lower, middle, and upper regions. The upper includes the Rocky Mountains, with the head waters of most of the rivers running west and east, north and south, and extends west to the Blue and Spokan ranges of mountains. The lower includes the belt of country bounded on the west by the Pacific, and on the east by the Nesqually, Cascade, and California Mountains. The middle region lies between the two, and embraces probably far the greatest extent of country, and is in some respects the most desirable for settlers.

The number of rainy days, during the winter season, in the lower country, is thought to be about eighty-five one-hundredths; while the number of rainy days during the same season in the upper (or middle) country, is about fifteen one-hundredths. [166] There is but little more snow during the winter season in the middle than in the lower region of the Columbia river, or upon the plains. Of course the depth of snow upon the mountains, depends upon their height.

The lower country is subject to inundations, to a greater or less extent, from the Columbia river, which gathering into standing pools, with the great amount of vegetable decay consequent upon low prairie countries, produces to some extent unhealthy fogs during the summer season. This, however, is greatly moderated by the sea breezes from the Pacific. The middle region is entirely free from these evils, and has probably one of the most pacific, healthy, and every way most desirable climates in the world. This, with its extensive prairies, covered with a superior quality of grass tuft, or bunch grass, which springs fresh twice a year, and spotted and streaked everywhere with springs and streams of the purest, sweetest water, renders it admirably adapted to the herding system. The lower country will ever have greatly the advantage in its proximity to market, its extensive sea coast, and from the fact that it contains one of the largest and best harbors in the world, viz. Puget's sound, running far inland, the mouth of which is protected by Vancouver's island, easy of access at all seasons and under all winds.

But to go into detail. Myself and wife were appointed missionaries by the American Board of Commissioners for Foreign Missions, and destined to this field, and with our worthy associates, Dr. Whitman, and lady, arrived in this country in the fall of 1836. The Doctor settled among the Cayuses near fort Wallawalla, and myself at this place, where we have ever since continued to dwell. Our duties have called us to travel more or less every year to visit the distant bands and tribes, as also to pack our supplies. I have traversed this middle region in seventeen different routes, of from 60 to 300 miles. Over many of the routes I have passed probably in every month in the year, have marked the progress of vegetation from its earliest shooting forth; the effects of this climate [167] upon the animal constitution; the rapidity with which exhausted poor animals regain their flesh and activity, when turned upon the plains; and have kept tables under some of these heads, as also a meteorological table for several years.

Let me here observe that my views of the country have been materially changed by a more accurate acquaintance with its true nature. I once thought the valleys only susceptible of habitation; considering the plains too dry for cultivation. But I am now prepared to say this is not the case. The plains suffer far less from drought than the valleys, on account of the reflection of heat from the surrounding hills. The country, however, is nowhere peculiarly subject to drought, as was once thought. My place is one of the deepest valleys, and consequently the most exposed to the reflection from the high bluffs around, which rise from two to three thousand feet; but my farm, though prepared for irrigation, has remained without it for the last four years. I find the ground becomes more moist by cultivation. Three years ago I raised six hundred bushels of shelled corn from six acres, and good crops of wheat on the same piece the two following years, without irrigation. Eight years ago I raised 1500 bushels of potatoes from one acre and a half; measuring some of the bags in which they were brought to the cellars, and so judging of the whole amount. I gave every eleventh bag for digging and fetching, and kept a strict account of what every person brought, so that I was able to make a pretty accurate estimate of the whole amount. My potatoes and corn are always planted in drills.

Every kind of grain or vegetable which I have tried or seen tried in this upper country, grows well. Wheat is sown in the fall, and harvested in June at this place; at Dr. Whitman's in July, being a more open country. Corn is planted in April and ripens in July; peas the same.

EXTENT OF COUNTRY

The southern boundary of Oregon territory is the 42d degree of north latitude. The northern boundary is not yet settled; [222] [168] both England and the United States claim north of the Columbia river to latitude 49°. But this vast fertile region, well timbered upon the mountains and river sources, and well watered, besides having the fine harbor above named, Puget's sound, must ever remain the most important portion of Oregon, especially on account of this harbor, which will naturally

---

[222] Since this letter was written, the forty-ninth parallel of north latitude has been established by treaty as the boundary line between the governments of Great Britain and the United States — except that portion of Vancouver's island south of 49°, which continues under the jurisdiction of Great Britain.— PALMER.

control these seas, and consequently the country. Should the British flag finally exclusively wave over its placid waters, it will be to the rest of Oregon as Quebec is to Canada, or Gibraltar to the Mediterranean. Vancouver's Island is doubtless another reason why Great Britain wishes to make the Columbia river her northern boundary. The line of 49° passes a little north of the southern half of the island. The whole island contains a territory considerably larger than England and Scotland, produces every kind of grain and vegetable well, and has a climate very similar to our Middle and Southern states. Whatever nation possesses this island, or the south portion of it, with its neighboring harbor, Puget's sound, possesses nearly all of a national consideration which pertains to Oregon, and will consequently control it. But if this island, or this portion of it, with this harbor, add their ever controlling influence to the undivided interests of Oregon, this young colony, but yesterday begun, and whose country and existence were but yesterday disputed, will at no distant day, under the softening, life-giving influence of civilization and our holy religion, take its place among the wealthiest, happiest, and best nations of the earth.

The country of Oregon, should it extend to 49° north latitude, is probably capable of sustaining as great a population as two-thirds of the territory of the States, and with far less hard labor.

CLIMATE

This is decidedly the inviting characteristic of the country, and is certainly a great inducement for all persons of delicate health. I speak of the middle region.

Free from marshes or standing water and vegetable
decay, the air is remarkably pure and serene; summers rather warm, especially in the valleys; the mercury
ranges, for some time during the hot season, from 100
to 109 degrees above zero. Nights cool, but no fog
or dew, except in a few places. Twice since I have
been in the country frost has injured vines, leaves, &c.,
first of May, but never in the fall till late; often my
melon vines, &c., are green till the first of December.
Four times since I have been here the mercury has
fallen below zero; once to 26 degrees. But usually
it ranges above 20 in the morning, and above 60 through
the day. During six of the ten winters I have passed
in the country, the rivers have not been frozen. The
Columbia river has been frozen nearly to its mouth,
twice since I have been in the country. The snow
sometimes falls a foot deep — I should judge about
once in five years. About half of my winters here
there has been no snow in the valleys, and but little on
the plains, except to whiten the earth for a short time.
It disappears in a few hours, especially on the south
face of the bluffs and hills. Last year I made a collection
of flowers and plants, which I purpose to send to Washington. I gathered two flowers in January, on the 22d
and 29th,[338] and during the month of February some
40 showed themselves, and by the first of March the
grass on the south faces of the bluffs was 14 inches
high. This year the season was about three weeks
later, judging by the appearance of flowers. I know
of no disease that can be said to be peculiar to the

[338] Flowers have been seen in the last winter, and winter before, from the
20th of January.— M. W.

country. The country is peculiarly free from sudden changes of weather, or violent storms. Persons who have wintered here from the south, tell me the winters are as mild as the winters [170] in the northern parts of North and South Carolina, and with less sudden changes.

ADVANTAGES FOR THE HERDING SYSTEM

The country is one extensive prairie, except the mountains, which are covered with several species of pine, cedar, and fir. The prairies are rolling, and with the exception of a narrow belt of sand and sedge upon the Columbia, and portions of the Snake river, are everywhere covered with the bunch grass, which, from observation, I judge to be a richer, heartier food for animals than corn, oats, and the best pastures of the States. It is a fine, solid stalk, growing two feet high, with fine leaves, holds its freshness through the winter; I mean the old stalk, which mingled with the young growth, that usually springs fresh in the fall, forms a food for animals through the winter, preferable to the best hay. Horses and oxen perform labor at all seasons upon this grass simply, without the aid of grain; which I now think disposes the animal system to various diseases.

When I pack, I usually travel from thirty-five to forty miles a day, each horse carrying two hundred pounds — rest an hour at noon, without taking down the packs; camp while the sun is yet two hours high; hobble the horses and drive them up in the morning at sunrise. I find that horses will endure such labor for twenty-five or thirty days, resting of course on the Sabbath, upon this grass, without injuring them. Their

wind is evidently better than that of horses fed on grain
and hay. I have rode from Dr. Whitman's station to
this, 125 miles, in nineteen hours, starting at 9 o'clock
in the night, and driving a spare horse for change; but
this was no advantage, for I find it is more fatiguing
to a horse to be drove than to be rode. You doubtless
recollect the man who overtook us on the head of Ala-
pausawi, Thursday morning. He had left the Dalles
or Long Narrows on the Columbia on Tuesday morning,
slept a short time Tuesday night below the Umatillo,
passed by Dr. Whitman's station, and slept Wednes-
day night on the Tukanan, [171] a distance from the
Dalles of two hundred and forty miles; and the day
he passed us he traveled fifty-five miles more.²²⁴ He
rode one horse and drove another for change. You
will probably even recollect those horses, as they left us
upon the round gallop. A man went from this place,
starting late, to Wallawalla, and returned on the third
day, sun two hours high, making the journey in about
two days and a half. The whole distance traveled was
two hundred and fifty miles, and but one horse was
used. None of these horses were injured.

Cattle, sheep, horses, and hogs feed out through the
winter, and continue fat. We very often kill our beef
in March, and always have the very best of meat. Often
an ox from the plains, killed in March, yields over one
hundred and fifty pounds of tallow. You have seen
two specimens, one killed at Dr. Whitman's, and one
at this place. Sheep need the care of a shepherd through

²²⁴ The first creek is that now called Alpowa, in Asotin and Garfield counties,
Washington; it is a southwestern tributary of the Lewis. Tukenon River, in
Columbia County, Washington, the largest southern affluent of the Lewis west
of Lewiston, was known by Lewis and Clark as the Kimooenem.— ED.

the winter, to protect the lambs from the prairie wolves. A band of mares should have a good stud that will herd them and protect the colts from the large wolves. Some thirty different kinds of roots grow abundantly upon the plains and bluffs, which, with the grass, furnish the best of food for hogs, and they are always good pork. The south faces of the extensive bluffs and hills are always free from snow, and, cut up into ten thousand little ravines, form the most desirable retreat imaginable for sheep during the winter. Here they have the best of fresh grass, and the young lambs, coming regularly twice a year, are protected from the winds and enlivened by the warm sun. We have a flock of sheep belonging to the Mission, received from the islands eight years ago; there are now about one hundred and fifty. Not one has yet died from disease, a thing of such frequent occurrence in the States. It must certainly become a great wool growing country.

I cannot but contrast the time, labor, and expense requisite to look after herds in this country, with that required in the States, especially in the Northern and Middle States, where two-thirds of every man's time, labor, and money is expended [172] on his animals, in preparing and fencing pasture grounds and meadows, building barns, sheds, stables, and granaries, cutting and securing hay and grains, and feeding and looking to animals through winter. In this country all this is superceded by Nature's own bountiful hand. In this country a single shepherd with his horse and dogs can protect and look after five thousand sheep.[226] A man with his horse and perhaps a dog can easily attend to

---

[226] At present it will require one man to a thousand in the winter to pro-

two thousand head of cattle and horses, without spending a dollar for barns, grain, or hay. Consider the vast amount of labor and expense such a number of animals would require in the States. Were I to select for my friends a location for a healthy happy life, and speedy wealth, it would be this country.

Timber is the great desideratum. But the country of which I am particularly speaking, extending every way perhaps four hundred miles, is everywhere surrounded by low mountains, which are thickly timbered, besides two or three small ridges passing through it; also the rivers Columbia, Snake, Spokan, Paluse, Clear Water, Yankiman, Okanakan, Salmon, Wailua, Tukanan, Wallawalla, Umatillo, John Day's and river De Shutes; and down most of these timber or lumber can be rafted in any quantities. So that but a very small portion of the country will be over ten or fifteen miles from timber; most of it in the immediate vicinity of timber. The numerous small streams which occur every five or six miles, affording most desirable locations for settlements, contain some cotton wood, alder and thorn. But timber is soon grown from sprouts. The streams everywhere run over a stony bottom, while the soil is entirely free from stone. Streams are rapid, affording the best of mill privileges.

MARKET, SEAS AND BAYS

The western shores of Oregon are washed by the placid [173] waters of the Pacific, which bring the 360,000,000 of China, the many millions of the vast

tect from wolves. But Strycknine is a sure poison with which to destroy them.— M. W.

Indies and of Australasia, and lay them at our doors
with opening hands to receive our produce; which, with
the numerous whale ships that literally whiten the
Northern Pacific, calling not only for provisions, but
harbors to winter in, must ever afford one of the most
extensive markets in the world for all kinds of produce,
and one concerning which there need be but little fear
that it will ever be overstocked. A market compared
with which, that offered by western Europe to the eastern section of the United States, will become as a drop
to the bucket. The United States' Commercial Agent
at Oahu, Sandwich Islands, is desirous to make a con-
tract for a certain amount of provisions to be supplied
to American shipping every year at Oregon city; but as
yet the supplies of the country over and above the home
consumption, are not sufficient to warrant a dependence
of our whale shipping upon the country. In fact for
many years, while the United States continue to pour
their inhabitants by tens of thousands, every year, into
this young republic, the home market must continue
in competition with the foreign. But the day is not
distant when this country, settled by an industrious,
virtuous, Sabbath-loving people, governed by whole-
some laws, blessed with schools, and the institutions
of our holy religion, will hold out abundant encourage-
ments for the numerous whale and merchant ships of
the Pacific to leave their heavy lading of three years'
supply of provisions at home, and depend upon the
market in the immediate vicinity of their fishing grounds.
Others following in their track, learning of this new
world, and finding out our ample harbors, soon this little
obscure point upon the map of the world will become

a second North American Republic — her commerce whitening every sea, and her crowded ports fanned by the flags of every nation. From this upper country, a distance of three hundred or four hundred miles, droves of cattle and sheep can be driven to the lower portions of the Columbia river, [174] with far less expense and labor than they are driven the same distances in the States, always being in the midst of grass upon which they may feed every night without charge.

The principal harbors are Puget's Sound, mouths of Columbia, Frazier's, Shahales, Umpqua, Rose and Clamet rivers.[226] Doubtless others will be discovered, as the country becomes more known. A dangerous bar extends nearly across the mouth of the Columbia, leaving but a narrow obscure channel, difficult of access or egress, except with favorable winds. Vessels sometimes find it impossible to enter the river by reason of contrary winds; and sometimes are detained in the river two or three months, there not being sea room enough to go out against a head wind. This difficulty could be greatly obviated, and perhaps removed, by a pilot boat. Concerning the other rivers I have no certain knowledge, but have been informed that some of them are navigable for vessels from forty to sixty miles, and afford convenient harbors. Puget's Sound, as before observed, is one of the safest and best harbors in the world, it can be entered or left under any winds and at any season of the year. The scenery around is said to be most enchanting. Two lakes near sending off a small stream of pure water. A considerable river runs

---

[226] These rivers have all been noted in the text, *ante*. By "Rose" the author intends Rogue River.— ED.

into the sound, making a fall of some twenty-five feet just as it plunges into the sea, affording the opportunity of building mills upon the wharfs.

But very little has been known by Americans concerning the extensive country north of the Columbia, till last winter. I have several times been told by British subjects that the countries bordering on Frazier's river and Puget's Sound were too sterile for cultivation, and but poor crops could be raised on the Cowlitz. Whereas, the exploring party who left Oregon city, last winter, report that they found a very extensive country north of the Columbia river, of apparently good soil, well timbered with pine and oak, and well watered with the following rivers and their tributaries, viz.: the Cowlitz, emptying into the Columbia river from the north; the Shahales, [175] running into a small bay north of the Columbia river; the Nesqualla, rising near the source of the Cowlitz, and running north into Puget's Sound; Frazier's river north of this, and several smaller ones not named.

On the Cowlitz, Nesqualla and Frazier's rivers, the Hudson Bay Company have large establishments, and are producing vast quantities of wool, beef, pork, and all kinds of grain, for British whale ships which frequent the harbors. Besides these establishments, they have extensive farms and herds at Vancouver, in the Willamette valley and Colvile, and trading posts on Vancouver island, and at the mouth of the Columbia river, Umpqua, Vancouver, Wallawalla, Okanakan and Colvile, Boise and fort Hall, with very many at the north. Some of these are strongly fortified, and are being well supplied with cannon and other munitions of war, by almost every ship that arrives. So I have been informed by persons from these ships.

With the extensive valley watered by the Willamette and its numerous tributaries, you are better acquainted than myself, as I have never visited that country. I cannot, however, deny myself the pleasure of expressing my opinion of the country, formed from information derived yearly from scores of persons who have dwelt long in, or traveled more or less through its extensive territory, at all seasons of the year.

On the west the great valley is separated from the Pacific by a low range of well timbered mountains, that give rise to numerous streams and small rivers, some of which are lately found sufficient to admit vessels. On the east it is bounded by the Cascade or President's range, everywhere abounding with white pine and cedar. The Willamette river rises in latitude 42°, and runs north and empties itself into the Columbia river 85 miles above its mouth. The falls of the Willamette are about thirty miles above its mouth, and must ever add a vast interest to the country. The power for mills and machinery that may be erected on each side of the river, and on the island in the middle of the falls, is adequate for almost any conceivable demand.

[176] Oregon city, situated at the falls on the east side of the river, contains over five hundred souls, about eighty houses, viz.: two churches, two blacksmith shops, one cooper shop, two cabinet shops, four tailor shops, one hatter's shop, one tannery, three shoe shops, two silver smiths, four stores, two taverns, two flouring and two saw mills, and a lathe machine. Directly opposite, on the west side, are two towns laid out, and buildings are going up. The face of the country in the Willa-

mette valley is rolling, very equally divided into prairie
and timbered countries, with frequent oak openings.
Wheat produces well; corn, potatoes, &c. produce
well in some places, and probably would everywhere
do well with good cultivation; soil everywhere considered of a superior quality. Less snow during the
winter season than in the middle district, but much
more rain, with fogs, on the low lands during the summer, which render the country less healthy than this
middle region; but still the country cannot be considered
an unhealthy country. The face of the country is everywhere covered with bunch grass,[227] and animals feed
out through the winter, as in the middle region.

The rivers Umpqua, Rose and Clamet, which empty
into the Pacific, south of the Columbia, are said to
water extensive fertile countries; but as yet very little
is known of these regions. Ships come up the Willamette river within a few miles of Oregon city. Concerning the road for wagons commenced south of Mount
Hood, and which is to be completed this summer, to be
in readiness for the next emigration, you are better
acquainted than myself.

I am happy to recommend to future emigrants your
directions and advice as to the best mode of traveling;
number of wagons desirable to travel together; quantity
of provisions required for each person; best route;
distance to be traveled each day. You will also be
able to give the prices for which the Hudson Bay company sells flour, at Forts Hall [177] and Bois, and for
which it is brought from the Willamette to the Dalles
and sold.

You are acquainted with the fact that the Mission

---

[227] Clover (native) is more abundant in June.— M. W.

station at this place, and at Waiilatpu, have been in the habit of furnishing provisions to immigrants. We are willing to do so as long as there are no other sources of supplies in this vicinity, and therefore seems a duty. But our object in the country is to civilize and Christianize the Indian tribes among whom we are located. We are stewards of the property of others. We receive no salaries, but simply our living and clothing. We therefore feel it to be our duty to endeavour to make the receipts for provisions sold, net their expenses. For this end, Mr. Gilbert, a gentleman from New York, has taken charge of the secular affairs of this station, and will furnish provisions to immigrants on the most reasonable terms. He will give you their probable prices, and the names of such things as will be taken in exchange. You have seen the quantity and quality of flour and beef at this place, as also at Waiilatpu.

Yours very sincerely,

H. H. SPALDING.

P. S. During last season, commencing 22d of January, I collected and preserved over two thousand different species of flowers, plants and grasses,[219] many of which I think are rare, but I am no botanist.

---

[219] Probably what are called species here, are in many cases only a variety of the same species.— M. W.

ORGANIC LAWS OF OREGON
(WITH AMENDMENTS)

The Legislative Committee recommend that the following Laws be adopted.

PREAMBLE

WE, the people of Oregon Territory, for purposes of mutual protection, and to secure peace and prosperity among ourselves, agree to adopt the following laws and regulations, until such time as the United States of America extend their jurisdiction over us.

Be it enacted, therefore, by the free citizens of Oregon Territory, that the said territory, for purposes of temporary government, be divided into not less than three nor more than five districts, subject to be extended to a greater number when an increase of population shall require.

For the purpose of fixing the principles of civil and religious liberty, as the basis of all laws and constitutions of government that may hereafter be adopted —

Be it enacted, That the following articles be considered articles of compact among the free citizens of this territory:

ARTICLE I

§ 1. No person demeaning himself in a peaceable and orderly manner, shall ever be molested on account of his mode of worship or religious sentiments.

[180] § 2. The inhabitants of said territory shall always be entitled to the benefits of the writ of habeas

corpus and trial by jury, of a proportionate representation of the people in the legislature, and of judicial proceedings, according to the course of common law. All persons shall be bailable, unless for capital offences, where the proof shall be evident or the presumption great. All fines shall be moderate, and no cruel or unusual punishments shall be inflicted. No man shall be deprived of his liberty but by the judgment of his peers, or the law of the land; and should the public exigencies make it necessary for the common preservation to take any person's property, or to demand his particular services, full compensation shall be made for the same; and in the just preservation of rights and property, it is understood and declared that no law ought ever to be made, or have force in said territory, that shall, in any manner whatever, interfere with or affect private contracts or engagements, " bona fide" and without fraud previously formed.

§ 3. Religion, morality and knowledge being necessary — to good government and the happiness of mankind, schools and the means of education shall forever be encouraged. The utmost good faith shall always be observed towards the Indians; their lands and property shall never be taken from them without their consent; and in their property, rights or liberty they shall never be invaded or disturbed, unless in just and lawful wars, authorised by the representatives of the people; but laws founded in justice and humanity shall, from time to time, be made for preventing injustice being done to them, and for preserving peace and friendship with them.

§ 4. There shall be no slavery nor involuntary servitude in said territory otherwise than for the punishment

of crimes, whereof the party shall have been duly convicted.

§ 5.   No person shall be deprived of the right of bearing
arms in his own defence; no unreasonable searches or
seizures shall be granted; the freedom of the press shall
not be restrained; [181] no person shall be twice tried for
the same offence; nor the people deprived of the right of
peaceably assembling and discussing any matter they
may think proper; nor shall the right of petition ever
be denied.

§ 6.   The powers of the government shall be divided
into three distinct departments — the legislative, executive, and judicial; and no person, belonging to one of
these departments, shall exercise any of the powers
properly belonging to either of the others, except in
cases herein directed or permitted.

ARTICLE II

§ 1.   The legislative power shall be vested in a House
of Representatives, which shall consist of not less than
thirteen nor more than sixty-one members, whose numbers
shall not be increased more than five at any one session, to
be elected by the qualified electors at the annual election,
giving to each district a representation in proportion to
its population, (excluding Indians,) and the said members shall reside in the district for which they shall be
chosen; and in case of vacancy by death, resignation
or otherwise, the executive shall issue his writ to the
district where such vacancy has occurred, and cause a
new election to be held, giving sufficient notice at least
ten days previously, of the time and place of holding
said election.

§ 2. The House of Representatives, when assembled, shall choose a speaker and its other officers, be judges of the qualifications and election of its members, and sit upon its own adjournment from day to day. Two-thirds of the House shall constitute a quorum to transact business, but a smaller number may adjourn from day to day, and may be authorised by law to compel the attendance of absent members.

§ 3. The House may determine the rules of its proceedings, punish its members for disorderly behavior, and with the concurrence of two-thirds, expel a member, but not a second time for the same offence; and shall have all powers necessary for [182] a legislature of a temporary government, not in contravention with the restrictions imposed in this Organic Law.

§ 4. The House of Representatives shall, from time to time, fix the salaries of the different officers appointed or elected under this compact, provided the pay of no officer shall be altered during the term of his service; nor shall the pay of the House be increased by any law taking effect during the session at which such alteration is made.

§ 5. The House of Representatives shall have the sole power of impeaching; three-fourths of all the members must concur in an impeachment. The governor and all civil officers under these articles of compact, shall be liable to impeachment for treason, bribery, or any high crime or misdemeanor in office. Judgment in such cases shall not extend further than removal from office, and disqualification to hold any office of honor, trust or profit under this compact; but the party convicted may be dealt with according to law.

§ 6. The House of Representatives shall have power to lay out the territory into suitable districts, and apportion the representation in their own body. They shall have power to pass laws for raising a revenue either by the levying and collecting of taxes, or the imposing license on merchandize, ferries, or other objects — to open roads and canals, either by the levying a road tax, or the chartering of companies; to regulate the intercourse of the people with the Indian tribes; to establish post offices and post roads; to declare war, suppress insurrection or repel invasion; to provide for the organizing, arming, and disciplining the militia, and for calling forth the militia to execute the laws of Oregon; to pass laws to regulate the introduction, manufacture, or sale of ardent spirits; to regulate the currency and internal police of the country; to create inferior offices necessary and not provided for by these articles of compact; and generally to pass such laws to promote the general welfare of the people of Oregon, not contrary to the spirit of this instrument; and all powers not hereby expressly delegated, [183] remain with the people. The House of Representatives shall convene annually on the first Tuesday in December, at such place as may be provided by law, and shall, upon their first meeting after the adoption of this instrument of compact, proceed to elect and define the duties of a secretary, recorder, treasurer, auditor, marshal, or other officers necessary to carry into effect the provisions of this compact.

§ 7. The executive power shall be vested in one person, elected by the qualified voters at the annual election, who shall have power to fill vacancies; to remit fines and forfeitures; to grant pardons and reprieves for offences against the laws of the territory; to call out the military force of the country to repel invasion or suppress insurrection; to take care that the laws are faithfully executed, and to recommend such laws as he may consider necessary to the representatives of the people for their action. Every bill which shall have been passed by the House of Representatives, shall, before it becomes a law, be presented to the governor for his approbation. If he approve, he shall sign it; if not, he shall return it, with his objections, to the House, and the House shall cause the objections to be entered at large on its journals, and shall proceed to reconsider the bill; if, after such reconsideration, a majority of two-thirds of the House shall agree to pass the same, it shall become a law. In such cases the vote shall be taken by ayes and noes, and be entered upon the journal. If any bill shall not be returned by the governor to the House of Representatives within three days (Sundays excepted) after it shall have been presented to him, the same shall become a law in like manner as if the governor had signed it, unless the House of Representatives, by its adjournment, shall prevent its return; in which case it shall not become a law. The governor shall continue in office two years, and until his successor is duly elected and qualified; and in case of the office becoming vacant by death, resignation, or otherwise, the secretary shall exercise the duties of the office until the vacancy shall be filled by [184] election. The governor shall receive the sum of   dollars per annum, as full compensation for his services, which sum may be increased or diminished at any time by law, provided the salary of no governor shall be altered during his term of service. The governor shall have power to convene the legislature on extraordinary occasions.

§ 8. The judicial power shall be vested in a supreme court, and such inferior courts of law, equity, and arbitration, as may, by law from time to time be established. The supreme court shall consist of one judge, who shall be elected by the House of Representatives, and hold his office for four years, and until his successor is duly elected and qualified. The supreme court, except in cases otherwise directed by this compact, shall have appellate jurisdiction only, which shall be co-extensive with this territory, and shall hold two sessions annually, beginning on the first Mondays in June and September, and at such places as by law may be directed. The supreme court shall have a general superintending control over all inferior courts of law. It shall have power to issue writs of habeas corpus, mandamus, quo warranto, certiorari, and other original remedial writs, and hear and determine the same. The supreme court shall have power to decide upon and annul any laws contrary to the provisions of these articles of compact, and whenever called upon by the House of Representatives, the supreme judge shall give his opinion touching the validity of any pending measure. The House of Representatives may, hereafter, provide by law for the supreme court having original jurisdiction in criminal cases.

§ 9. All officers under this compact, shall take an oath, as follows, to wit: I do solemnly swear, that I will support the Organic Laws of the provisional Government of Oregon, so far as said Organic Laws are consistent with my duties as a citizen of the United States, or a subject of Great Britain,[220] and faithfully demean myself in office. So help me God.

---

[220] This clause was introduced into the "Organic Law" of the provisional

§ 10. Every free male descendant of a white man, inhabitant [185] of this territory, of the age of twenty-one years and upwards, who shall have been an inhabitant of this territory at the time of its organization, shall be entitled to vote at the election of officers, civil and military, and be eligible to any office in the territory, provided, that all persons of the description entitled to vote by the provisions of this section, who shall emigrate to this territory after its organization, shall be entitled to the rights of citizens after having resided six months in the territory.

§ 11. The election for all civil officers, provided for by this compact, shall be held the first Monday in June annually.

ARTICLE III — LAND LAW

§ 1. Any person now holding, or hereafter wishing to establish a claim to land in this territory, shall designate the extent of his claim by natural boundaries, or by marks at the corners and upon the lines of such claim, and have the extent and boundaries of said claim recorded in the office of the territorial recorder, in a book to be kept by him for that purpose, within twenty days from the time of making said claim: provided, that those who shall be already in possession of land, shall be allowed twelve months from the passage of this act to file a descrip-

government in order to secure the Hudson's Bay traders, and hold their allegiance to the newly-established league of order. A copy was sent to Governor McLoughlin, who having examined the document and finding "that this compact does not interfere with our duties and allegiance to our respective governments," wrote "we the officers of the Hudson's Bay Company, consent to become parties to the articles of compact." See H. H. Bancroft, *History of Oregon*, i, p. 495, note 31.— ED.

tion of his claim in the recorder's office: and provided further, that the said claimant shall state in his record, the size, shape, and locality of such claim, and give the names of the adjoining claimants; and the recorder may require the applicant for such record to be made to answer, on his oath, touching the facts.

§ 2.   All claimants shall, within six months from the time of recording their claims, make permanent improvements upon the same, by building or enclosing, and also become an occupant upon said claim within one year from the date of such record, or in case not occupied, the person holding said claim shall pay into the treasury the sum of five dollars annually, and in case of failure to occupy, or on failure of payment of [186] the sum above stated, the claim shall be considered as abandoned: provided, that no non-resident of this territory shall have the benefit of this law: and, provided further, that any resident of this territory, absent on private business for two years, may hold his claim by paying five dollars annually to the treasury.

§ 3.   No individual shall be allowed to hold a claim of more than one square mile, or six hundred and forty acres, in a square or oblong form, according to the natural situation of the premises.   Nor shall any individual be allowed to hold more than one claim at the same time. Any person complying with the provisions of these ordinances, shall be entitled to the same recourse against trespass as in other cases by law provided.

§ 4.   Partnerships of two or more persons shall be allowed to take up a tract of land not exceeding six hundred and forty acres to each person in said partnership, subject to all the provisions of the law; and whenever such partnership is dissolved, the members shall each record the particular parts of said tract as may be allotted to him: provided that no member of said partnership shall hold a separate claim at the time of the existence of said partnership.

§ 5.   The boundary lines of all claims shall hereafter conform, as near as may be, to the cardinal points.

§ 6.   The officers elected at the general election, held on the first Tuesday in June, 1845, shall be the officers to act under this organic law, and their official acts, so far as they are in accordance with this compact, are hereby declared valid and legal.

§ 7.   Amendments to this instrument may be proposed by the House of Representatives, two-thirds of the members concurring therein; which amendments shall be made public in all parts of Oregon, and be read at the polls at the next succeeding general election, and a concurrence of two-thirds of all [187] the members elected at said election, may pass said amendments, and they shall become a part of this compact.

CERTIFICATE

I, John E. Long,[220] secretary of Oregon territory, do hereby certify, that the foregoing is a true and correct copy of the original law, as passed by the representatives of the people of Oregon, on the fifth day of July, A. D. 1845, and submitted to the people on the twenty-sixth day of the same month, and by them adopted and now on file in my office.   J. E. LONG, *Secretary.*

[220] For note on Long, see De Smet's *Oregon Missions* in our volume xxix, p. 280, note 174.— ED.

N. B. At the December Session, 1845, of the House of Representatives, two-thirds of the members concurring therein, the following amendments to the Organic Law were proposed, to wit: Strike out in the 4th section of said law, the words "or more." Also, to amend the land law so as to "permit claimants to hold six hundred acres in the prairie, and forty acres in the timber, though said tracts do not join."

ARDENT SPIRITS

AN ACT to prevent the introduction, sale, and distillation of ardent spirits in Oregon.

§ 1. *Be it enacted by the House of Representatives of Oregon Territory*, That if any person shall hereafter import or introduce any ardent spirits into Oregon, with intent to sell, barter, give, or trade the same, and shall offer the same for sale, trade, barter, or gift, he shall be fined the sum of fifty dollars for each and every such offence, which may be recovered by indictment, or by trial before a justice of the peace, without the form of pleading.

§ 2. That if any person shall hereafter sell, barter, give, or trade any ardent spirits of any kind whatever, directly or indirectly, to any person within Oregon, he shall forfeit and pay [188] the sum of twenty dollars for each and every such sale, trade, barter, or gift, to be recovered by indictment in the county court, or before a justice of the peace, without the form of pleading.

§ 3. That if any person shall hereafter establish or carry on any manufactory or distillery of ardent spirits in Oregon, he shall be subject to be indicted before the county court, as for a nuisance, and if convicted, he shall be fined the sum of one hundred dollars; and the court shall issue an order to the sheriff, directing him to seize and destroy the distilling apparatus, which order the sheriff shall execute.

§ 4. Whenever it shall come to the knowledge of any officer of this government, or any private citizen, that any kind of spirituous liquors are being distilled or manufactured in Oregon, they are hereby authorised and required to proceed to the place where such illicit manufacture is known to exist, and seize the distilling apparatus, and deliver the same to the nearest district judge or justice of the peace, whose duty it shall be immediately to issue his warrant, and cause the house and premises of the person against whom such warrant shall be issued to be further searched; and in case any kind of spirituous liquors are found in or about said premises, or any implements or apparatus that have the appearance of having been used or constructed for the purpose of manufacturing any kind of spirituous liquors, the officer who shall have been duly authorised to execute said warrant, shall seize all such apparatus, implements, and spirituous liquors, and deliver the same to the judge or justice of the peace who issued the said warrant; said officer shall also arrest the person or persons in or about whose premises such apparatus, implements, or spirituous liquors are found, and conduct him or them to said judge or justice of the peace, whose duty it shall be to proceed against such criminal or criminals, and dispose of the articles seized, according to law.

§ 5. All fines and penalties imposed under this act, shall go, [189] one-half to the informant and witnesses, and the other half to the officers engaged in arresting and trying the criminal or criminals; and it shall be the duty of all officers into whose hands such fines and penalties may come, to pay over as directed in this section.

§ 6. This act shall not be so construed as to prevent any practising physician from selling such liquors for medicine, not to exceed half a pint at one time.

§ 7. That it shall be the duty of the secretary to publish this act in the first newspaper printed in Oregon.

CERTIFICATE

I, John E. Long, Secretary of Oregon, do hereby certify, that the foregoing act on ardent spirits, is truly and correctly revised by me.   J. E. LONG, *Secretary.*

Important
Historical Publications
OF
The Arthur H. Clark Company

Full descriptive circulars will be mailed
on application

The HISTORIC HIGH WAYS OF AMERICA

BY

ARCHER BUTLER HULBERT

*A series of monographs on the History of America as portraye
in the evolution of its highways of War, Commerce
and Social Expansion*

THE VOLUMES ARE

1—Paths of the Mound-Building Indians
and Great Game Animals: Part I, habitat and
migrations of the mound-builders; Part II, buffalo trails.

2—Indian Thoroughfares: An account of Indian
woodcraft and the five great Indian trails of the Eastern
States.

3—Washington's Road: The first chapter of
the Old French War. Washington's early life from an
original standpoint.

4—Braddock's Road: The famous campaign of
1755. This road from the Potomac to the Monon-
gahela was the first great highway of material progress
to the West.

5—Old Glade Road: Built by Forbes, Braddock's
successor. The campaign of 1758, resulting in the
capture of Fort Duquesne.

6—Boone's Wilderness Road: This highway
through Cumberland Gap was the scene of the memor-
able exploits of Boone, Walker, and Gist, which had
such far-reaching effects for Western settlement.

7—Portage Paths: The important portages which
were the "keys to the interior of the continent" for
explorers, missionaries, traders, and pioneers.

8—Military Roads: Such roads as those
by Maria, Bouquet, Lewis, McIntosh, George Rog
Clark, Crawford, Harmar, St. Clair, and Wayne
described.

9—Waterways of Westward Expansio
The history of the Ohio River and its tributaries; the
influence in the peopling of the Northwest Territory.

10—The Cumberland Road: From Maryla
to Illinois. "It carried thousands of population
millions of wealth into the West and, more than
other material structure in the land, served to harmoni
and strengthen, if not to save, the Union."

11-12—Pioneer Roads, two volumes: Tavern
stage lines, mail and express systems, the story of
famous turnpikes.

13-14—The Great American Canals,
volumes: The Erie Canal, Chesapeake and Ohi
Pennsylvania Canal, etc.

15—The Future of Road-Making: A sy
sium by the latest and best authorities on Good Road

16—Index to the Series: Constructed on an
cal principles and affording ready access to any
or topic in the entire work.

Sixteen volumes, crown octavo, cloth, uncut, gilt tops. A LIMITE
EDITION only, printed direct from type, and the type distributed. Eac
volume handsomely printed in large type on Dickinson's hand-mad
paper, and illustrated with maps, plates, and facsimiles.
Price, volumes 1 and 2, $2.00 net each; volumes 3 to 16, $2.50 net each

"The fruit not only of the study of original historical sources in documen
found here and in England, but of patient and enthusiastic topographical studies, i
the course of which every foot of these old historic highways has been traced an
traversed."—*The Living Age.*

Full descriptive circulars giving the contents of each volum

RECONSTRUCTIO

Political, Military, Social, Religious, Educational & Industrial
1865 to the Present Time

SELECTED AND EDITED BY
WALTER L. FLEMING, Ph. D.
PROFESSOR OF HISTORY IN WEST VIRGINIA UNIVERSITY

Printed on a specially made paper, illustrated with facsimiles, two volume large 8vo, (about 900 pages), cloth, uncut, gilt tops. Price per set, $10.00 ne

This work has been prepared in response to a demand on the part students and thoughtful readers for an adequate collection of historica material which shall

1st. *Present the original sources, which alone give the true contemporary conditions, and allow the reader to make his own interpretation of the facts.*

2nd. *Comprehend all phases of the progress and results of Reconstruction, social and economic, as well as political.*

3rd. *Exhibit not only the national aspects but also the local conditions of Reconstruction, in all the States.*

PROFESSOR FLEMING is recognized as one of the fore most authorities in the country on the Reconstructio Period. The excellence of his previous contributions o special topics in this field is sufficient guarantee of th value of the present comprehensive work.

"It is certainly a most interesting and important plan."—WOODROW WILSON.

"Every student . . . will rejoice over this addition to his facilities for intellige appreciation of the great interests involved in the sectional struggle of 1861.186 and its aftermath."—*Chicago Evening Post.*

"I feel sure that your work will be of great interest and benefit to the futu historian."—THOMAS NELSON PAGE.

uments

Pittman's Prefent State of the European Settlements on the Miſſiſippi

With folding Plans and Draughts

Edited with Introduction, Notes and Index, by
FRANK HEYWOOD HODDER
Profeſſor of American Hiſtory, Univerſity of Kanſas

THIS exceedingly rare work, issued in 1770, is so much in demand by and collectors of Americana that even imperfect copies of the original are no almost impossible to obtain at any price. It contains much valuable original material for the study of the French and Spanish Settlements of old Louisiana, West Florida, and the Illinois country, after the Peace of 1763.

> "Giving in a compact form, much useful and reliable information (nowhere else to be found) concerning the Mississippi Valley and its people at that transition period."—WALLACE.
>
> Dr. WILLIAM F. POOLE in Winsor's *Narrative and Critical History of America* says: "It is the earliest English account of these settlements, and, as an authority in early western history, is of the highest importance."
>
> "An authoritative and extremely rare source."—AMERICAN HISTORICAL REVIEW.

Professor Hodder has made a special study of American historical geography, and his notes embody the results of the latest researches in this field.

500 copies, each numbered, handsomely printed in large Caslon type on Dickinson's deckle-edged paper. Large 8vo, cloth, uncut, gilt top. Price $3.00 net.

"A real literary and historical find."

Personal Narrative of Travels
in Virginia, Maryland, Pennsylvania, Ohio, Indiana, Kentucky; and of a Residence in the Illinois Territory
(1817-1818) by
ELIAS PYM FORDHAM
With facsimiles of the author's sketches and plans

Edited with Notes, Introduction, Index, etc., by
FREDERIC AUSTIN OGG, A. M.
Author of "The Opening of the Mississippi"

THIS hitherto unpublished MS. was written in 1817-18 by a young Englishman emigrating to America. Landing at Baltimore, he visited Philadelphia, Pittsburg, and Cincinnati, and traveled through Indiana, Ohio, Kentucky, and Illinois, making frank and pointed comments on the people and the country.

The narrative is consequently rich in *personalia* of early settlers, remarks on contemporary history and politics, state of trade, agriculture, prices, and information on local history not obtainable elsewhere; it will therefore make accessible to historical students much new and important material, besides giving the general reader a book of vital and absorbing interest.

> "An artless but convincing narrative of life in what we now call the Middle West, but was then the very rugged edge of civilization."—*The Dial.*